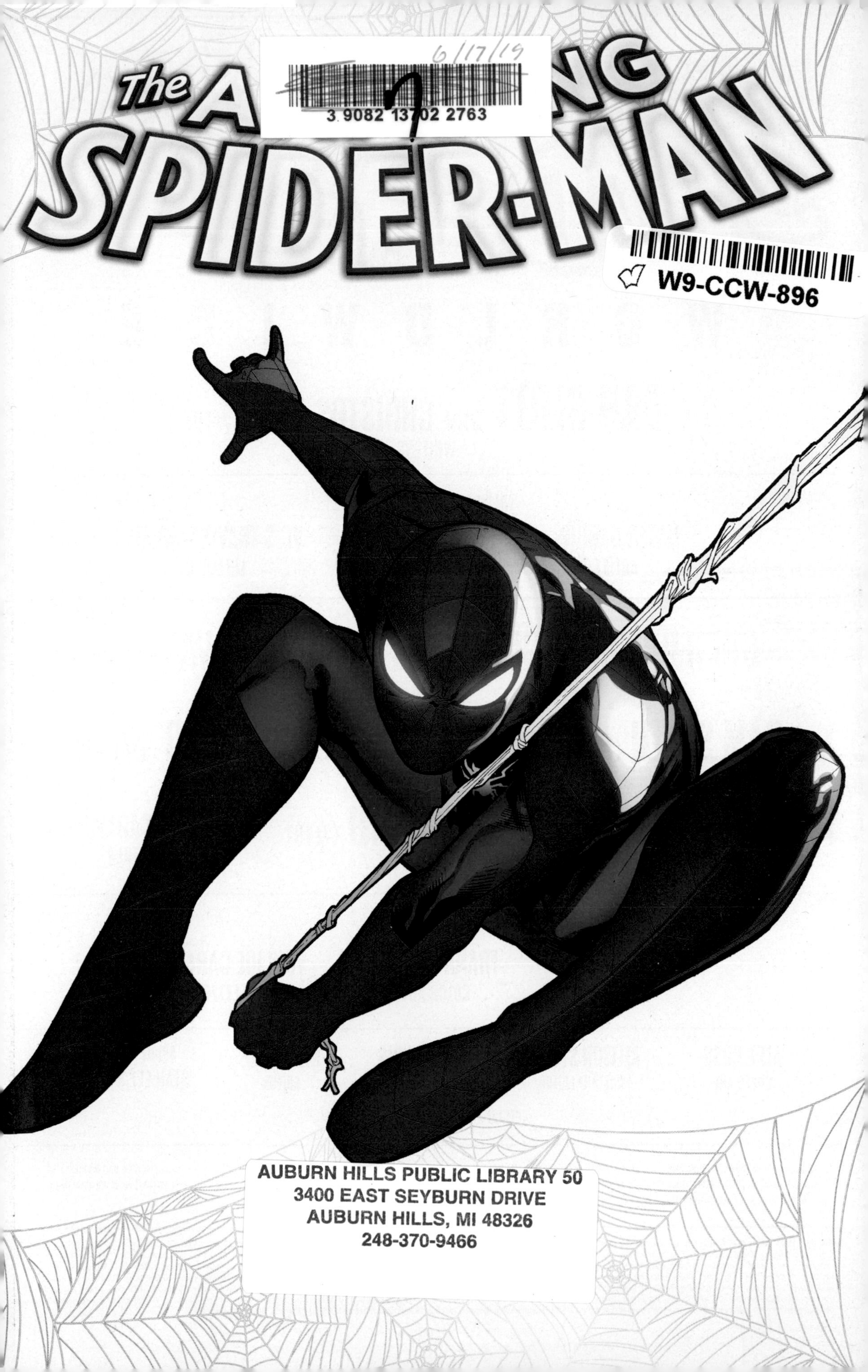
The A
NG
SPIDER-MAN

The AMAZING SPIDER-MAN

WORLDWIDE

DAN SLOTT WITH CHRISTOS GAGE (#19)
WRITERS

FREE COMIC BOOK DAY 2016

JAVIER GARRÓN
ARTIST

FRANK D'ARMATA
COLOR ARTIST

VC'S TRAVIS LANHAM
LETTERER

GIUSEPPE CAMUNCOLI (#16 & #19) & R.B. SILVA (#17-18)
PENCILERS

CAM SMITH (#16 & #19) & ADRIANO DI BENEDETTO (#17-18)
INKERS

MARTE GRACIA (#16-18) & JASON KEITH (#19)
COLORISTS

VC'S JOE CARAMAGNA
LETTERER

"KINGS RANSOM"

JAVIER GARRÓN
ARTIST

FRANK D'ARMATA
COLOR ARTIST

VC'S JOE CARAMAGNA
LETTERER

ALEX ROSS
COVER ART

ALLISON STOCK
ASSISTANT EDITOR

DEVIN LEWIS
ASSOCIATE EDITOR

NICK LOWE
EDITOR

SPIDER-MAN CREATED BY
STAN LEE & STEVE DITKO

SPECIAL THANKS TO DANIELE ORLANDINI

COLLECTION EDITOR: JENNIFER GRÜNWALD
ASSOCIATE MANAGING EDITOR: KATERI WOODY
ASSOCIATE EDITOR: SARAH BRUNSTAD

EDITOR, SPECIAL PROJECTS: MARK D. BEAZLEY
VP PRODUCTION & SPECIAL PROJECTS: JEFF YOUNGQUIST
SVP PRINT, SALES & MARKETING: DAVID GABRIEL

EDITOR IN CHIEF: AXEL ALONSO
CHIEF CREATIVE OFFICER: JOE QUESADA

PUBLISHER: DAN BUCKLEY
EXECUTIVE PRODUCER: ALAN FINE

AMAZING SPIDER-MAN: WORLDWIDE VOL. 4. Contains material originally published in magazine form as AMAZING SPIDER-MAN #16-19 and FREE COMIC BOOK DAY 2016 (CAPTAIN AMERICA) #1. First printing 2017. ISBN# 978-1-302-90237-7. Published by MARVEL WORLDWIDE, INC., a subsidiary of MARVEL ENTERTAINMENT, LLC. OFFICE OF PUBLICATION: 135 West 50th Street, New York, NY 10020. Copyright © 2017 MARVEL No similarity between any of the names, characters, persons, and/or institutions in this magazine with those of any living or dead person or institution is intended, and any such similarity which may exist is purely coincidental. **Printed in Canada.** ALAN FINE, President, Marvel Entertainment; DAN BUCKLEY, President, TV, Publishing & Brand Management; JOE QUESADA, Chief Creative Officer; TOM BREVOORT, SVP of Publishing; DAVID BOGART, SVP of Business Affairs & Operations, Publishing & Partnership; C.B. CEBULSKI, VP of Brand Management & Development, Asia; DAVID GABRIEL, SVP of Sales & Marketing, Publishing; JEFF YOUNGQUIST, VP of Production & Special Projects; DAN CARR, Executive Director of Publishing Technology; ALEX MORALES, Director of Publishing Operations; SUSAN CRESPI, Production Manager; STAN LEE, Chairman Emeritus. For information regarding advertising in Marvel Comics or on Marvel.com, please contact Vit DeBellis, Integrated Sales Manager, at vdebellis@marvel.com. For Marvel subscription inquiries, please call 888-511-5480. **Manufactured between 11/18/2016 and 12/26/2016 by SOLISCO PRINTERS, SCOTT, QC, CANADA.**

10 9 8 7 6 5 4 3 2 1

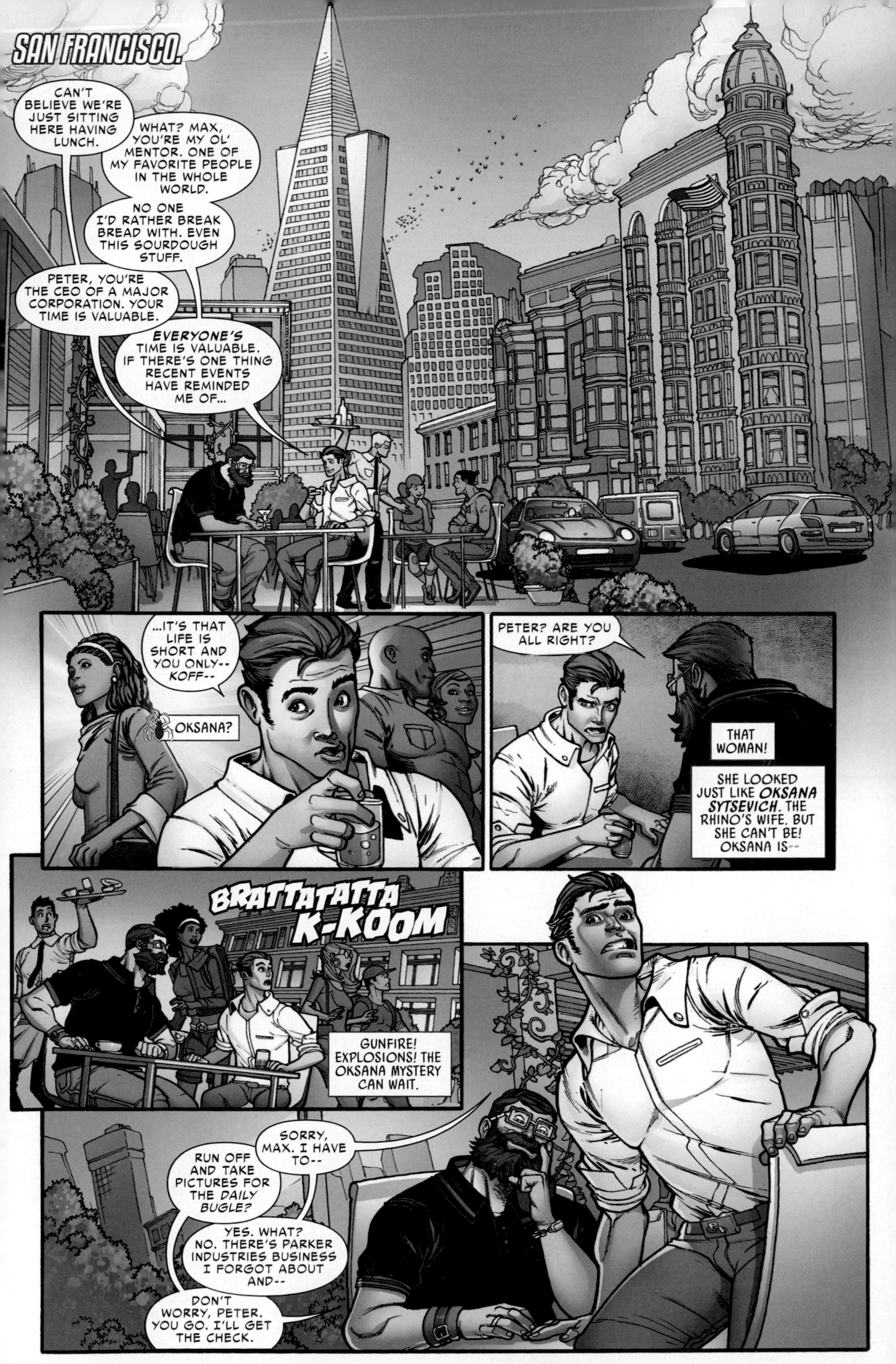
SAN FRANCISCO.
CAN'T BELIEVE WE'RE JUST SITTING HERE HAVING LUNCH.
WHAT? MAX, YOU'RE MY OL' MENTOR. ONE OF MY FAVORITE PEOPLE IN THE WHOLE WORLD.
NO ONE I'D RATHER BREAK BREAD WITH. EVEN THIS SOURDOUGH STUFF.
PETER, YOU'RE THE CEO OF A MAJOR CORPORATION. YOUR TIME IS VALUABLE.
EVERYONE'S TIME IS VALUABLE. IF THERE'S ONE THING RECENT EVENTS HAVE REMINDED ME OF...
...IT'S THAT LIFE IS SHORT AND YOU ONLY-- KOFF--
OKSANA?
PETER? ARE YOU ALL RIGHT?
THAT WOMAN!
SHE LOOKED JUST LIKE OKSANA SYTSEVICH. THE RHINO'S WIFE. BUT SHE CAN'T BE! OKSANA IS--
BRATTATATTA K-KOOM
GUNFIRE! EXPLOSIONS! THE OKSANA MYSTERY CAN WAIT.
SORRY, MAX. I HAVE TO--
RUN OFF AND TAKE PICTURES FOR THE DAILY BUGLE?
YES. WHAT? NO. THERE'S PARKER INDUSTRIES BUSINESS I FORGOT ABOUT AND--
DON'T WORRY, PETER. YOU GO. I'LL GET THE CHECK.

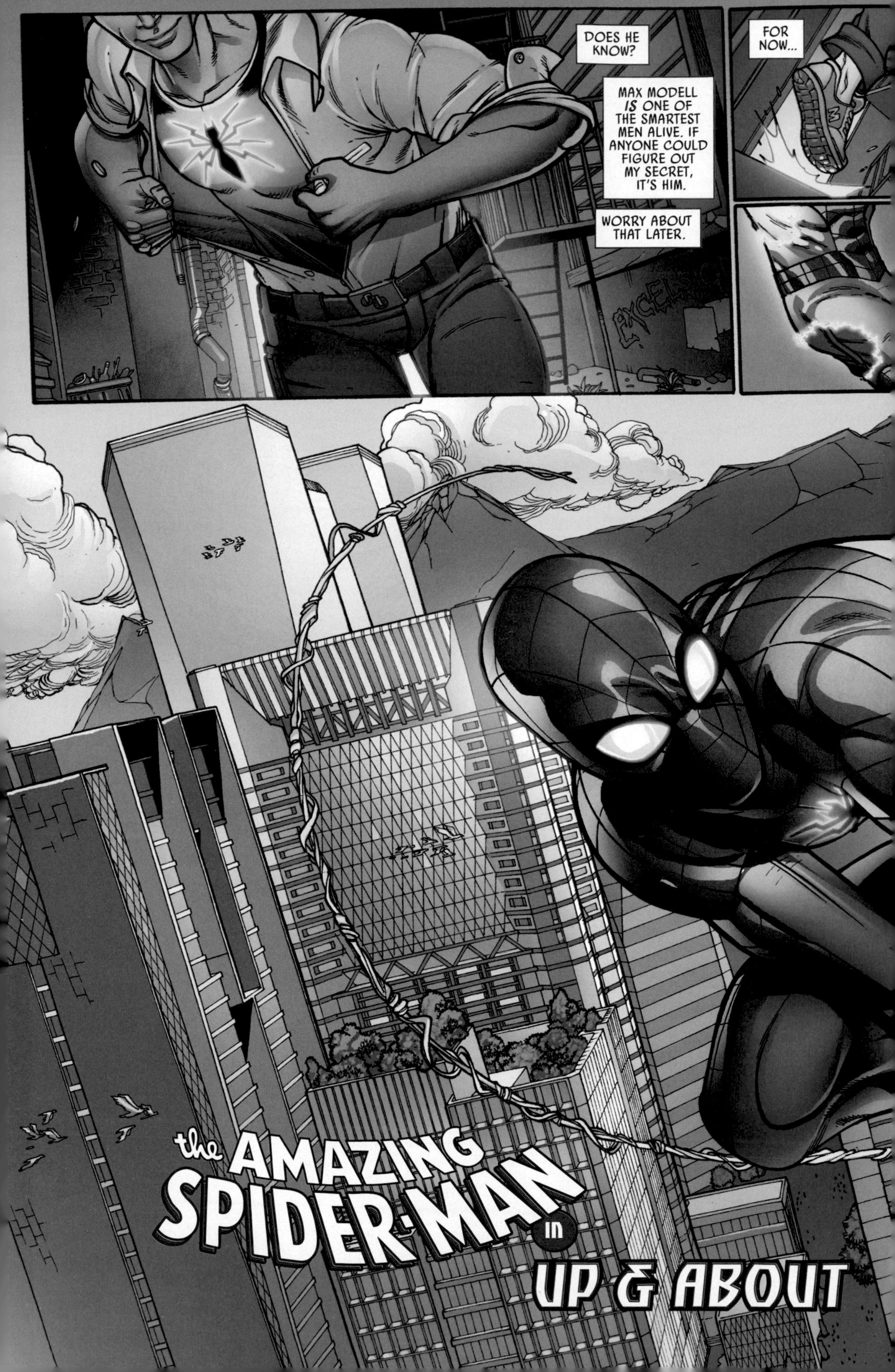
DOES HE KNOW?
MAX MODELL IS ONE OF THE SMARTEST MEN ALIVE. IF ANYONE COULD FIGURE OUT MY SECRET, IT'S HIM.
WORRY ABOUT THAT LATER.
FOR NOW...
the AMAZING SPIDER-MAN in
UP & ABOUT

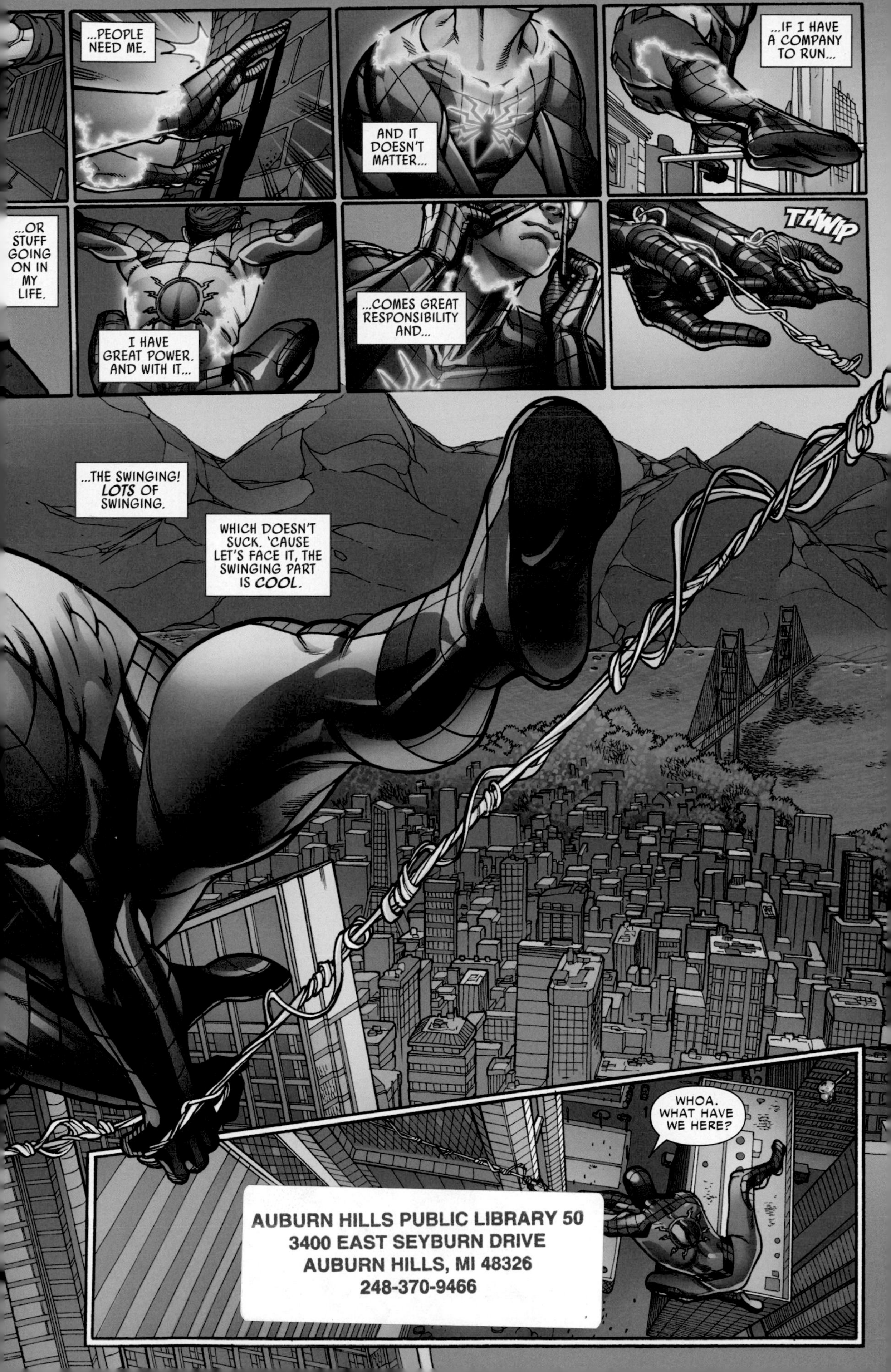
...PEOPLE NEED ME.
AND IT DOESN'T MATTER...
...IF I HAVE A COMPANY TO RUN...
...OR STUFF GOING ON IN MY LIFE.
I HAVE GREAT POWER. AND WITH IT...
...COMES GREAT RESPONSIBILITY AND...
THWIP
...THE SWINGING! LOTS OF SWINGING.
WHICH DOESN'T SUCK. 'CAUSE LET'S FACE IT, THE SWINGING PART IS COOL.
WHOA. WHAT HAVE WE HERE?

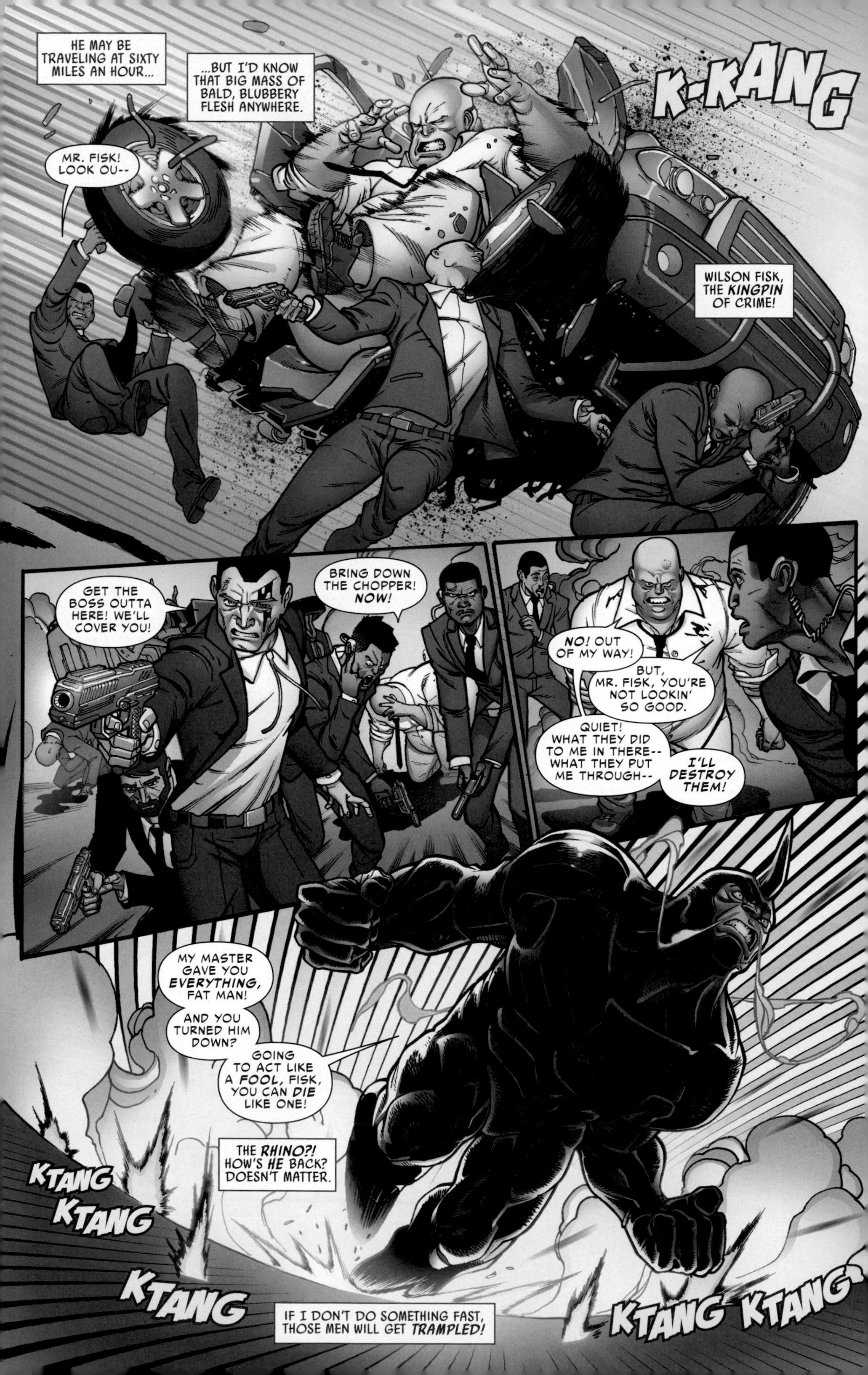
HE MAY BE TRAVELING AT SIXTY MILES AN HOUR...
...BUT I'D KNOW THAT BIG MASS OF BALD, BLUBBERY FLESH ANYWHERE.
K-KANG
MR. FISK! LOOK OU--
WILSON FISK, THE *KINGPIN* OF CRIME!
GET THE BOSS OUTTA HERE! WE'LL COVER YOU!
BRING DOWN THE CHOPPER! ***NOW!***
NO! OUT OF MY WAY!
BUT, MR. FISK, YOU'RE NOT LOOKIN' SO GOOD.
QUIET! WHAT THEY DID TO ME IN THERE-- WHAT THEY PUT ME THROUGH--
I'LL DESTROY THEM!
MY MASTER GAVE YOU ***EVERYTHING,*** FAT MAN!
AND YOU TURNED HIM DOWN?
GOING TO ACT LIKE A ***FOOL,*** FISK, YOU CAN ***DIE*** LIKE ONE!
THE *RHINO?!* HOW'S *HE* BACK? DOESN'T MATTER.
KTANG
KTANG
KTANG
IF I DON'T DO SOMETHING FAST, THOSE MEN WILL GET *TRAMPLED!*
KTANG KTANG

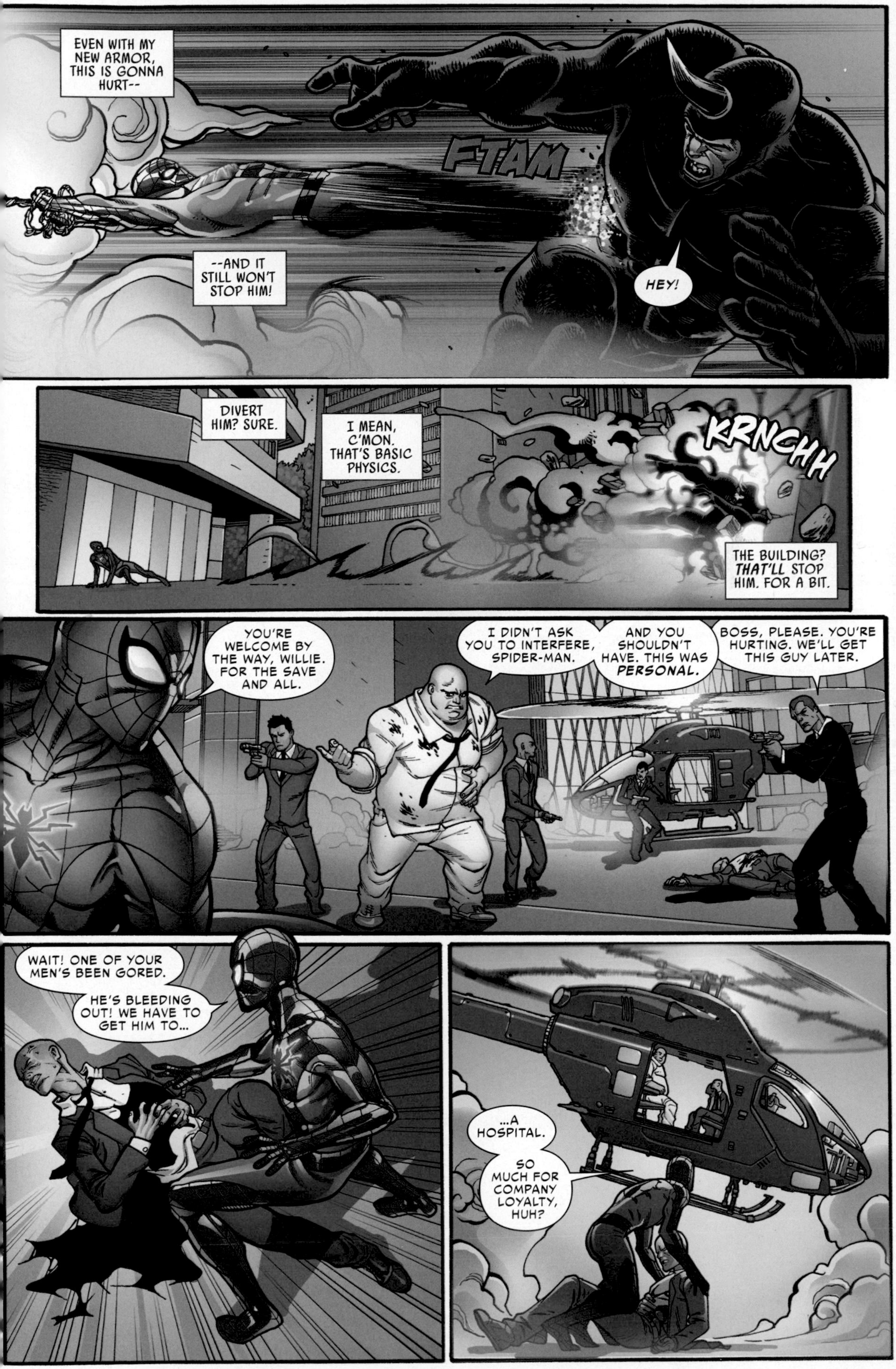

EVEN WITH MY NEW ARMOR, THIS IS GONNA HURT--
FTAM
--AND IT STILL WON'T STOP HIM!
HEY!
DIVERT HIM? SURE.
I MEAN, C'MON. THAT'S BASIC PHYSICS.
KRNCHH
THE BUILDING? THAT'LL STOP HIM. FOR A BIT.
YOU'RE WELCOME BY THE WAY, WILLIE. FOR THE SAVE AND ALL.
I DIDN'T ASK YOU TO INTERFERE, SPIDER-MAN.
AND YOU SHOULDN'T HAVE. THIS WAS PERSONAL.
BOSS, PLEASE. YOU'RE HURTING. WE'LL GET THIS GUY LATER.
WAIT! ONE OF YOUR MEN'S BEEN GORED.
HE'S BLEEDING OUT! WE HAVE TO GET HIM TO...
...A HOSPITAL.
SO MUCH FOR COMPANY LOYALTY, HUH?

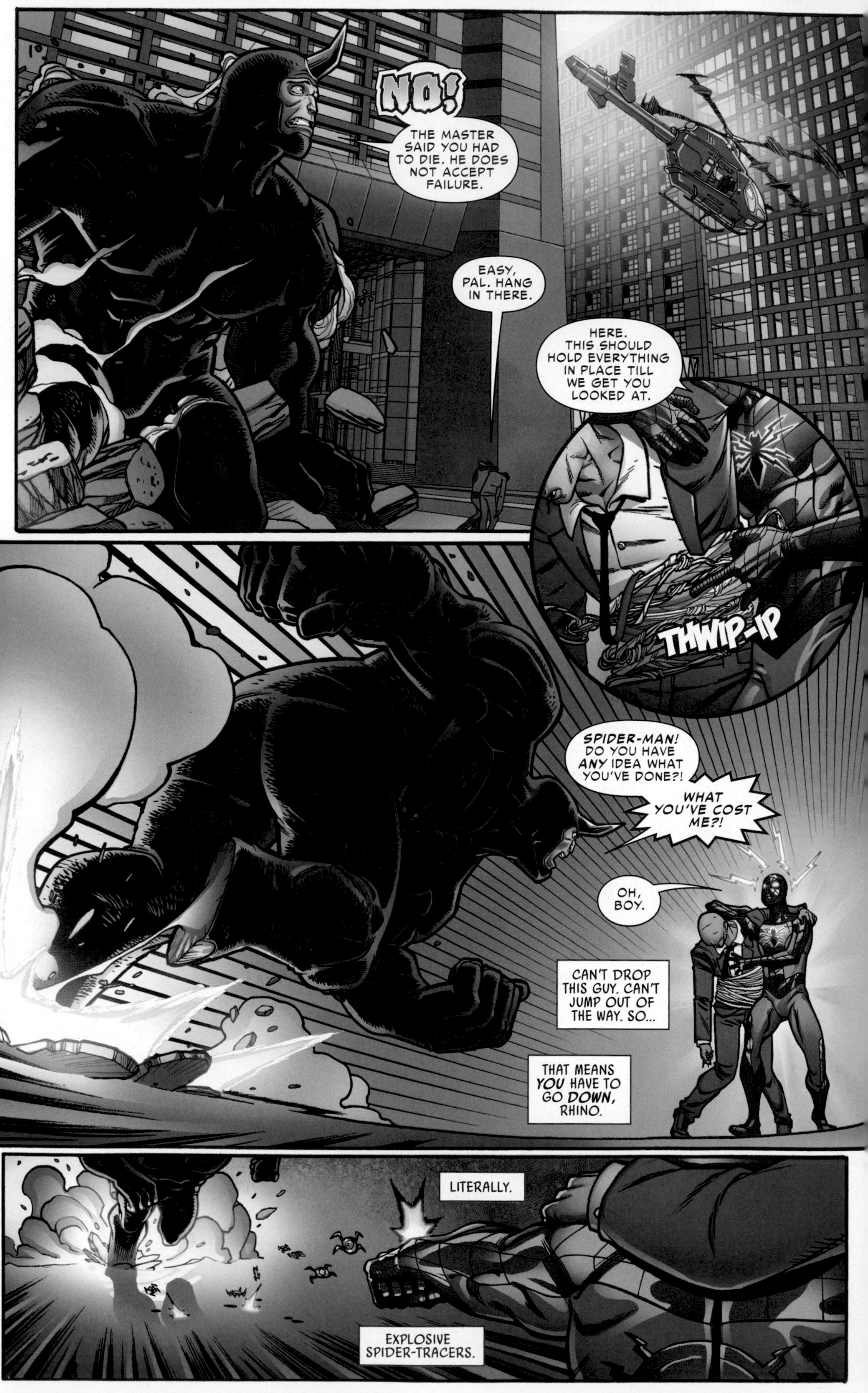
NO!
THE MASTER SAID YOU HAD TO DIE. HE DOES NOT ACCEPT FAILURE.
EASY, PAL. HANG IN THERE.
HERE. THIS SHOULD HOLD EVERYTHING IN PLACE TILL WE GET YOU LOOKED AT.
THWIP-IP
SPIDER-MAN! DO YOU HAVE ANY IDEA WHAT YOU'VE DONE?!
WHAT YOU'VE COST ME?!
OH, BOY.
CAN'T DROP THIS GUY. CAN'T JUMP OUT OF THE WAY. SO...
THAT MEANS YOU HAVE TO GO DOWN, RHINO.
LITERALLY.
EXPLOSIVE SPIDER-TRACERS.

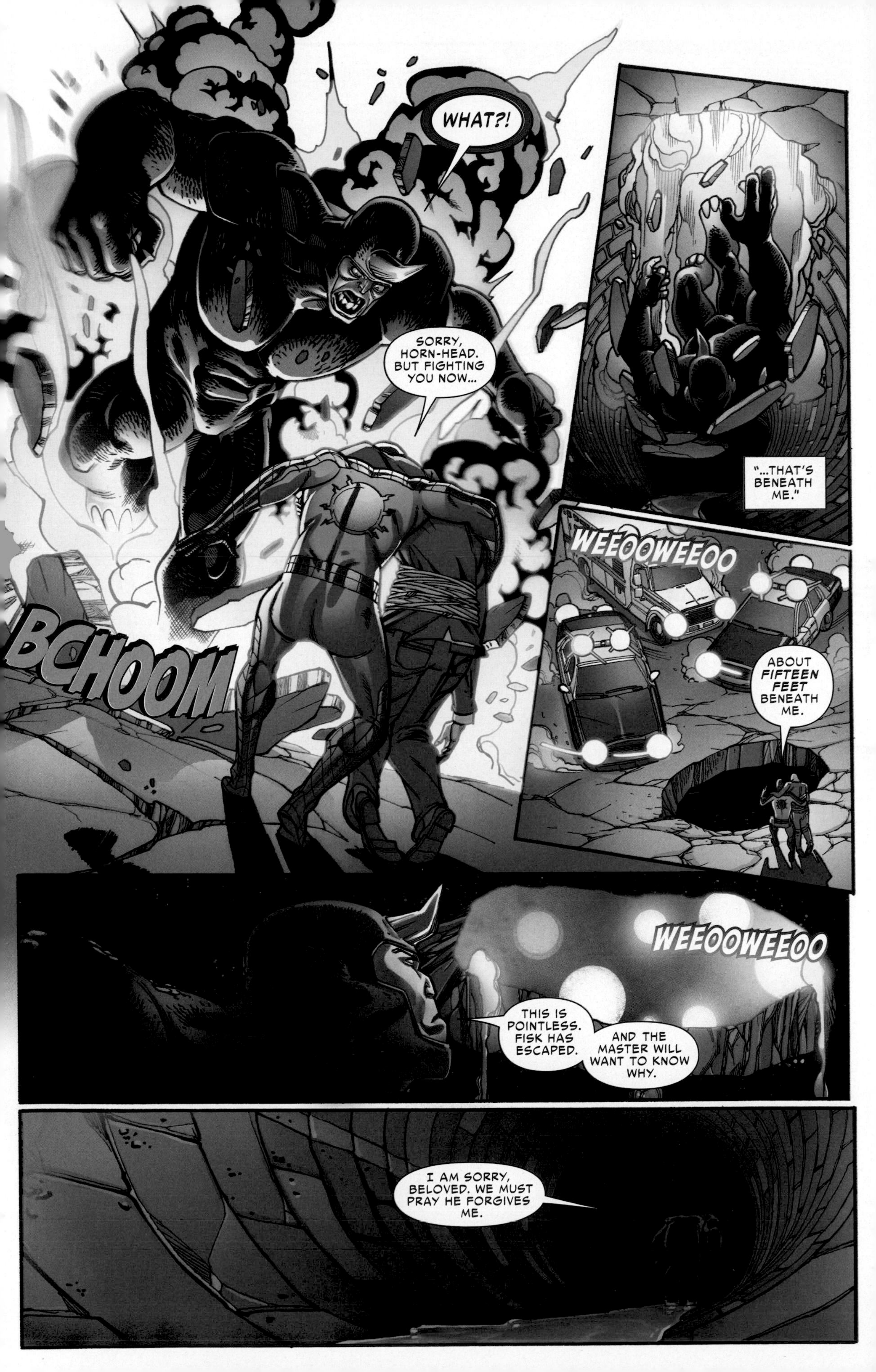
WHAT?!
SORRY, HORN-HEAD. BUT FIGHTING YOU NOW...
BCHOOM
"...THAT'S BENEATH ME."
WEEOOWEEOO
ABOUT FIFTEEN FEET BENEATH ME.
WEEOOWEEOO
THIS IS POINTLESS. FISK HAS ESCAPED.
AND THE MASTER WILL WANT TO KNOW WHY.
I AM SORRY, BELOVED. WE MUST PRAY HE FORGIVES ME.

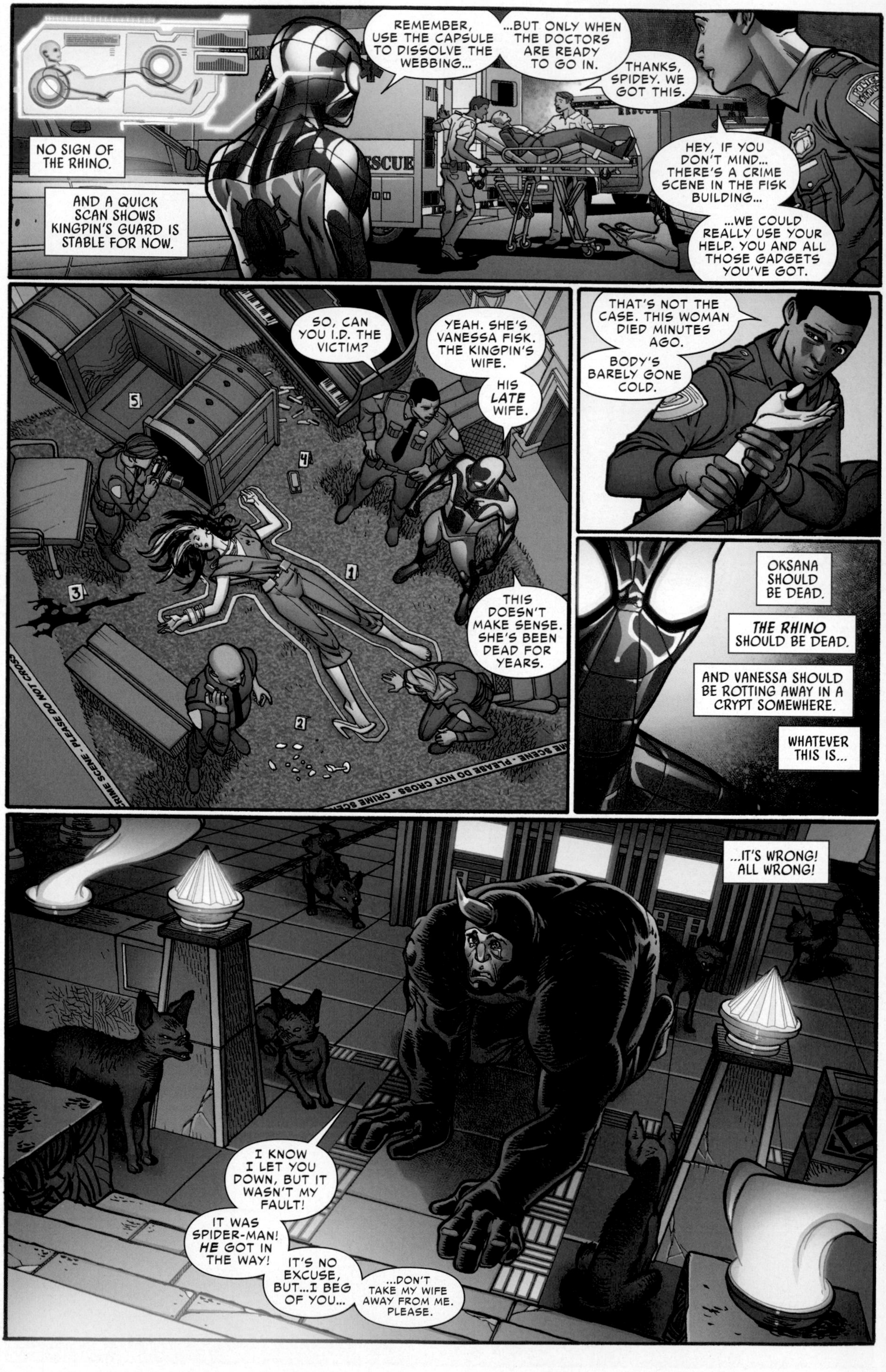
NO SIGN OF THE RHINO.
AND A QUICK SCAN SHOWS KINGPIN'S GUARD IS STABLE FOR NOW.
REMEMBER, USE THE CAPSULE TO DISSOLVE THE WEBBING...
...BUT ONLY WHEN THE DOCTORS ARE READY TO GO IN.
THANKS, SPIDEY. WE GOT THIS.
RESCUE
HEY, IF YOU DON'T MIND... THERE'S A CRIME SCENE IN THE FISK BUILDING...
...WE COULD REALLY USE YOUR HELP. YOU AND ALL THOSE GADGETS YOU'VE GOT.
SO, CAN YOU I.D. THE VICTIM?
YEAH. SHE'S VANESSA FISK. THE KINGPIN'S WIFE.
HIS *LATE* WIFE.
THIS DOESN'T MAKE SENSE. SHE'S BEEN DEAD FOR YEARS.
CRIME SCENE - PLEASE DO NOT CROSS - CRIME SCENE
THAT'S NOT THE CASE. THIS WOMAN DIED MINUTES AGO.
BODY'S BARELY GONE COLD.
OKSANA SHOULD BE DEAD.
THE RHINO SHOULD BE DEAD.
AND VANESSA SHOULD BE ROTTING AWAY IN A CRYPT SOMEWHERE.
WHATEVER THIS IS...
...IT'S WRONG! ALL WRONG!
I KNOW I LET YOU DOWN, BUT IT WASN'T MY FAULT!
IT WAS SPIDER-MAN! ***HE*** GOT IN THE WAY!
IT'S NO EXCUSE, BUT...I BEG OF YOU...
...DON'T TAKE MY WIFE AWAY FROM ME. PLEASE.

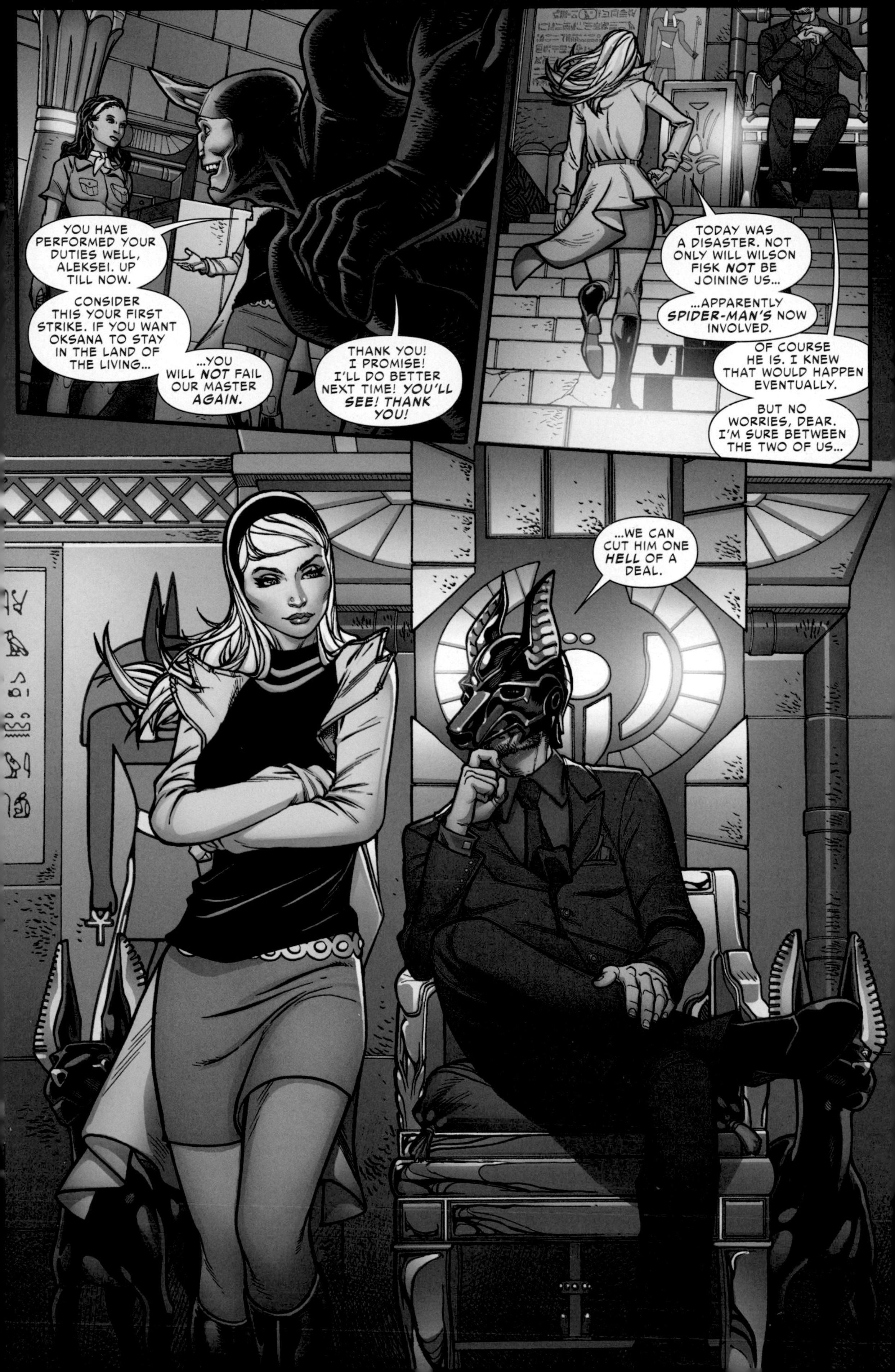
YOU HAVE PERFORMED YOUR DUTIES WELL, ALEKSEI. UP TILL NOW.
CONSIDER THIS YOUR FIRST STRIKE. IF YOU WANT OKSANA TO STAY IN THE LAND OF THE LIVING...
...YOU WILL NOT FAIL OUR MASTER AGAIN.
THANK YOU! I PROMISE! I'LL DO BETTER NEXT TIME! YOU'LL SEE! THANK YOU!
TODAY WAS A DISASTER. NOT ONLY WILL WILSON FISK NOT BE JOINING US...
...APPARENTLY SPIDER-MAN'S NOW INVOLVED.
OF COURSE HE IS. I KNEW THAT WOULD HAPPEN EVENTUALLY.
BUT NO WORRIES, DEAR. I'M SURE BETWEEN THE TWO OF US...
...WE CAN CUT HIM ONE HELL OF A DEAL.

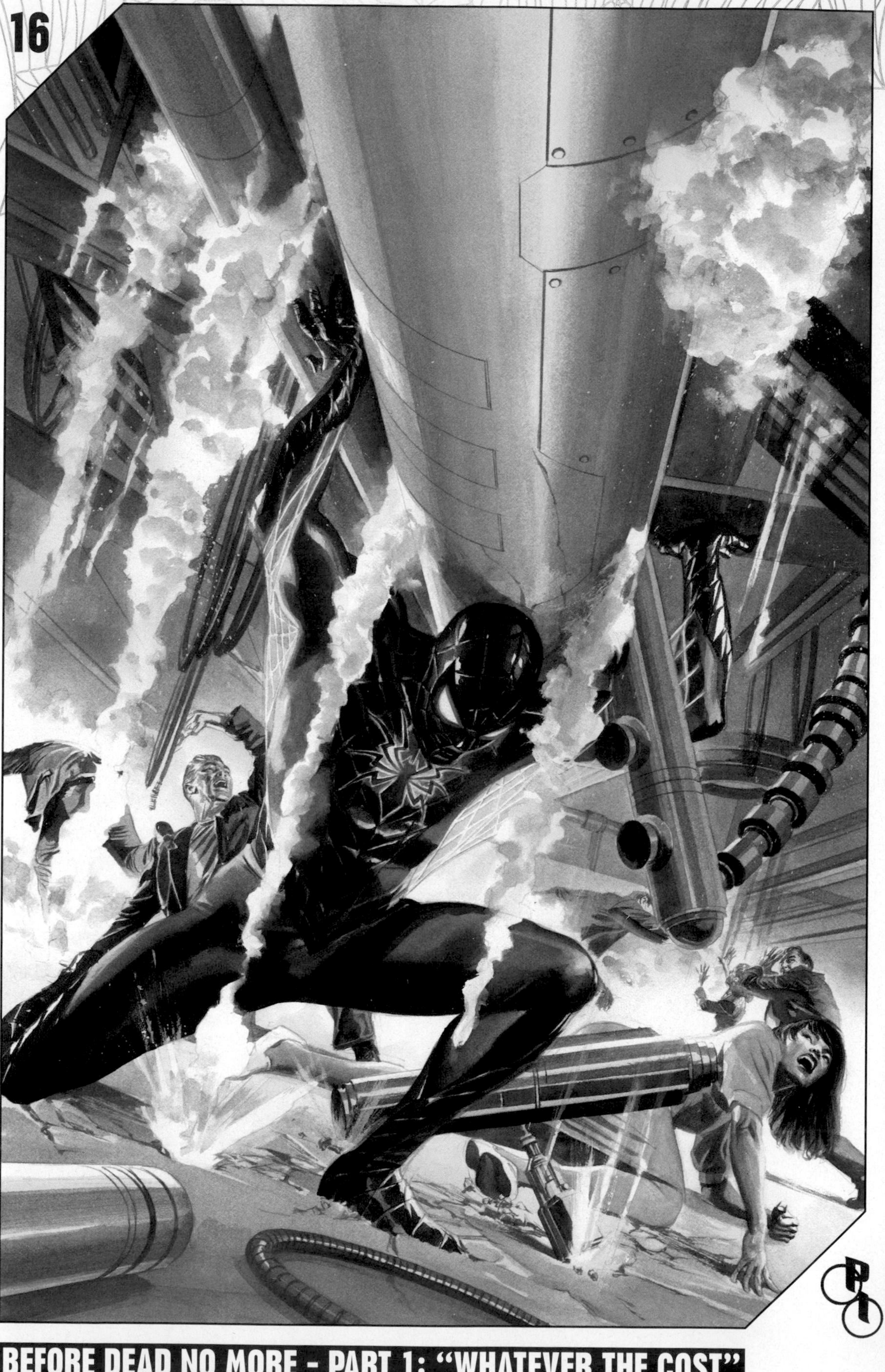

BEFORE DEAD NO MORE - PART 1: "WHATEVER THE COST"

PREVIOUSLY:
FOR MONTHS, PETER PARKER HAS BEEN LEADING A DOUBLE LIFE AS THE C.E.O. OF A MAJOR TECHNOLOGY CORPORATION, PARKER INDUSTRIES, AND AS THE WEB-SLINGING WONDER SPIDER-MAN.

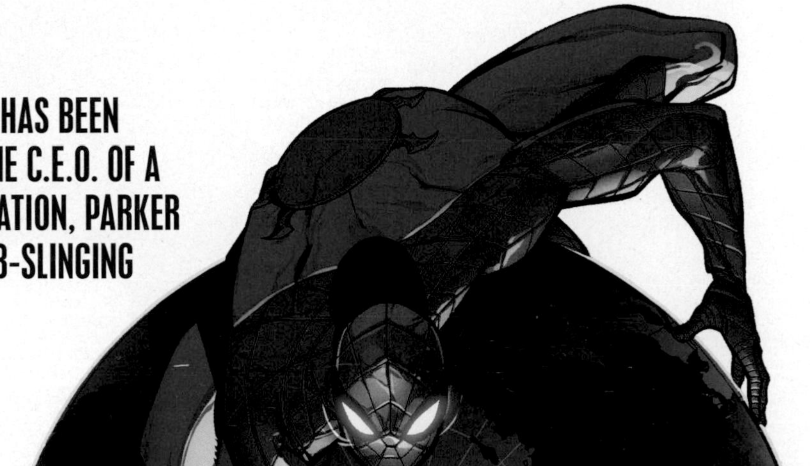

THAT HAS LEFT A VOID IN PETER'S LIFE: HE HASN'T HAD MUCH TIME WITH HIS FAMILY. IN AN EFFORT TO RECONNECT, HE RECENTLY HOSTED A PARTY AT HIS FAVORITE NEW YORK COFFEE SHOP FOR ALL OF HIS FRIENDS AND FAMILY.

THINGS TOOK A TRAGIC TURN, THOUGH, WHEN HIS AUNT MAY'S HUSBAND, JAY JAMESON, SUDDENLY COLLAPSED.

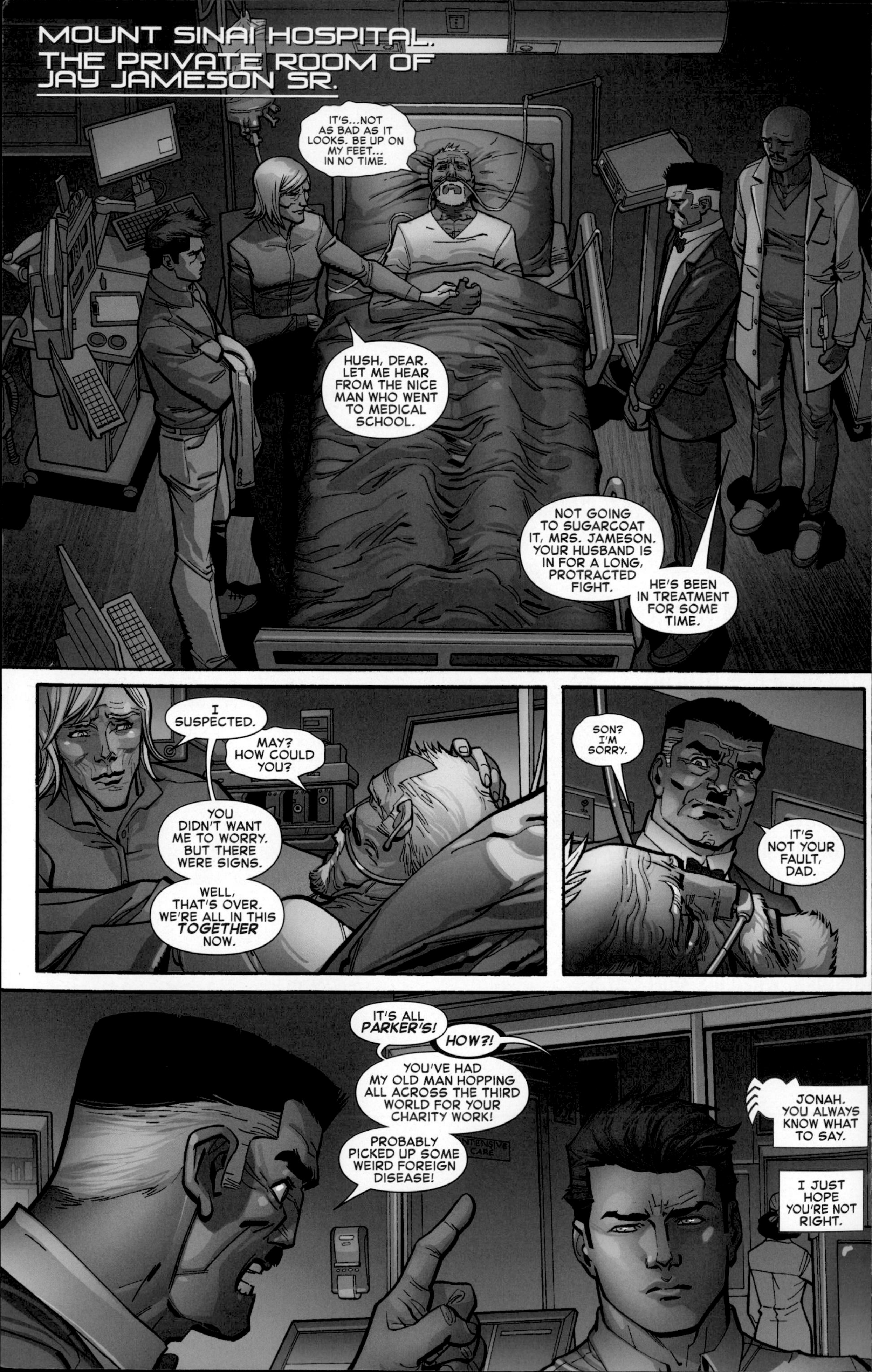
MOUNT SINAI HOSPITAL. THE PRIVATE ROOM OF JAY JAMESON SR.
IT'S...NOT AS BAD AS IT LOOKS. BE UP ON MY FEET... IN NO TIME.
HUSH, DEAR. LET ME HEAR FROM THE NICE MAN WHO WENT TO MEDICAL SCHOOL.
NOT GOING TO SUGARCOAT IT, MRS. JAMESON. YOUR HUSBAND IS IN FOR A LONG, PROTRACTED FIGHT.
HE'S BEEN IN TREATMENT FOR SOME TIME.
I SUSPECTED.
MAY? HOW COULD YOU?
YOU DIDN'T WANT ME TO WORRY. BUT THERE WERE SIGNS.
WELL, THAT'S OVER. WE'RE ALL IN THIS TOGETHER NOW.
SON? I'M SORRY.
IT'S NOT YOUR FAULT, DAD.
IT'S ALL PARKER'S!
HOW?!
YOU'VE HAD MY OLD MAN HOPPING ALL ACROSS THE THIRD WORLD FOR YOUR CHARITY WORK!
PROBABLY PICKED UP SOME WEIRD FOREIGN DISEASE!
INTENSIVE CARE
JONAH. YOU ALWAYS KNOW WHAT TO SAY.
I JUST HOPE YOU'RE NOT RIGHT.

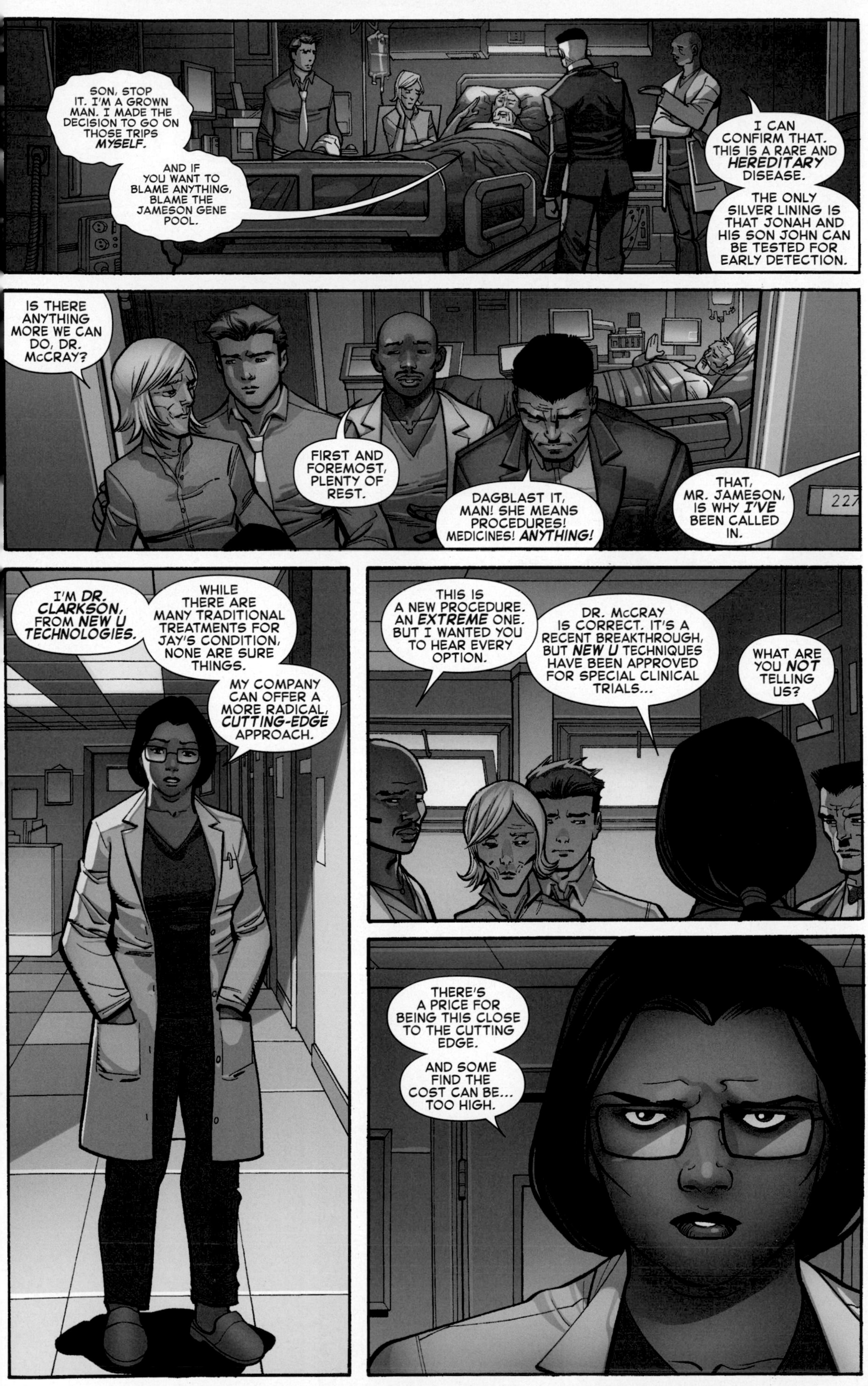
SON, STOP IT. I'M A GROWN MAN. I MADE THE DECISION TO GO ON THOSE TRIPS *MYSELF*.
AND IF YOU WANT TO BLAME ANYTHING, BLAME THE JAMESON GENE POOL.
I CAN CONFIRM THAT. THIS IS A RARE AND *HEREDITARY* DISEASE.
THE ONLY SILVER LINING IS THAT JONAH AND HIS SON JOHN CAN BE TESTED FOR EARLY DETECTION.
IS THERE ANYTHING MORE WE CAN DO, DR. McCRAY?
FIRST AND FOREMOST, PLENTY OF REST.
DAGBLAST IT, MAN! SHE MEANS PROCEDURES! MEDICINES! *ANYTHING!*
THAT, MR. JAMESON, IS WHY *I'VE* BEEN CALLED IN.
227
I'M *DR. CLARKSON*, FROM *NEW U TECHNOLOGIES*.
WHILE THERE ARE MANY TRADITIONAL TREATMENTS FOR JAY'S CONDITION, NONE ARE SURE THINGS.
MY COMPANY CAN OFFER A MORE RADICAL, *CUTTING-EDGE* APPROACH.
THIS IS A NEW PROCEDURE. AN *EXTREME* ONE. BUT I WANTED YOU TO HEAR EVERY OPTION.
DR. McCRAY IS CORRECT. IT'S A RECENT BREAKTHROUGH, BUT *NEW U* TECHNIQUES HAVE BEEN APPROVED FOR SPECIAL CLINICAL TRIALS...
WHAT ARE YOU *NOT* TELLING US?
THERE'S A PRICE FOR BEING THIS CLOSE TO THE CUTTING EDGE.
AND SOME FIND THE COST CAN BE... TOO HIGH.

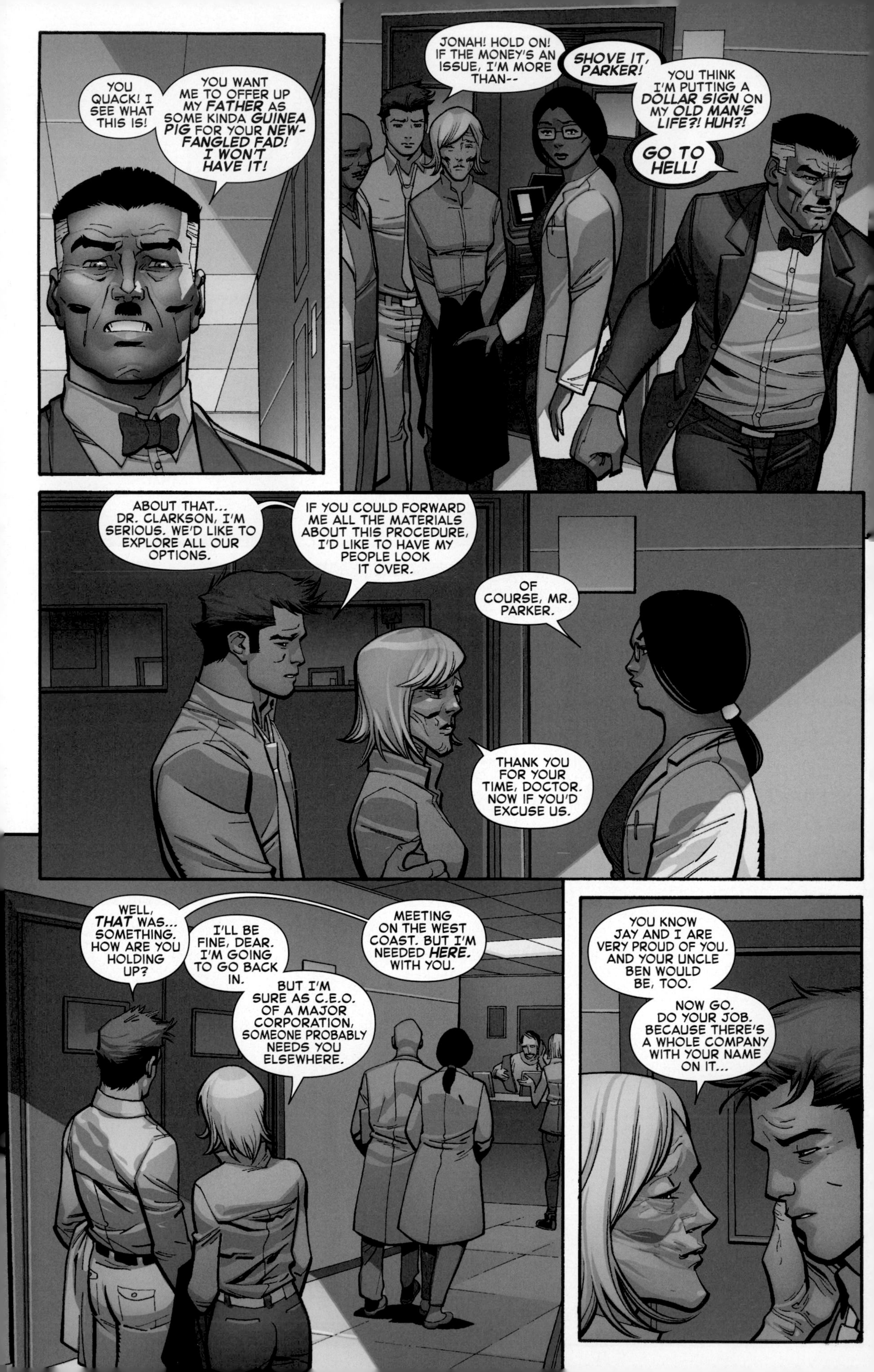
YOU QUACK! I SEE WHAT THIS IS!
YOU WANT ME TO OFFER UP MY FATHER AS SOME KINDA GUINEA PIG FOR YOUR NEW-FANGLED FAD! I WON'T HAVE IT!
JONAH! HOLD ON! IF THE MONEY'S AN ISSUE, I'M MORE THAN--
SHOVE IT, PARKER!
YOU THINK I'M PUTTING A DOLLAR SIGN ON MY OLD MAN'S LIFE?! HUH?!
GO TO HELL!
ABOUT THAT... DR. CLARKSON, I'M SERIOUS. WE'D LIKE TO EXPLORE ALL OUR OPTIONS.
IF YOU COULD FORWARD ME ALL THE MATERIALS ABOUT THIS PROCEDURE, I'D LIKE TO HAVE MY PEOPLE LOOK IT OVER.
OF COURSE, MR. PARKER.
THANK YOU FOR YOUR TIME, DOCTOR. NOW IF YOU'D EXCUSE US.
WELL, THAT WAS... SOMETHING. HOW ARE YOU HOLDING UP?
I'LL BE FINE, DEAR. I'M GOING TO GO BACK IN.
BUT I'M SURE AS C.E.O. OF A MAJOR CORPORATION, SOMEONE PROBABLY NEEDS YOU ELSEWHERE.
MEETING ON THE WEST COAST. BUT I'M NEEDED HERE. WITH YOU.
YOU KNOW JAY AND I ARE VERY PROUD OF YOU. AND YOUR UNCLE BEN WOULD BE, TOO.
NOW GO. DO YOUR JOB. BECAUSE THERE'S A WHOLE COMPANY WITH YOUR NAME ON IT...

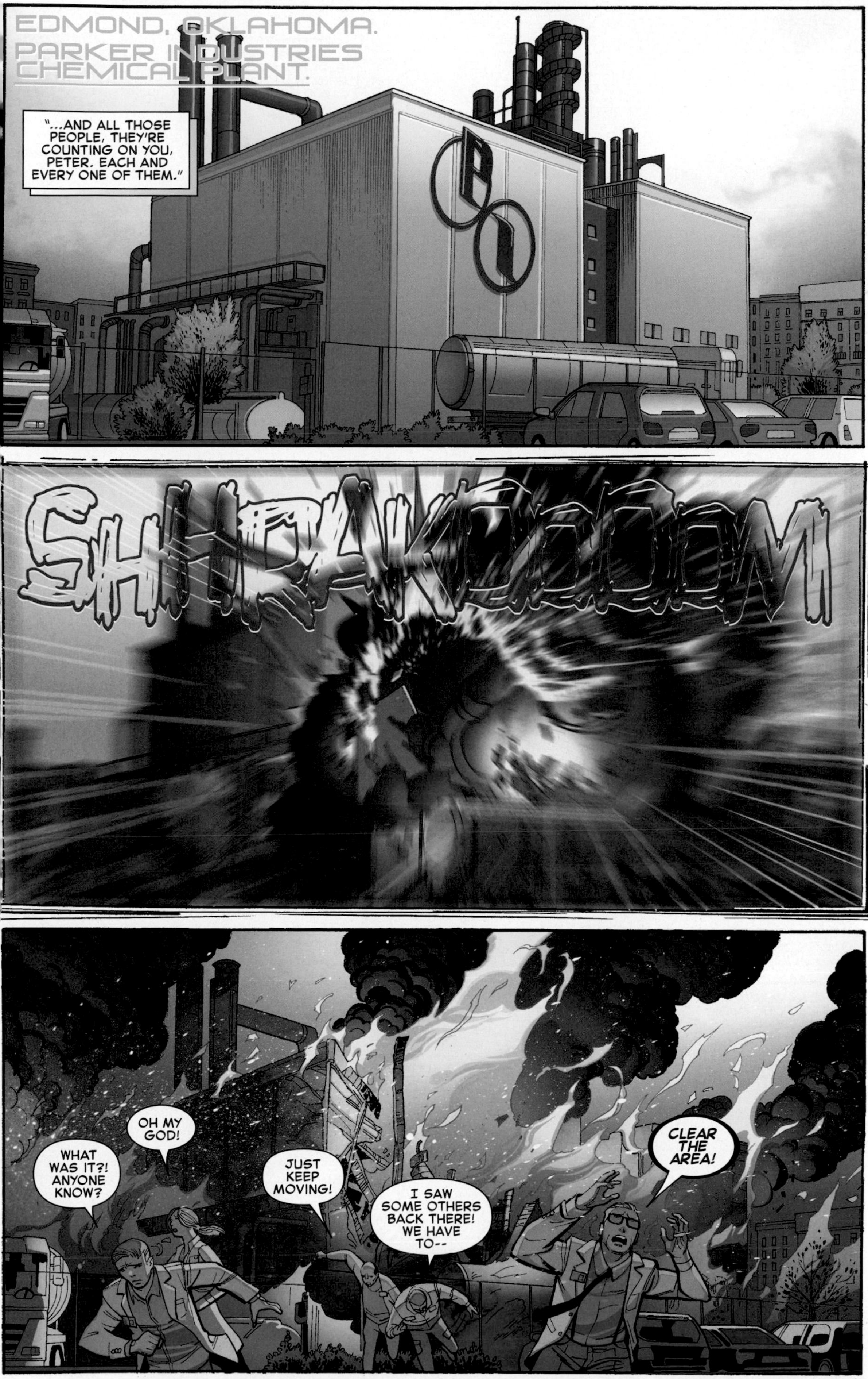
EDMOND, OKLAHOMA.
PARKER INDUSTRIES CHEMICAL PLANT.
"...AND ALL THOSE PEOPLE, THEY'RE COUNTING ON YOU, PETER. EACH AND EVERY ONE OF THEM."
OH MY GOD!
WHAT WAS IT?! ANYONE KNOW?
JUST KEEP MOVING!
I SAW SOME OTHERS BACK THERE! WE HAVE TO--
CLEAR THE AREA!

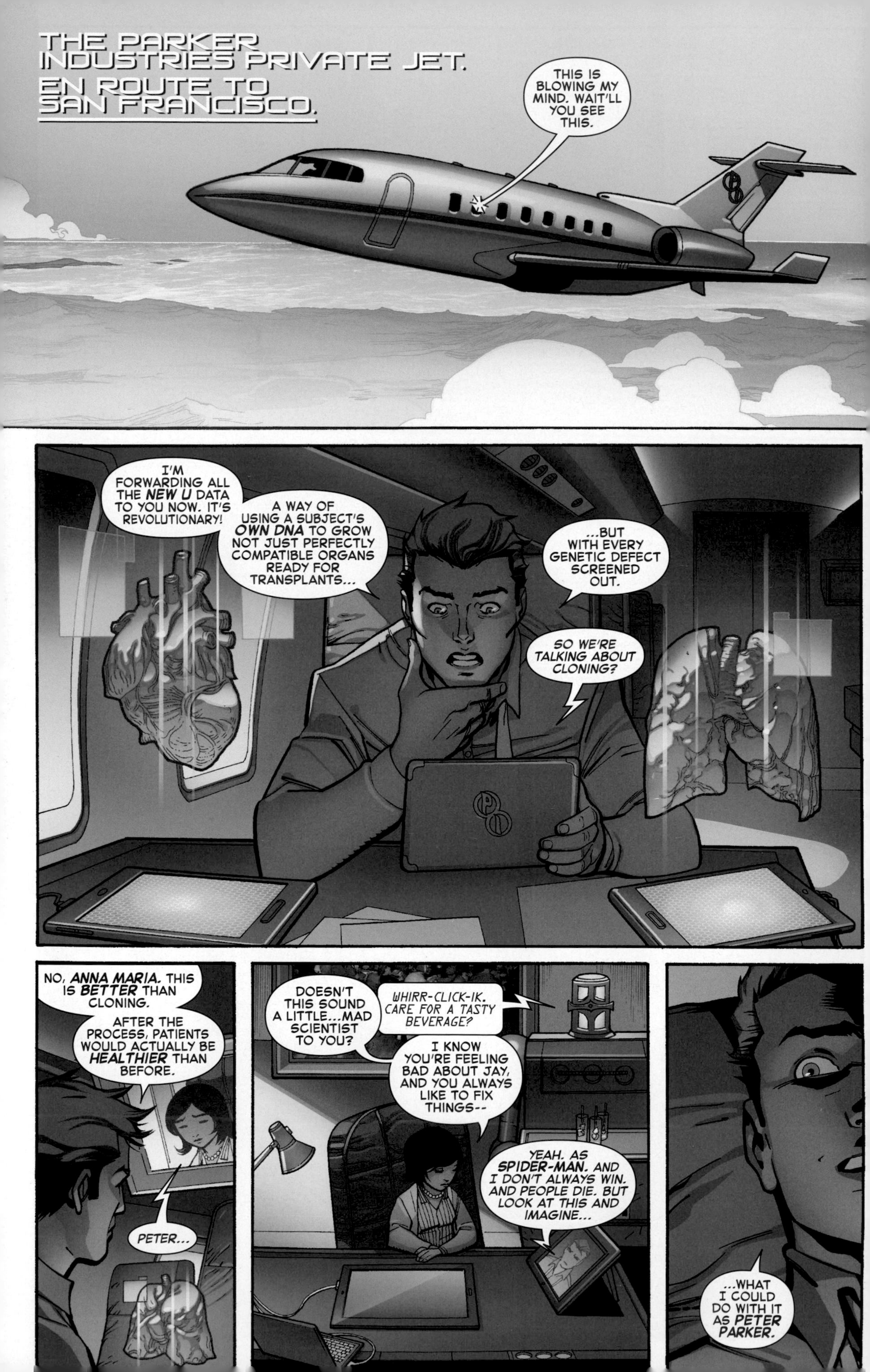
THE PARKER INDUSTRIES PRIVATE JET.
EN ROUTE TO SAN FRANCISCO.
THIS IS BLOWING MY MIND. WAIT'LL YOU SEE THIS.
I'M FORWARDING ALL THE NEW U DATA TO YOU NOW. IT'S REVOLUTIONARY!
A WAY OF USING A SUBJECT'S OWN DNA TO GROW NOT JUST PERFECTLY COMPATIBLE ORGANS READY FOR TRANSPLANTS...
...BUT WITH EVERY GENETIC DEFECT SCREENED OUT.
SO WE'RE TALKING ABOUT CLONING?
NO, ANNA MARIA. THIS IS BETTER THAN CLONING.
AFTER THE PROCESS, PATIENTS WOULD ACTUALLY BE HEALTHIER THAN BEFORE.
PETER...
DOESN'T THIS SOUND A LITTLE...MAD SCIENTIST TO YOU?
WHIRR-CLICK-IK. CARE FOR A TASTY BEVERAGE?
I KNOW YOU'RE FEELING BAD ABOUT JAY, AND YOU ALWAYS LIKE TO FIX THINGS--
YEAH. AS SPIDER-MAN. AND I DON'T ALWAYS WIN. AND PEOPLE DIE. BUT LOOK AT THIS AND IMAGINE...
...WHAT I COULD DO WITH IT AS PETER PARKER.

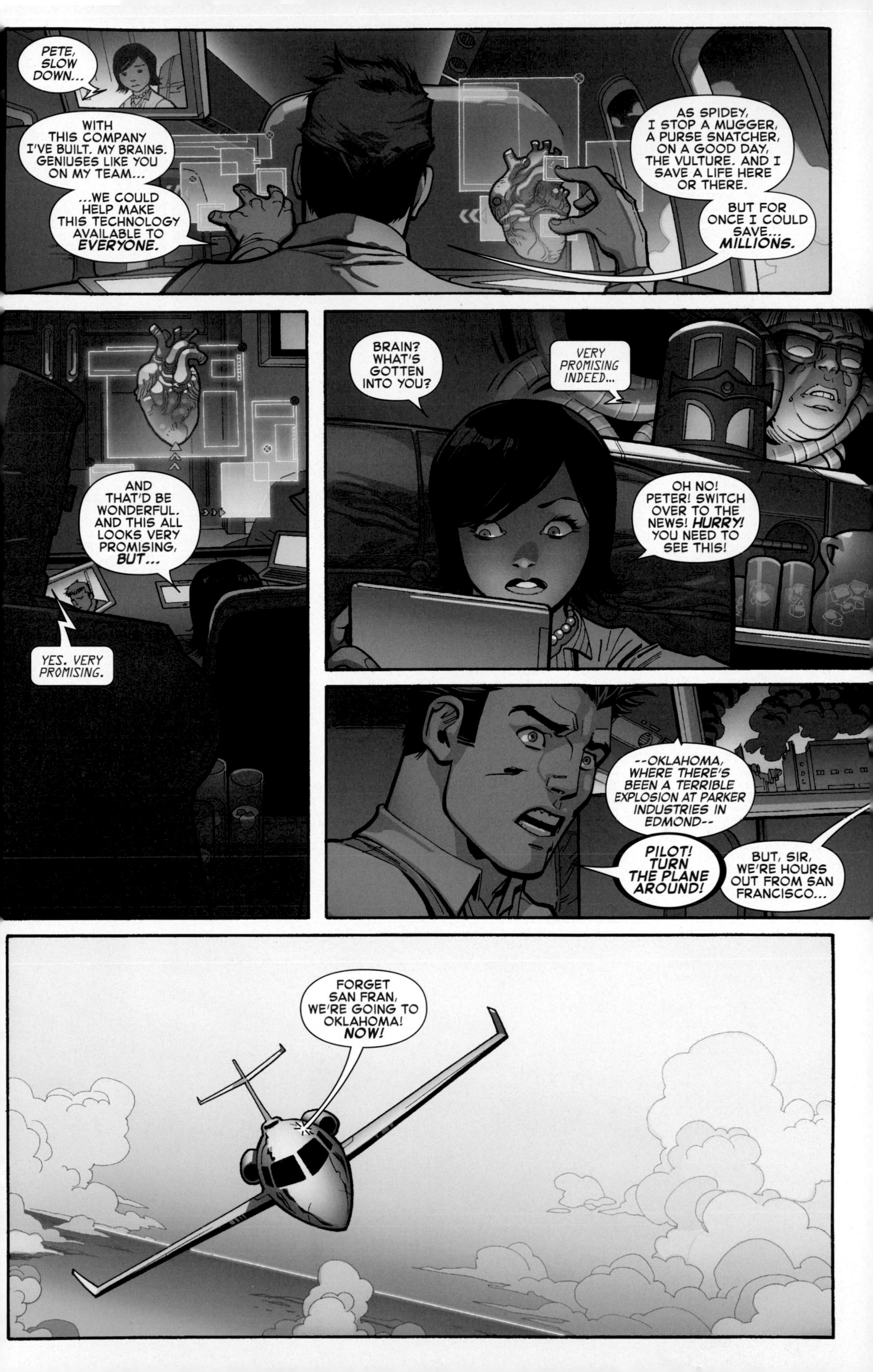
PETE, SLOW DOWN...
WITH THIS COMPANY I'VE BUILT. MY BRAINS. GENIUSES LIKE YOU ON MY TEAM...
...WE COULD HELP MAKE THIS TECHNOLOGY AVAILABLE TO EVERYONE.
AS SPIDEY, I STOP A MUGGER, A PURSE SNATCHER, ON A GOOD DAY, THE VULTURE. AND I SAVE A LIFE HERE OR THERE.
BUT FOR ONCE I COULD SAVE... MILLIONS.
AND THAT'D BE WONDERFUL. AND THIS ALL LOOKS VERY PROMISING, BUT...
YES. VERY PROMISING.
BRAIN? WHAT'S GOTTEN INTO YOU?
VERY PROMISING INDEED...
OH NO! PETER! SWITCH OVER TO THE NEWS! HURRY! YOU NEED TO SEE THIS!
--OKLAHOMA, WHERE THERE'S BEEN A TERRIBLE EXPLOSION AT PARKER INDUSTRIES IN EDMOND--
PILOT! TURN THE PLANE AROUND!
BUT, SIR, WE'RE HOURS OUT FROM SAN FRANCISCO...
FORGET SAN FRAN, WE'RE GOING TO OKLAHOMA! NOW!

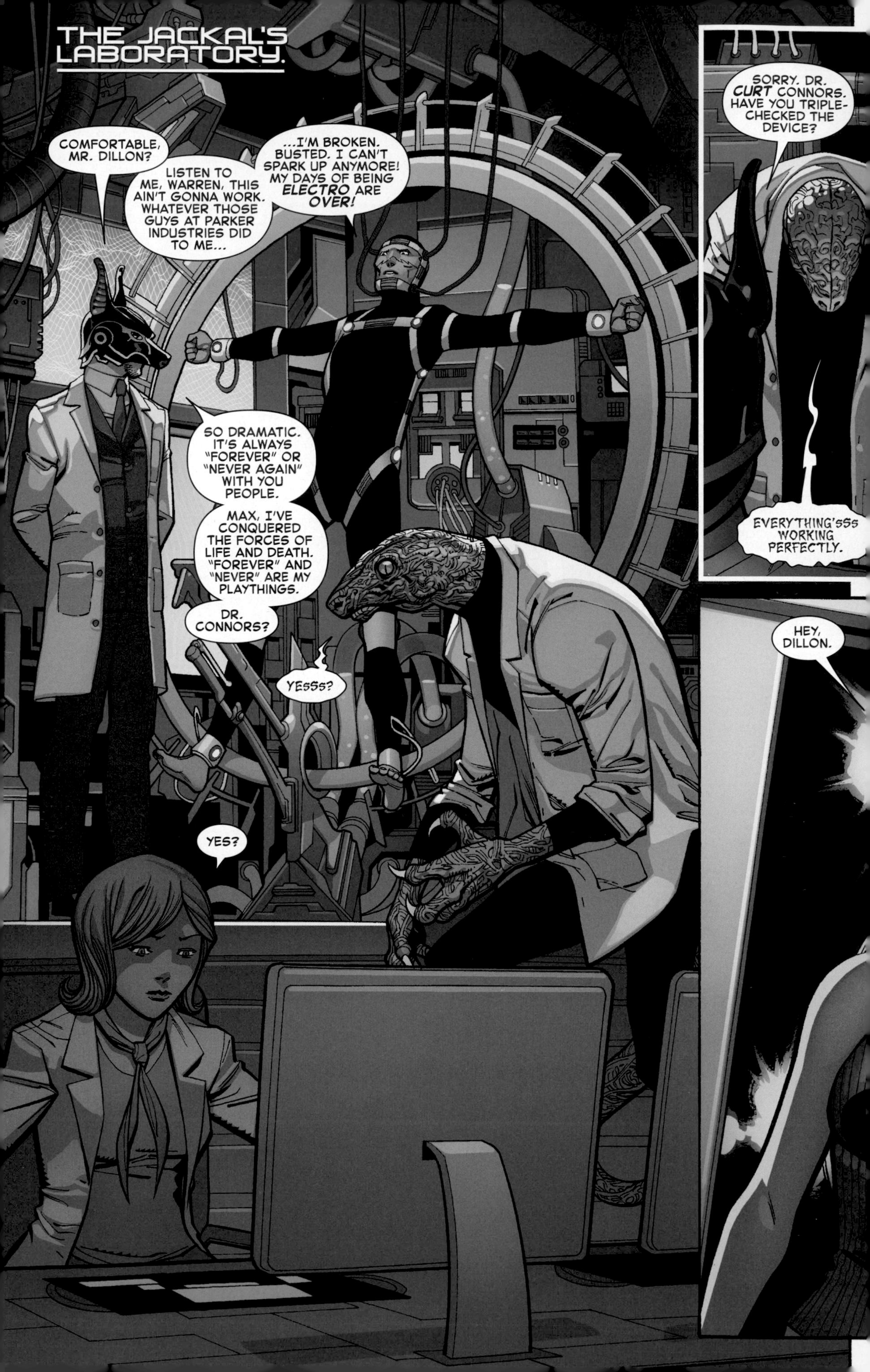
THE JACKAL'S LABORATORY.
COMFORTABLE, MR. DILLON?
LISTEN TO ME, WARREN, THIS AIN'T GONNA WORK. WHATEVER THOSE GUYS AT PARKER INDUSTRIES DID TO ME...
...I'M BROKEN. BUSTED. I CAN'T SPARK UP ANYMORE! MY DAYS OF BEING ELECTRO ARE OVER!
SO DRAMATIC. IT'S ALWAYS "FOREVER" OR "NEVER AGAIN" WITH YOU PEOPLE.
MAX, I'VE CONQUERED THE FORCES OF LIFE AND DEATH. "FOREVER" AND "NEVER" ARE MY PLAYTHINGS.
DR. CONNORS?
YESSS?
YES?
SORRY. DR. CURT CONNORS. HAVE YOU TRIPLE-CHECKED THE DEVICE?
EVERYTHING'SSS WORKING PERFECTLY.
HEY, DILLON.

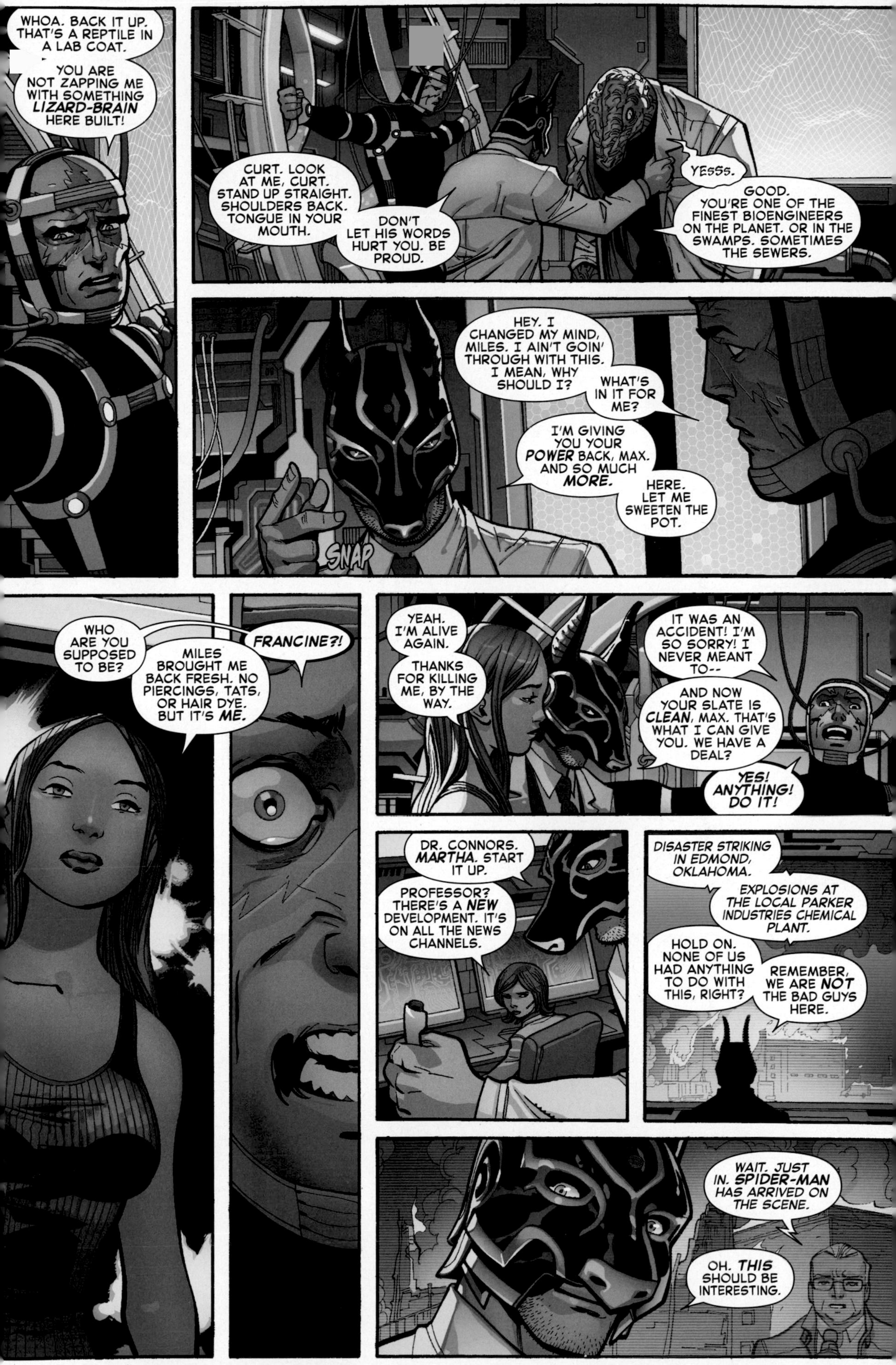
WHOA. BACK IT UP. THAT'S A REPTILE IN A LAB COAT.
YOU ARE NOT ZAPPING ME WITH SOMETHING LIZARD-BRAIN HERE BUILT!
CURT. LOOK AT ME, CURT. STAND UP STRAIGHT. SHOULDERS BACK. TONGUE IN YOUR MOUTH.
DON'T LET HIS WORDS HURT YOU. BE PROUD.
YESSS.
GOOD. YOU'RE ONE OF THE FINEST BIOENGINEERS ON THE PLANET. OR IN THE SWAMPS. SOMETIMES THE SEWERS.
HEY. I CHANGED MY MIND, MILES. I AIN'T GOIN' THROUGH WITH THIS. I MEAN, WHY SHOULD I?
WHAT'S IN IT FOR ME?
I'M GIVING YOU YOUR POWER BACK, MAX. AND SO MUCH MORE.
HERE. LET ME SWEETEN THE POT.
SNAP
WHO ARE YOU SUPPOSED TO BE?
FRANCINE?!
MILES BROUGHT ME BACK FRESH. NO PIERCINGS, TATS, OR HAIR DYE. BUT IT'S ME.
YEAH. I'M ALIVE AGAIN.
THANKS FOR KILLING ME, BY THE WAY.
IT WAS AN ACCIDENT! I'M SO SORRY! I NEVER MEANT TO--
AND NOW YOUR SLATE IS CLEAN, MAX. THAT'S WHAT I CAN GIVE YOU. WE HAVE A DEAL?
YES! ANYTHING! DO IT!
DR. CONNORS. MARTHA. START IT UP.
PROFESSOR? THERE'S A NEW DEVELOPMENT. IT'S ON ALL THE NEWS CHANNELS.
DISASTER STRIKING IN EDMOND, OKLAHOMA.
EXPLOSIONS AT THE LOCAL PARKER INDUSTRIES CHEMICAL PLANT.
HOLD ON. NONE OF US HAD ANYTHING TO DO WITH THIS, RIGHT?
REMEMBER, WE ARE NOT THE BAD GUYS HERE.
WAIT. JUST IN. SPIDER-MAN HAS ARRIVED ON THE SCENE.
OH. THIS SHOULD BE INTERESTING.

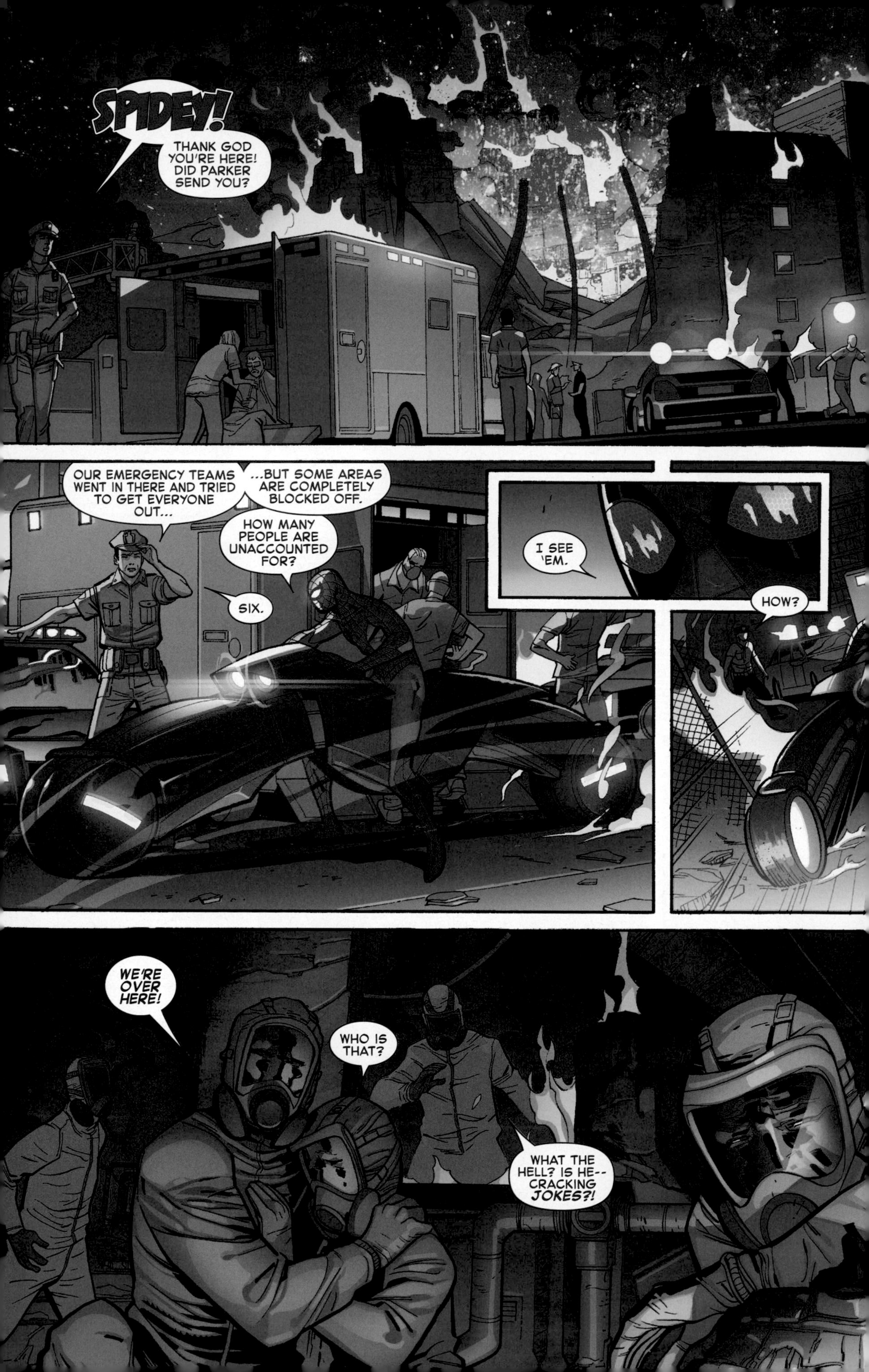
SPIDEY!
THANK GOD YOU'RE HERE! DID PARKER SEND YOU?
OUR EMERGENCY TEAMS WENT IN THERE AND TRIED TO GET EVERYONE OUT...
...BUT SOME AREAS ARE COMPLETELY BLOCKED OFF.
HOW MANY PEOPLE ARE UNACCOUNTED FOR?
SIX.
I SEE 'EM.
HOW?
WE'RE OVER HERE!
WHO IS THAT?
WHAT THE HELL? IS HE-- CRACKING JOKES?!

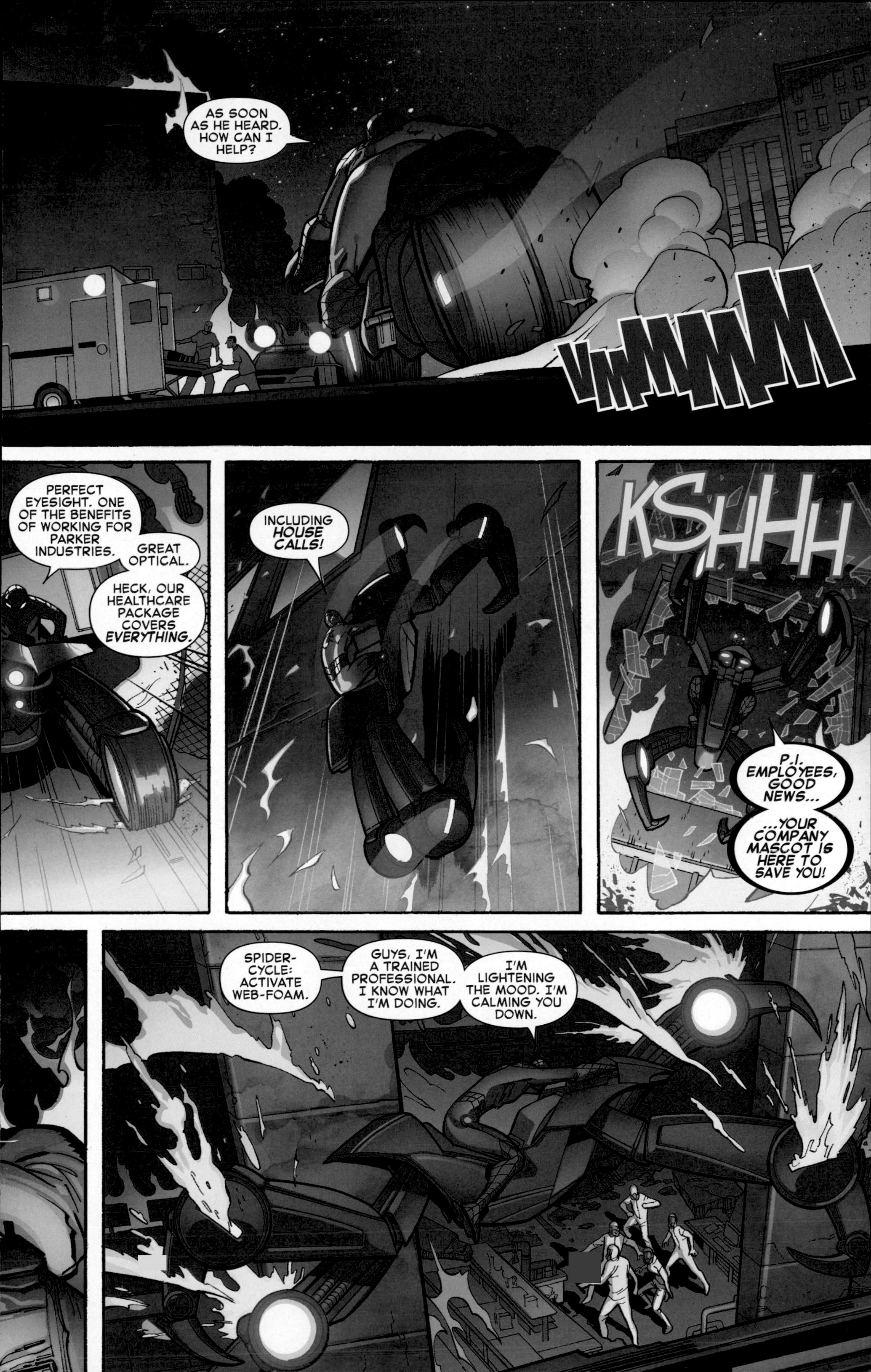

AS SOON AS HE HEARD. HOW CAN I HELP?
VMMMMMM
PERFECT EYESIGHT. ONE OF THE BENEFITS OF WORKING FOR PARKER INDUSTRIES.
GREAT OPTICAL.
HECK, OUR HEALTHCARE PACKAGE COVERS *EVERYTHING.*
INCLUDING *HOUSE CALLS!*
KSHHH
P.I. EMPLOYEES, GOOD NEWS...
...YOUR COMPANY MASCOT IS HERE TO SAVE YOU!
SPIDER-CYCLE: ACTIVATE WEB-FOAM.
GUYS, I'M A TRAINED PROFESSIONAL. I KNOW WHAT I'M DOING.
I'M LIGHTENING THE MOOD. I'M CALMING YOU DOWN.

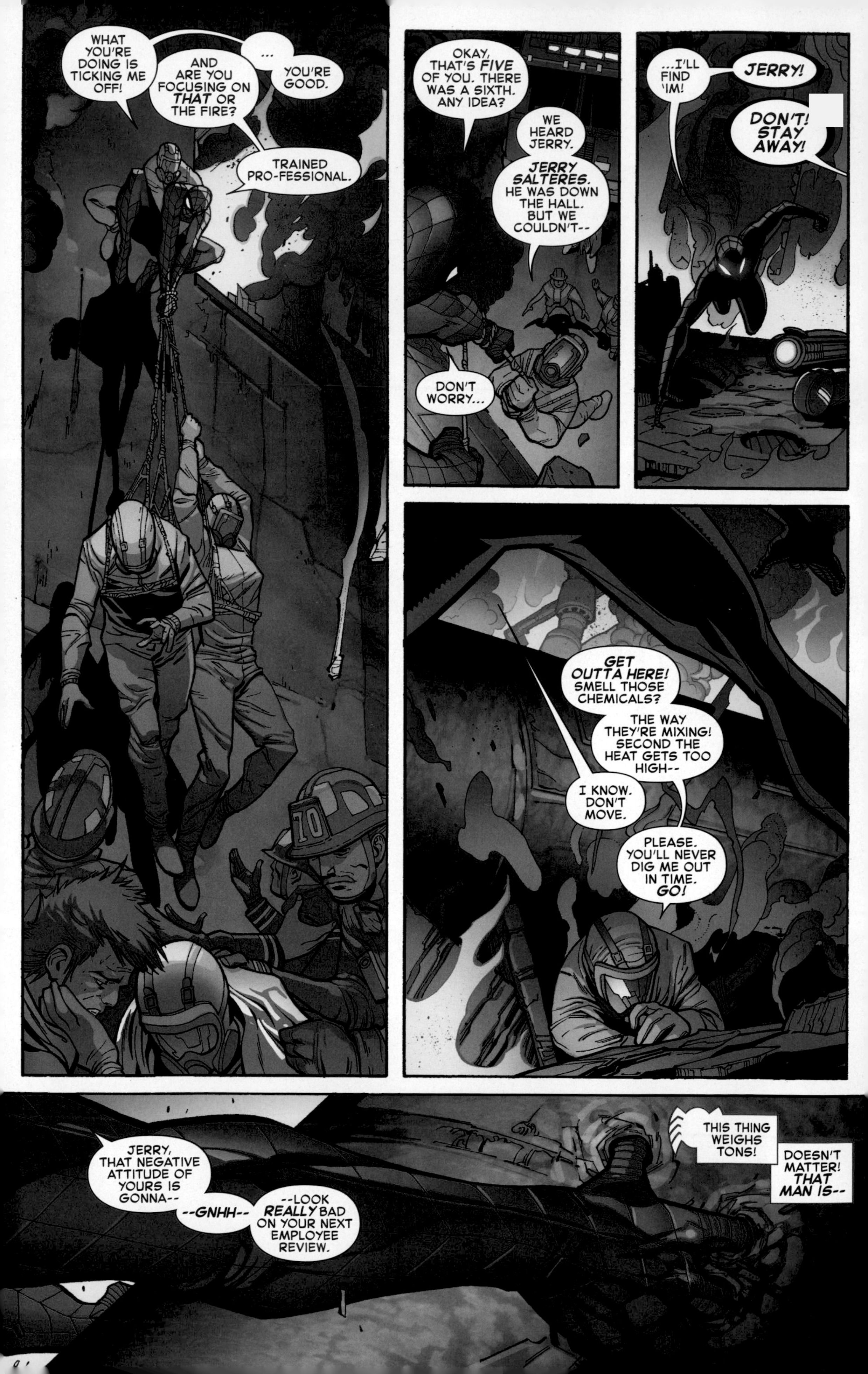
WHAT YOU'RE DOING IS TICKING ME OFF!
...
AND ARE YOU FOCUSING ON THAT OR THE FIRE?
YOU'RE GOOD.
TRAINED PRO-FESSIONAL.
OKAY, THAT'S FIVE OF YOU. THERE WAS A SIXTH. ANY IDEA?
WE HEARD JERRY.
JERRY SALTERES. HE WAS DOWN THE HALL. BUT WE COULDN'T--
DON'T WORRY...
...I'LL FIND 'IM!
JERRY!
DON'T! STAY AWAY!
GET OUTTA HERE! SMELL THOSE CHEMICALS?
THE WAY THEY'RE MIXING! SECOND THE HEAT GETS TOO HIGH--
I KNOW. DON'T MOVE.
PLEASE. YOU'LL NEVER DIG ME OUT IN TIME. GO!
JERRY, THAT NEGATIVE ATTITUDE OF YOURS IS GONNA--
--GNHH--
--LOOK REALLY BAD ON YOUR NEXT EMPLOYEE REVIEW.
THIS THING WEIGHS TONS!
DOESN'T MATTER! THAT MAN IS--

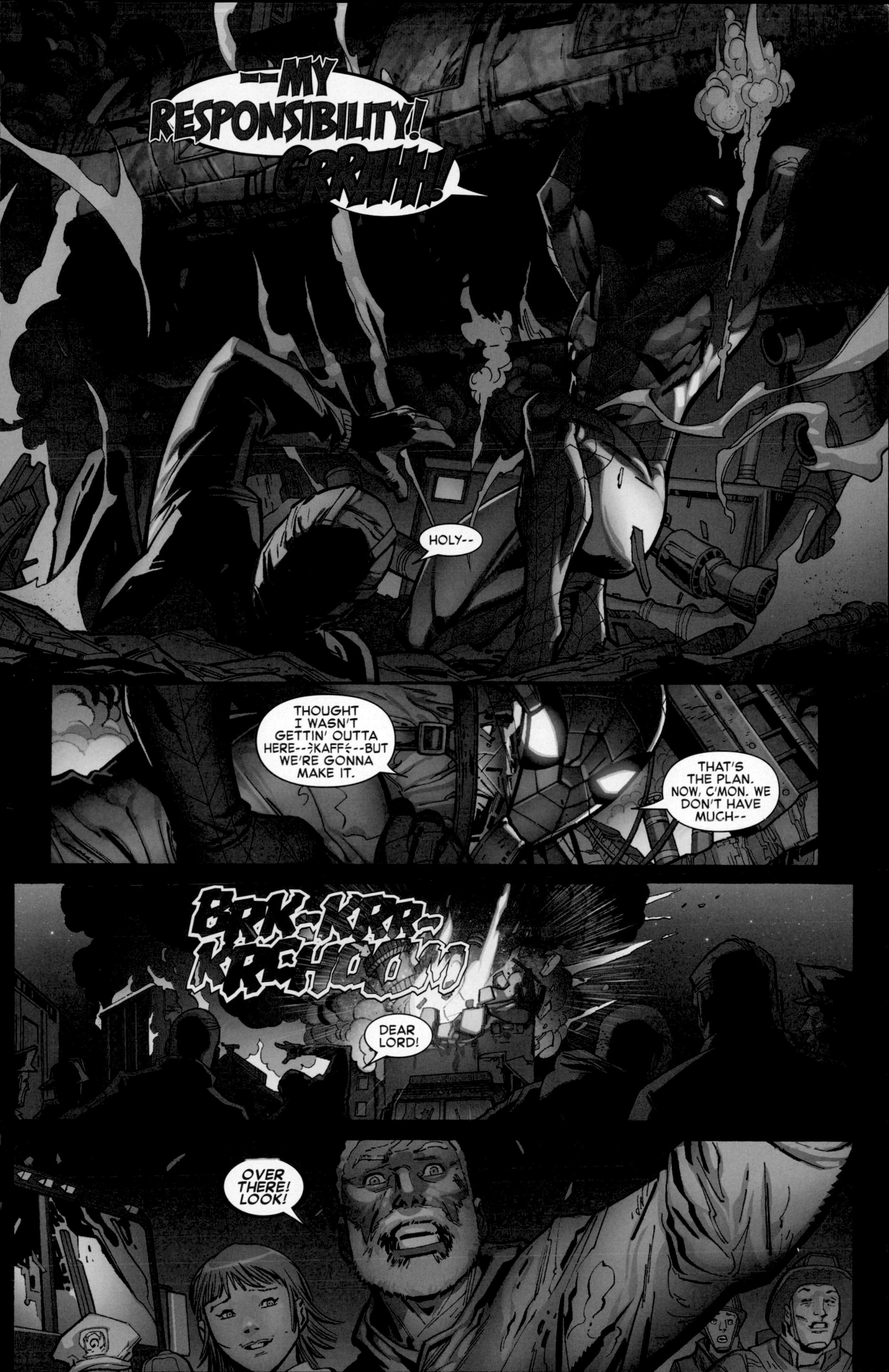
--MY RESPONSIBILITY! GRRAHH!
HOLY--
THOUGHT I WASN'T GETTIN' OUTTA HERE--KAFF--BUT WE'RE GONNA MAKE IT.
THAT'S THE PLAN. NOW, C'MON. WE DON'T HAVE MUCH--
BRK-KRR-KRCHOOM
DEAR LORD!
OVER THERE! LOOK!

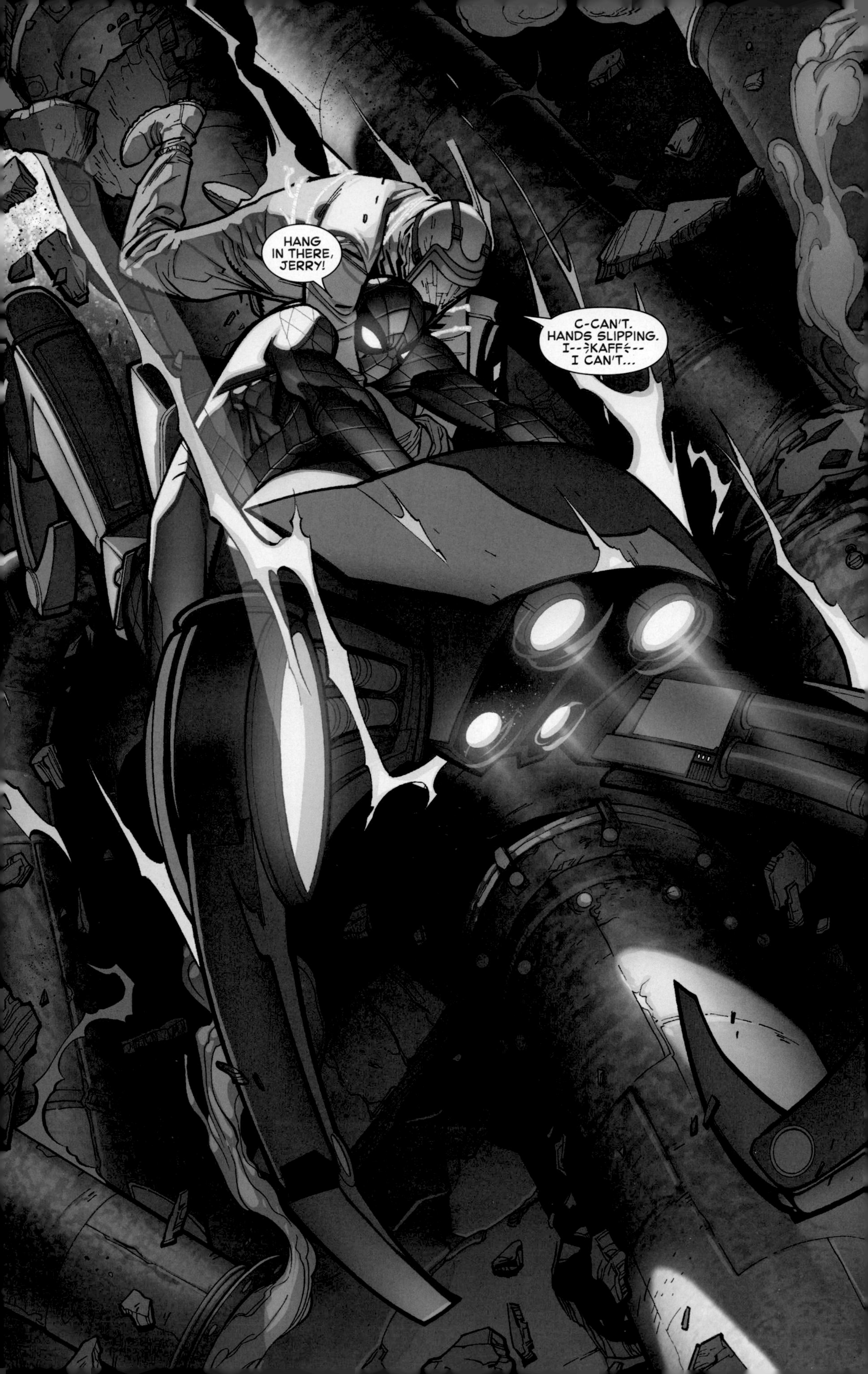
HANG IN THERE, JERRY!
C-CAN'T. HANDS SLIPPING. I--KAFF--I CAN'T...

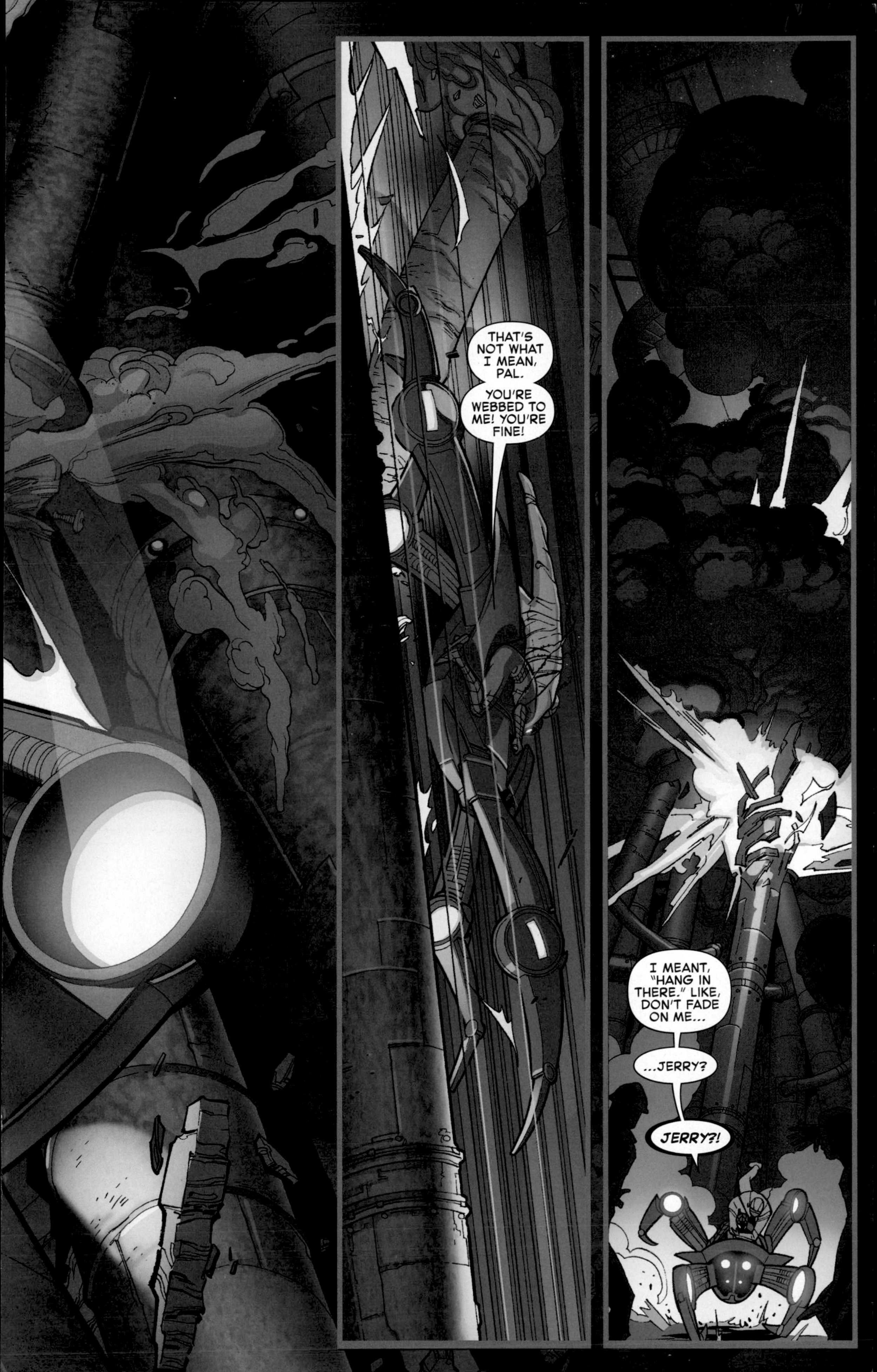
THAT'S NOT WHAT I MEAN, PAL.
YOU'RE WEBBED TO ME! YOU'RE FINE!
I MEANT, "HANG IN THERE." LIKE, DON'T FADE ON ME...
...JERRY?
JERRY?!

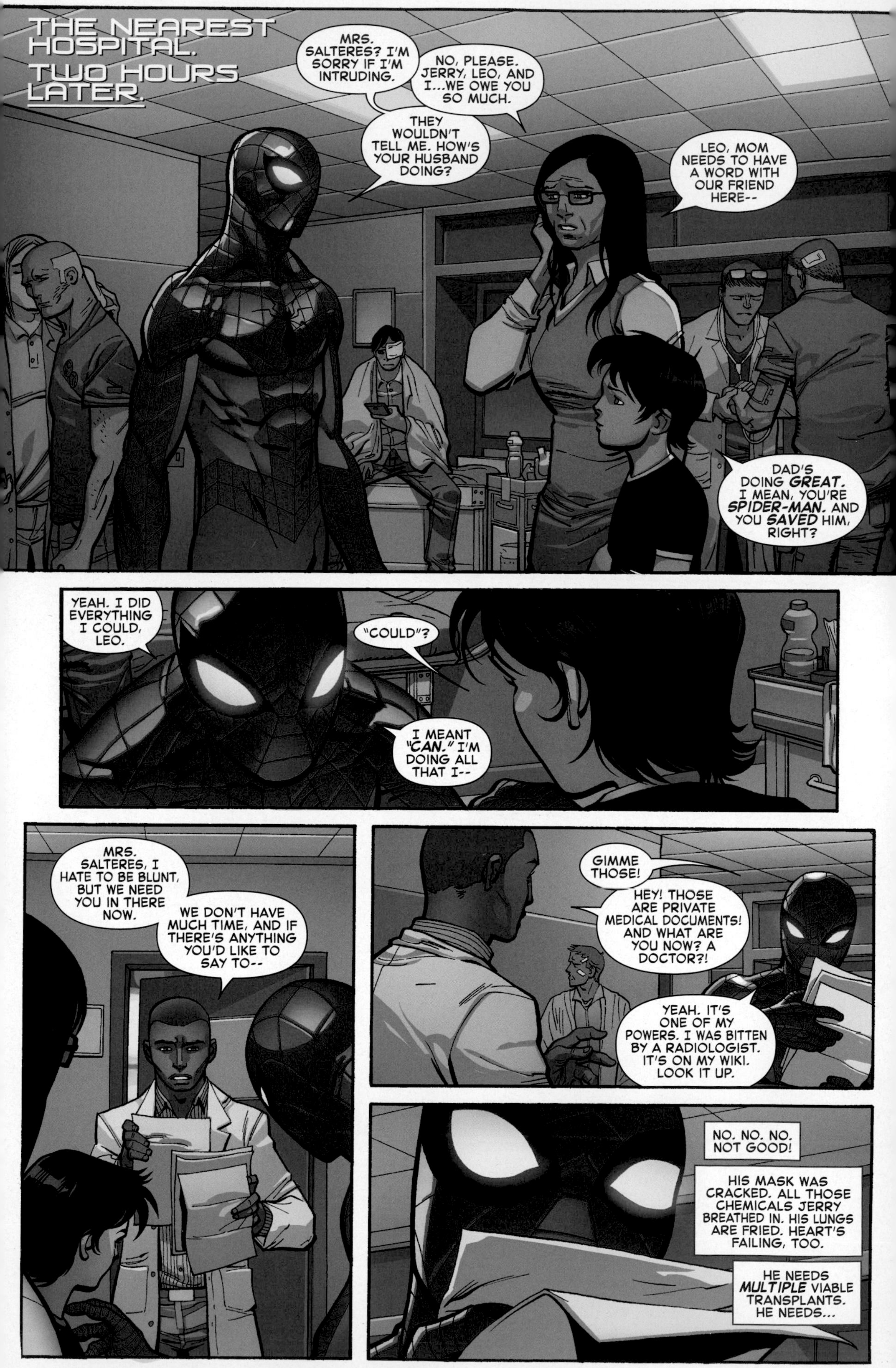
THE NEAREST HOSPITAL. TWO HOURS LATER.
MRS. SALTERES? I'M SORRY IF I'M INTRUDING.
THEY WOULDN'T TELL ME. HOW'S YOUR HUSBAND DOING?
NO, PLEASE. JERRY, LEO, AND I...WE OWE YOU SO MUCH.
LEO, MOM NEEDS TO HAVE A WORD WITH OUR FRIEND HERE--
DAD'S DOING GREAT. I MEAN, YOU'RE SPIDER-MAN. AND YOU SAVED HIM, RIGHT?
YEAH. I DID EVERYTHING I COULD, LEO.
"COULD"?
I MEANT "CAN." I'M DOING ALL THAT I--
MRS. SALTERES, I HATE TO BE BLUNT, BUT WE NEED YOU IN THERE NOW.
WE DON'T HAVE MUCH TIME, AND IF THERE'S ANYTHING YOU'D LIKE TO SAY TO--
GIMME THOSE!
HEY! THOSE ARE PRIVATE MEDICAL DOCUMENTS! AND WHAT ARE YOU NOW? A DOCTOR?!
YEAH. IT'S ONE OF MY POWERS. I WAS BITTEN BY A RADIOLOGIST. IT'S ON MY WIKI. LOOK IT UP.
NO. NO. NO. NOT GOOD!
HIS MASK WAS CRACKED. ALL THOSE CHEMICALS JERRY BREATHED IN. HIS LUNGS ARE FRIED. HEART'S FAILING, TOO.
HE NEEDS MULTIPLE VIABLE TRANSPLANTS. HE NEEDS...

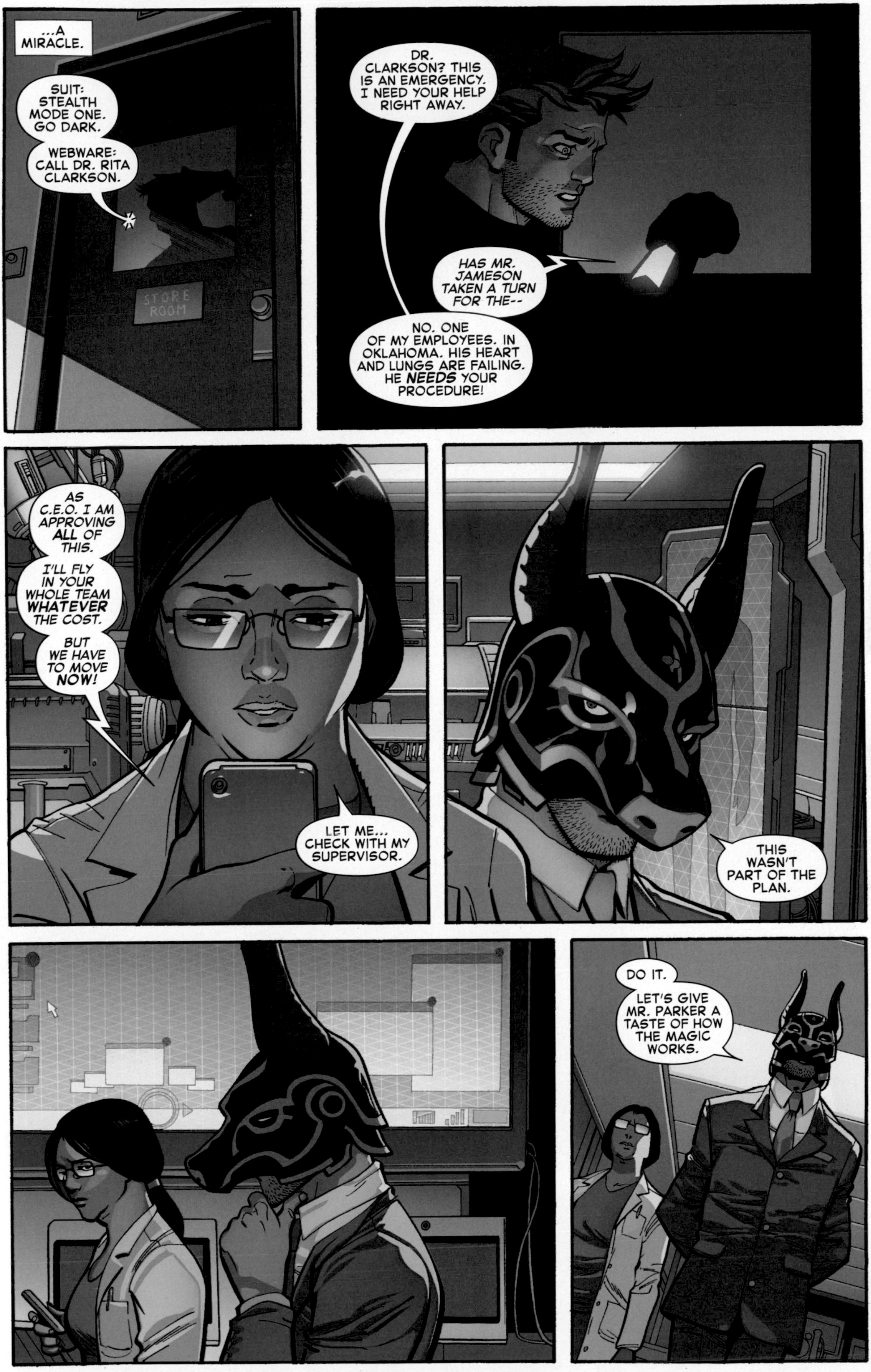
...A MIRACLE.
SUIT: STEALTH MODE ONE. GO DARK.
WEBWARE: CALL DR. RITA CLARKSON.
STORE ROOM
DR. CLARKSON? THIS IS AN EMERGENCY. I NEED YOUR HELP RIGHT AWAY.
HAS MR. JAMESON TAKEN A TURN FOR THE--
NO. ONE OF MY EMPLOYEES. IN OKLAHOMA. HIS HEART AND LUNGS ARE FAILING. HE **NEEDS** YOUR PROCEDURE!
AS C.E.O. I AM APPROVING **ALL** OF THIS.
I'LL FLY IN YOUR WHOLE TEAM **WHATEVER** THE COST.
BUT WE HAVE TO MOVE **NOW!**
LET ME... CHECK WITH MY SUPERVISOR.
THIS WASN'T PART OF THE PLAN.
DO IT.
LET'S GIVE MR. PARKER A TASTE OF HOW THE MAGIC WORKS.

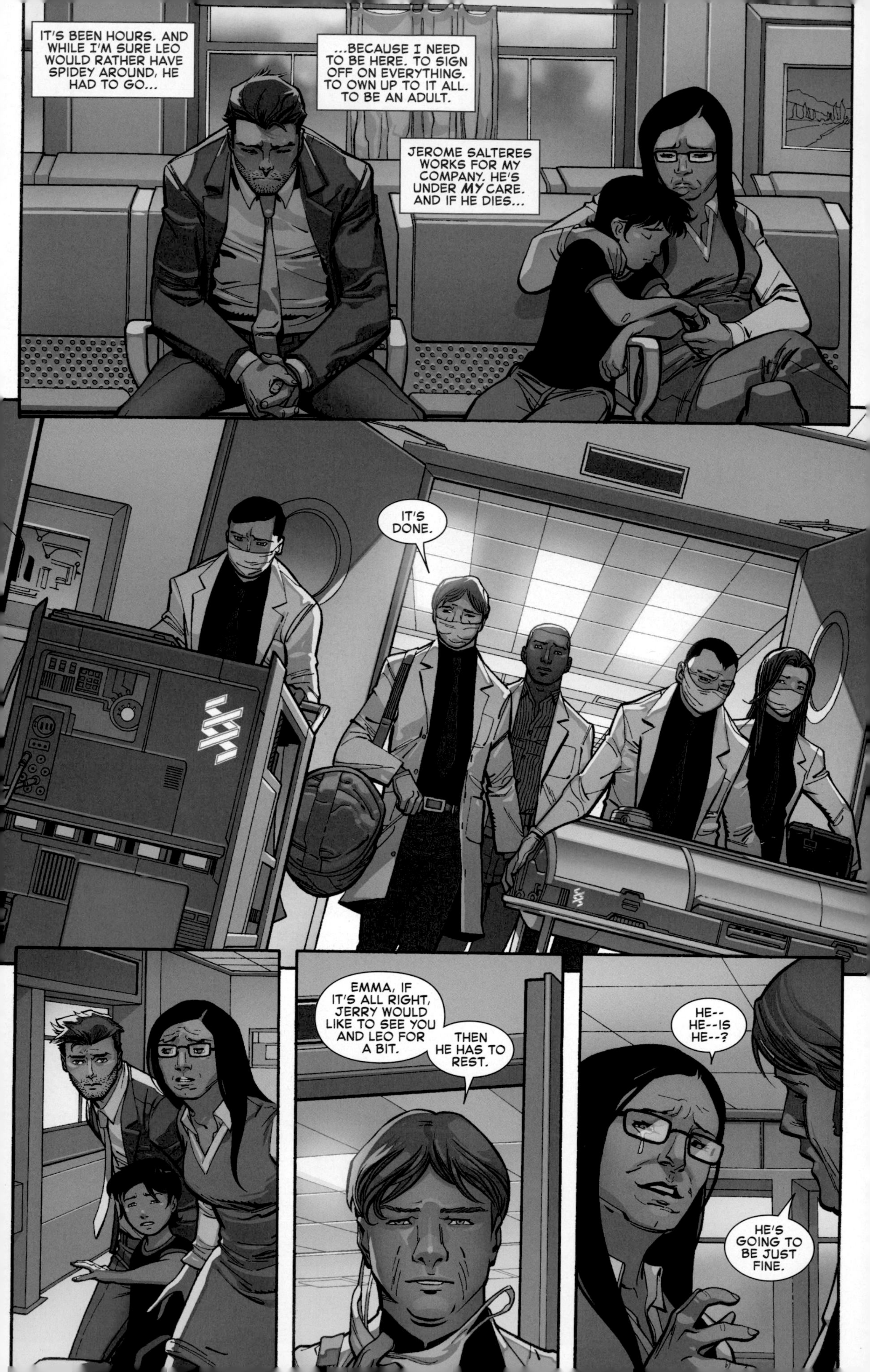
IT'S BEEN HOURS. AND WHILE I'M SURE LEO WOULD RATHER HAVE SPIDEY AROUND, HE HAD TO GO...
...BECAUSE I NEED TO BE HERE. TO SIGN OFF ON EVERYTHING. TO OWN UP TO IT ALL. TO BE AN ADULT.
JEROME SALTERES WORKS FOR MY COMPANY. HE'S UNDER MY CARE. AND IF HE DIES...
IT'S DONE.
EMMA, IF IT'S ALL RIGHT, JERRY WOULD LIKE TO SEE YOU AND LEO FOR A BIT.
THEN HE HAS TO REST.
HE-- HE--IS HE--?
HE'S GOING TO BE JUST FINE.

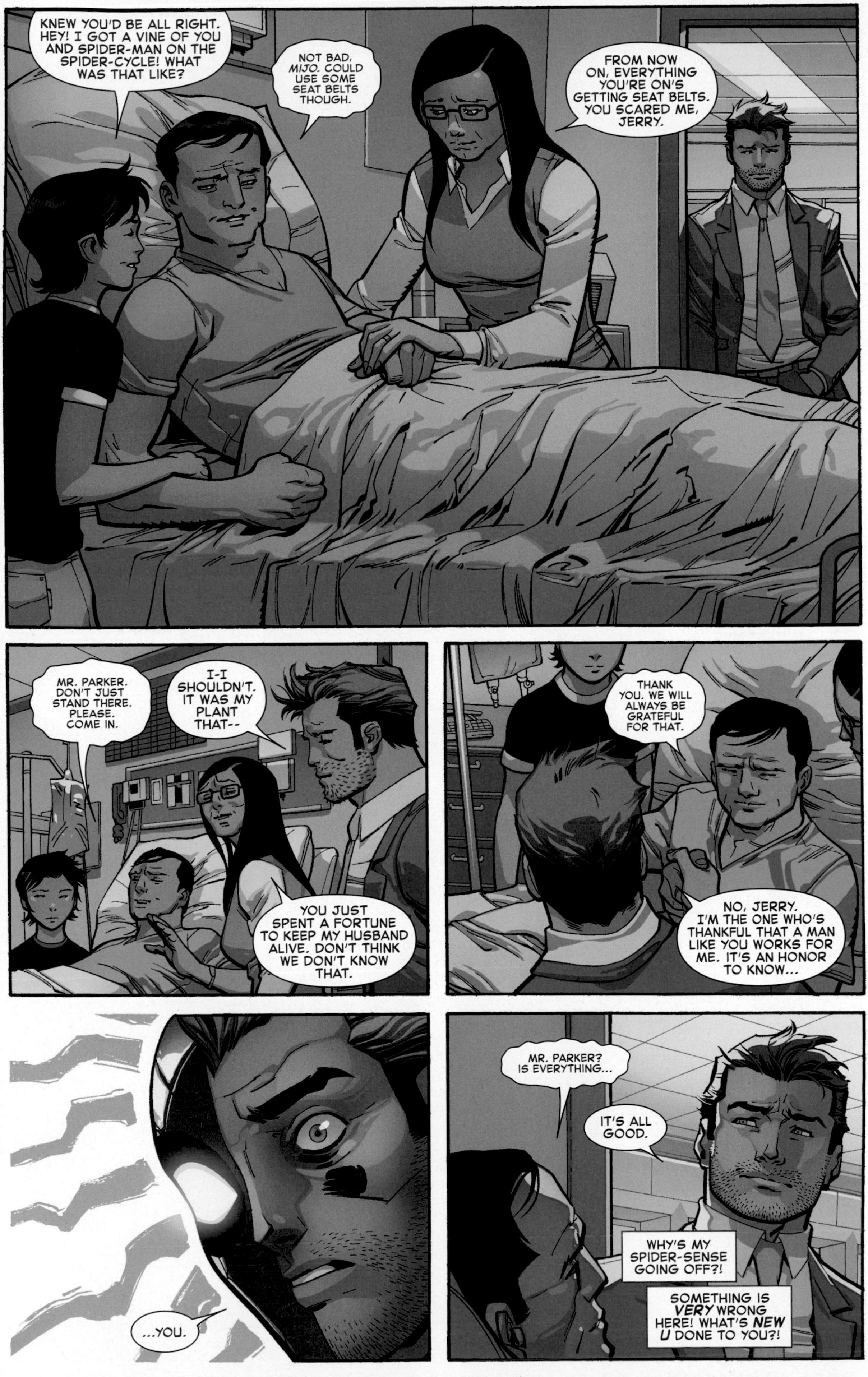
KNEW YOU'D BE ALL RIGHT. HEY! I GOT A VINE OF YOU AND SPIDER-MAN ON THE SPIDER-CYCLE! WHAT WAS THAT LIKE?
NOT BAD, *MIJO.* COULD USE SOME SEAT BELTS THOUGH.
FROM NOW ON, EVERYTHING YOU'RE ON'S GETTING SEAT BELTS. YOU SCARED ME, JERRY.
MR. PARKER. DON'T JUST STAND THERE. PLEASE. COME IN.
I-I SHOULDN'T. IT WAS MY PLANT THAT--
YOU JUST SPENT A FORTUNE TO KEEP MY HUSBAND ALIVE. DON'T THINK WE DON'T KNOW THAT.
THANK YOU. WE WILL ALWAYS BE GRATEFUL FOR THAT.
NO, JERRY. I'M THE ONE WHO'S THANKFUL THAT A MAN LIKE YOU WORKS FOR ME. IT'S AN HONOR TO KNOW...
...YOU.
MR. PARKER? IS EVERYTHING...
IT'S ALL GOOD.
WHY'S MY SPIDER-SENSE GOING OFF?!
SOMETHING IS ***VERY*** WRONG HERE! WHAT'S ***NEW U*** DONE TO YOU?!

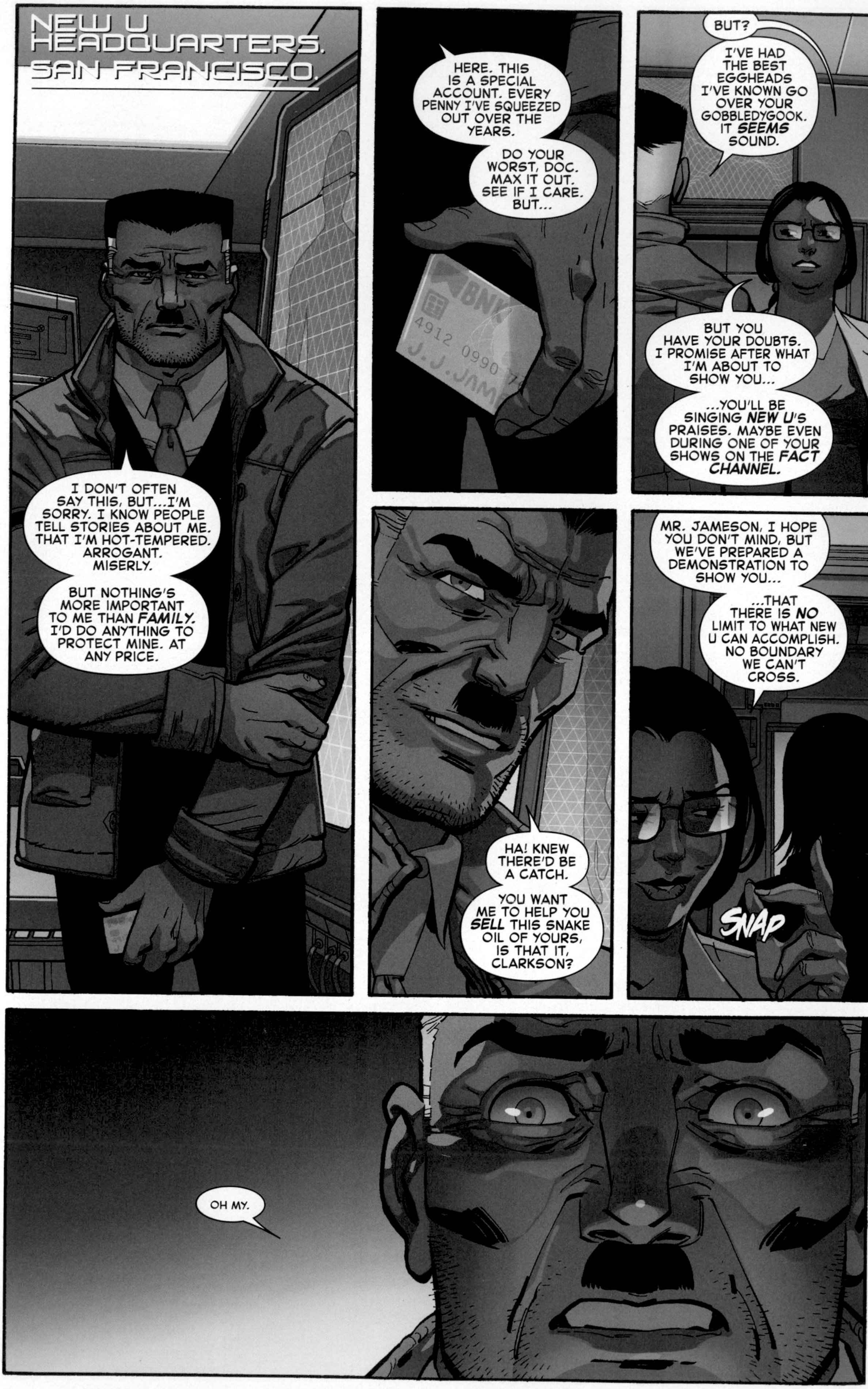
NEW U HEADQUARTERS. SAN FRANCISCO.
I DON'T OFTEN SAY THIS, BUT...I'M SORRY. I KNOW PEOPLE TELL STORIES ABOUT ME. THAT I'M HOT-TEMPERED. ARROGANT. MISERLY.
BUT NOTHING'S MORE IMPORTANT TO ME THAN FAMILY. I'D DO ANYTHING TO PROTECT MINE. AT ANY PRICE.
HERE. THIS IS A SPECIAL ACCOUNT. EVERY PENNY I'VE SQUEEZED OUT OVER THE YEARS.
DO YOUR WORST, DOC. MAX IT OUT. SEE IF I CARE. BUT...
BNK
4912 0990
J.J.JAM
BUT?
I'VE HAD THE BEST EGGHEADS I'VE KNOWN GO OVER YOUR GOBBLEDYGOOK. IT SEEMS SOUND.
BUT YOU HAVE YOUR DOUBTS. I PROMISE AFTER WHAT I'M ABOUT TO SHOW YOU...
...YOU'LL BE SINGING NEW U'S PRAISES. MAYBE EVEN DURING ONE OF YOUR SHOWS ON THE FACT CHANNEL.
HA! KNEW THERE'D BE A CATCH.
YOU WANT ME TO HELP YOU SELL THIS SNAKE OIL OF YOURS, IS THAT IT, CLARKSON?
MR. JAMESON, I HOPE YOU DON'T MIND, BUT WE'VE PREPARED A DEMONSTRATION TO SHOW YOU...
...THAT THERE IS NO LIMIT TO WHAT NEW U CAN ACCOMPLISH. NO BOUNDARY WE CAN'T CROSS.
SNAP
OH MY.

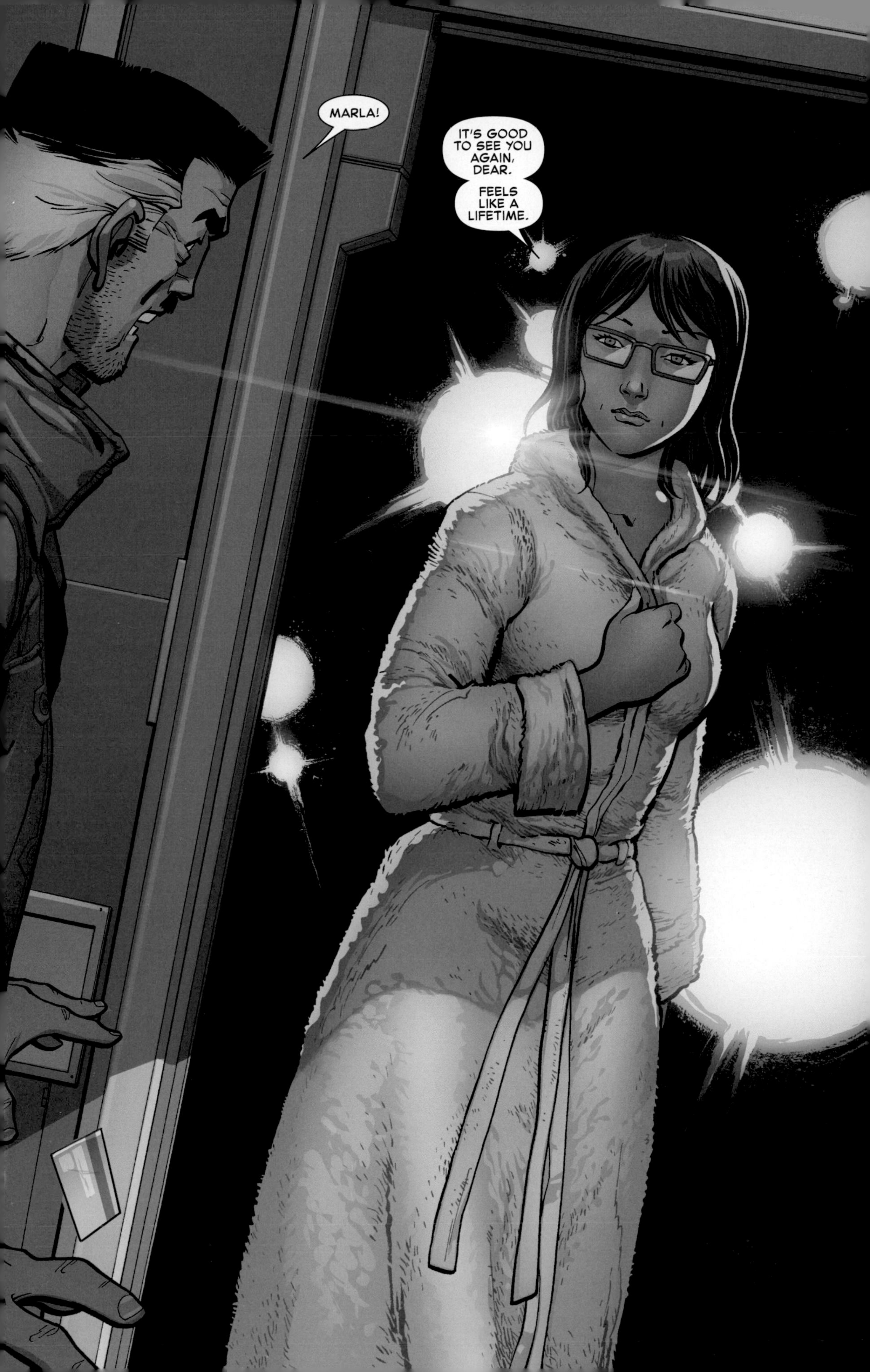
MARLA!
IT'S GOOD TO SEE YOU AGAIN, DEAR.
FEELS LIKE A LIFETIME.

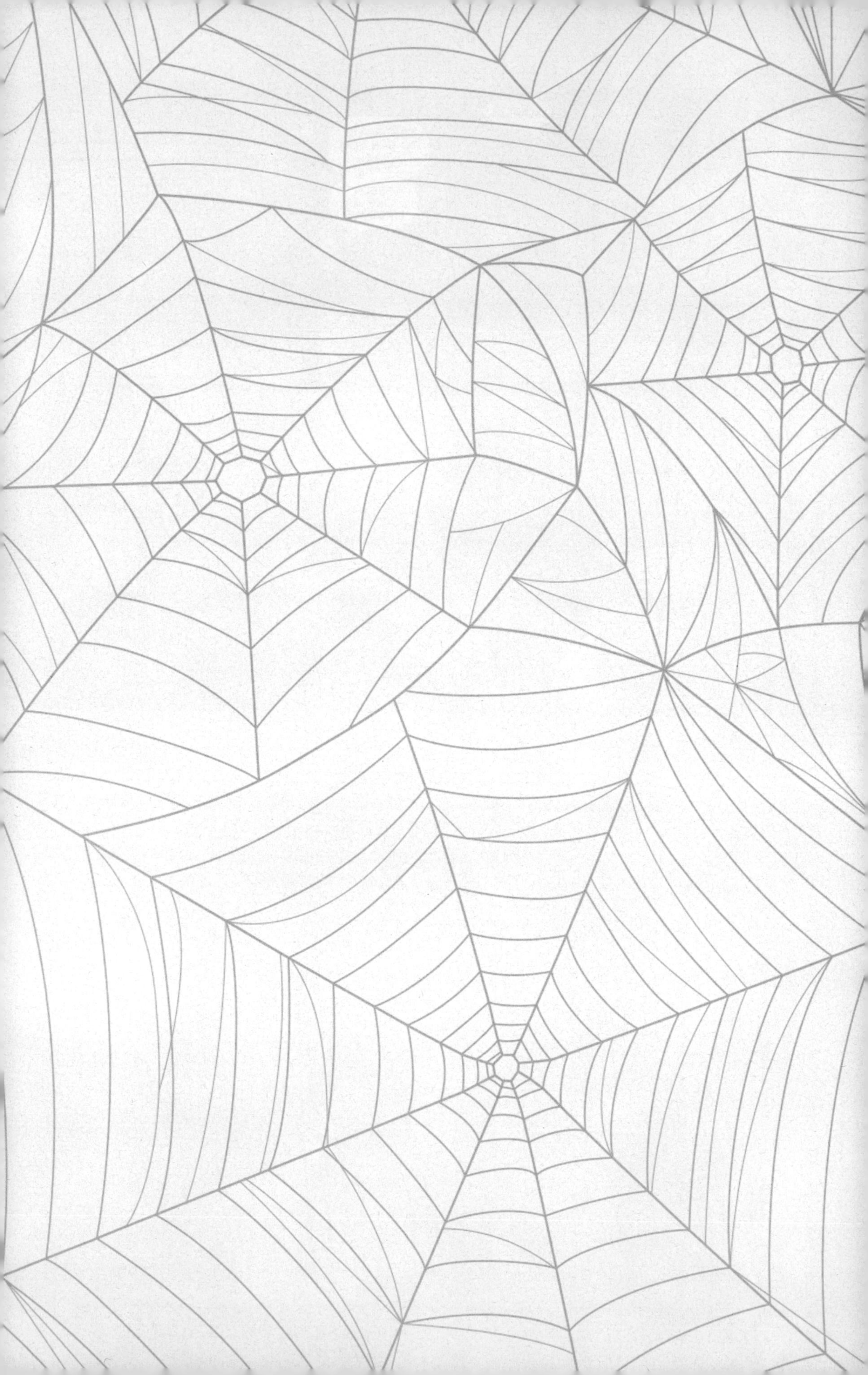

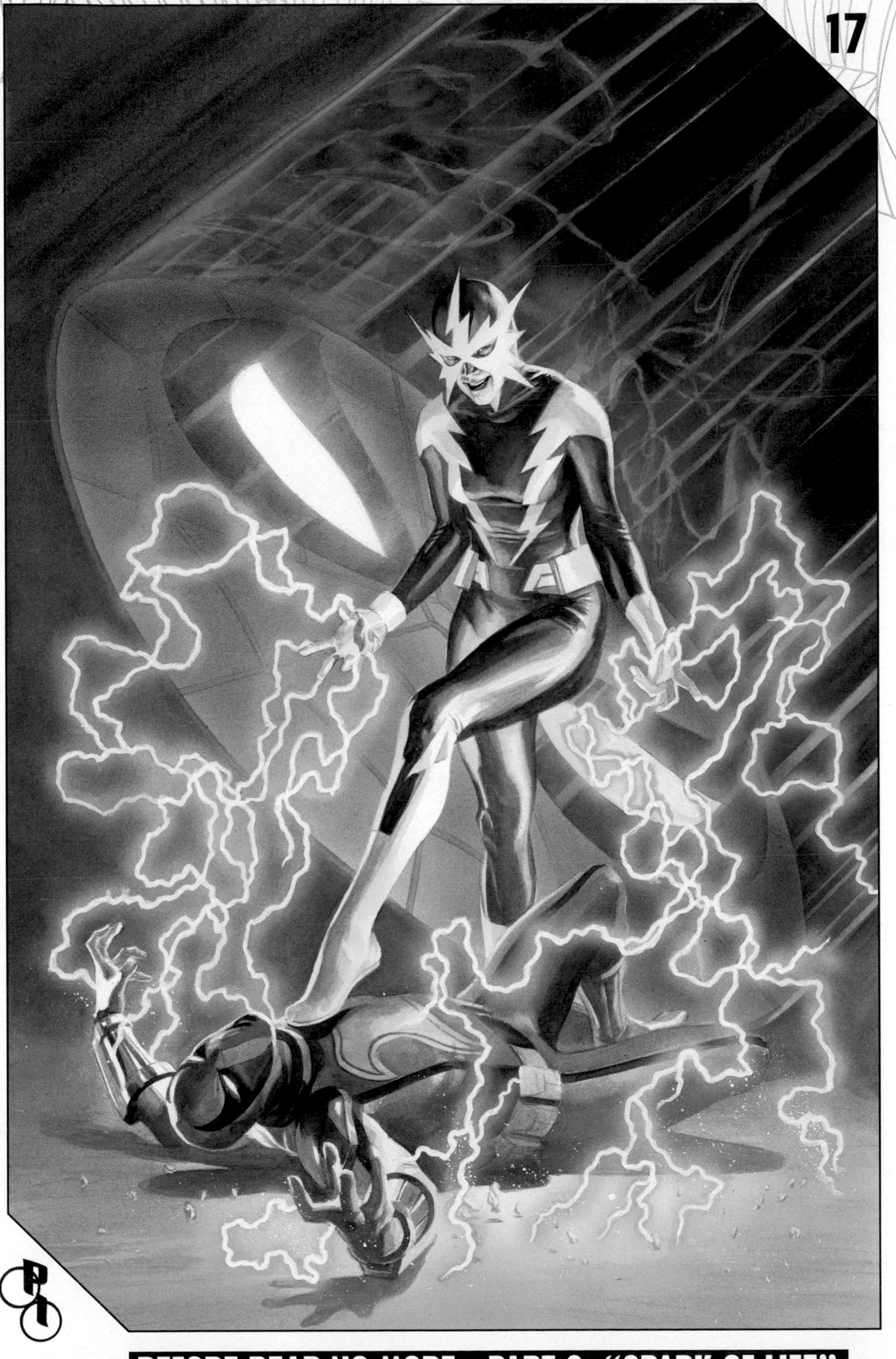

BEFORE DEAD NO MORE - PART 2: "SPARK OF LIFE"

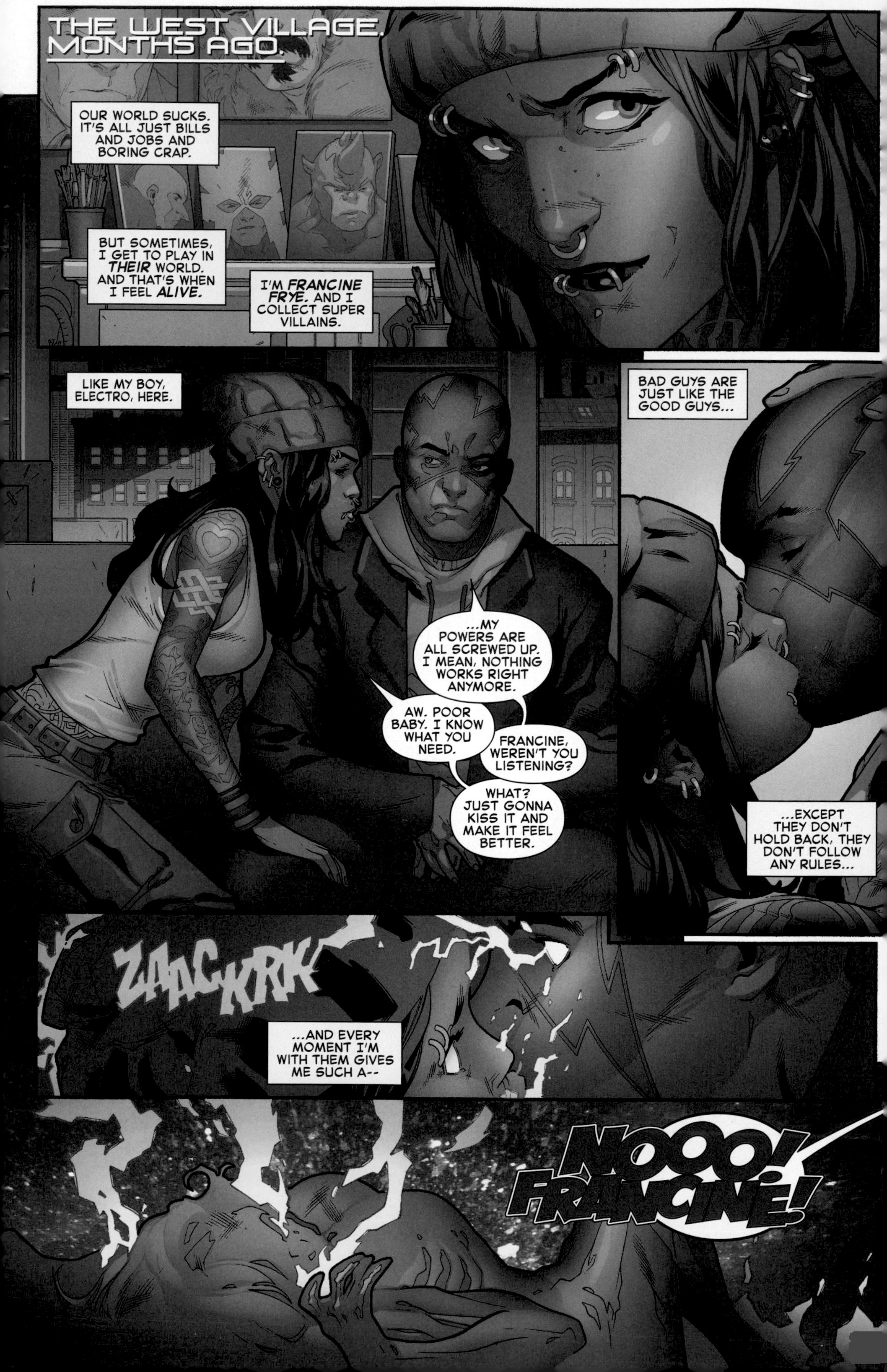
THE WEST VILLAGE. MONTHS AGO.
OUR WORLD SUCKS. IT'S ALL JUST BILLS AND JOBS AND BORING CRAP.
BUT SOMETIMES, I GET TO PLAY IN THEIR WORLD. AND THAT'S WHEN I FEEL ALIVE.
I'M FRANCINE FRYE. AND I COLLECT SUPER VILLAINS.
LIKE MY BOY, ELECTRO, HERE.
...MY POWERS ARE ALL SCREWED UP. I MEAN, NOTHING WORKS RIGHT ANYMORE.
AW. POOR BABY. I KNOW WHAT YOU NEED.
FRANCINE, WEREN'T YOU LISTENING?
WHAT? JUST GONNA KISS IT AND MAKE IT FEEL BETTER.
BAD GUYS ARE JUST LIKE THE GOOD GUYS...
...EXCEPT THEY DON'T HOLD BACK, THEY DON'T FOLLOW ANY RULES...
ZAACKRK
...AND EVERY MOMENT I'M WITH THEM GIVES ME SUCH A--
NOOO! FRANCINE!

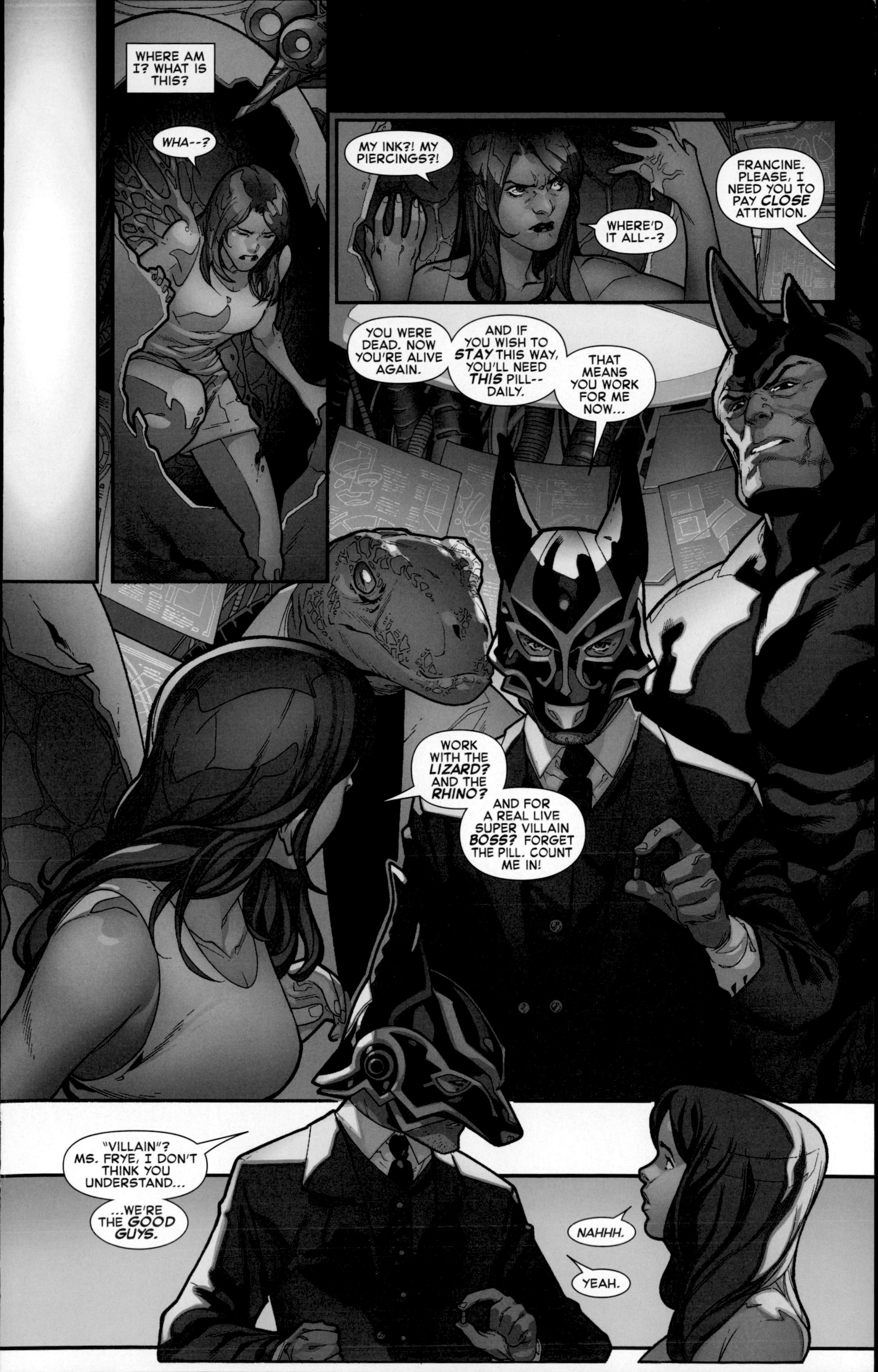
WHERE AM I? WHAT IS THIS?
WHA--?
MY INK?! MY PIERCINGS?!
WHERE'D IT ALL--?
FRANCINE. PLEASE, I NEED YOU TO PAY CLOSE ATTENTION.
YOU WERE DEAD. NOW YOU'RE ALIVE AGAIN.
AND IF YOU WISH TO STAY THIS WAY, YOU'LL NEED THIS PILL-- DAILY.
THAT MEANS YOU WORK FOR ME NOW...
WORK WITH THE LIZARD? AND THE RHINO?
AND FOR A REAL LIVE SUPER VILLAIN BOSS? FORGET THE PILL. COUNT ME IN!
"VILLAIN"? MS. FRYE, I DON'T THINK YOU UNDERSTAND...
...WE'RE THE GOOD GUYS.
NAHHH.
YEAH.

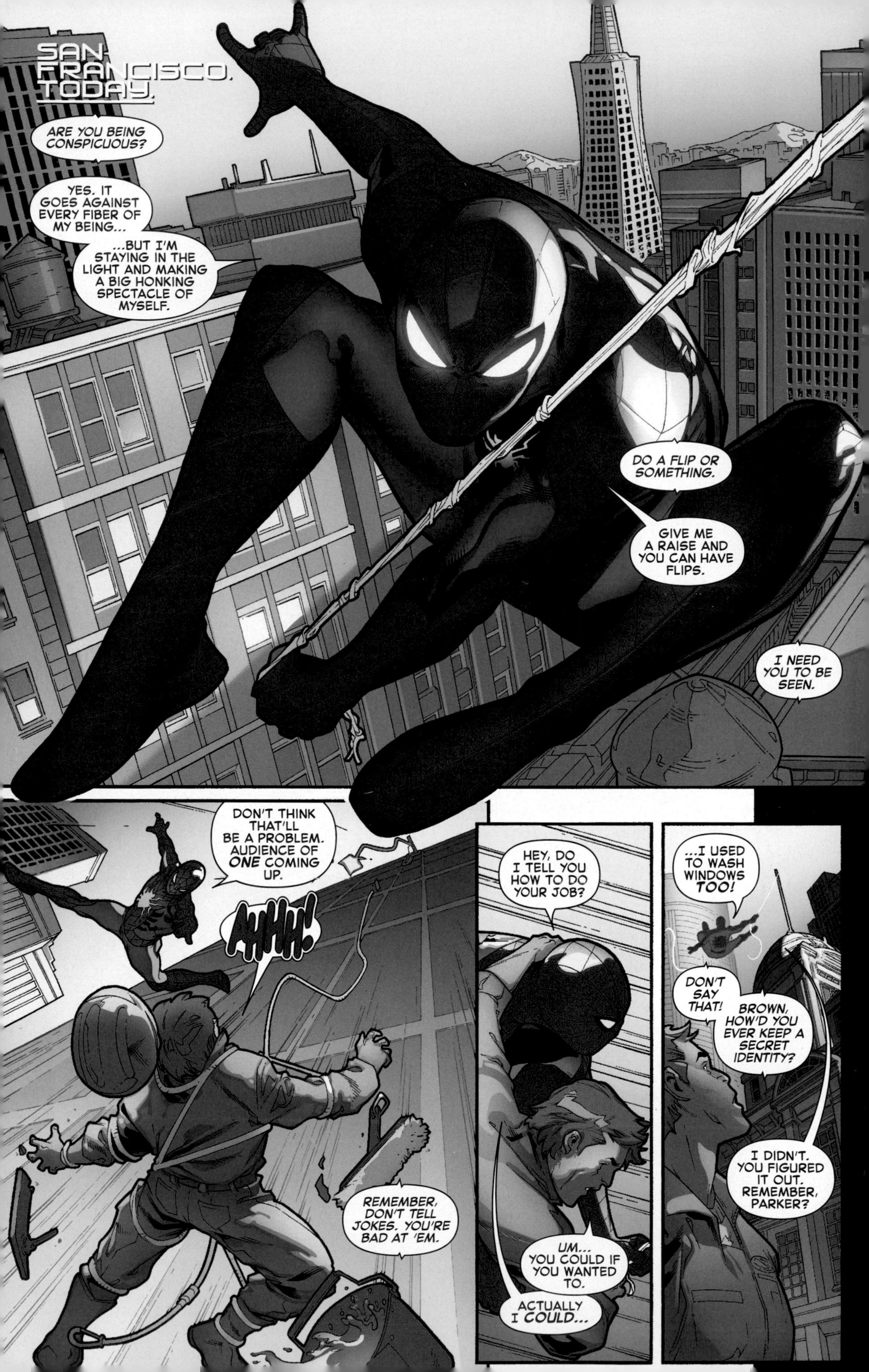
SAN-FRANCISCO. TODAY.
ARE YOU BEING CONSPICUOUS?
YES. IT GOES AGAINST EVERY FIBER OF MY BEING...
...BUT I'M STAYING IN THE LIGHT AND MAKING A BIG HONKING SPECTACLE OF MYSELF.
DO A FLIP OR SOMETHING.
GIVE ME A RAISE AND YOU CAN HAVE FLIPS.
I NEED YOU TO BE SEEN.
DON'T THINK THAT'LL BE A PROBLEM. AUDIENCE OF ONE COMING UP.
AHHH!
REMEMBER, DON'T TELL JOKES. YOU'RE BAD AT 'EM.
HEY, DO I TELL YOU HOW TO DO YOUR JOB?
UM... YOU COULD IF YOU WANTED TO.
ACTUALLY I COULD...
...I USED TO WASH WINDOWS TOO!
DON'T SAY THAT!
BROWN, HOW'D YOU EVER KEEP A SECRET IDENTITY?
I DIDN'T. YOU FIGURED IT OUT. REMEMBER, PARKER?

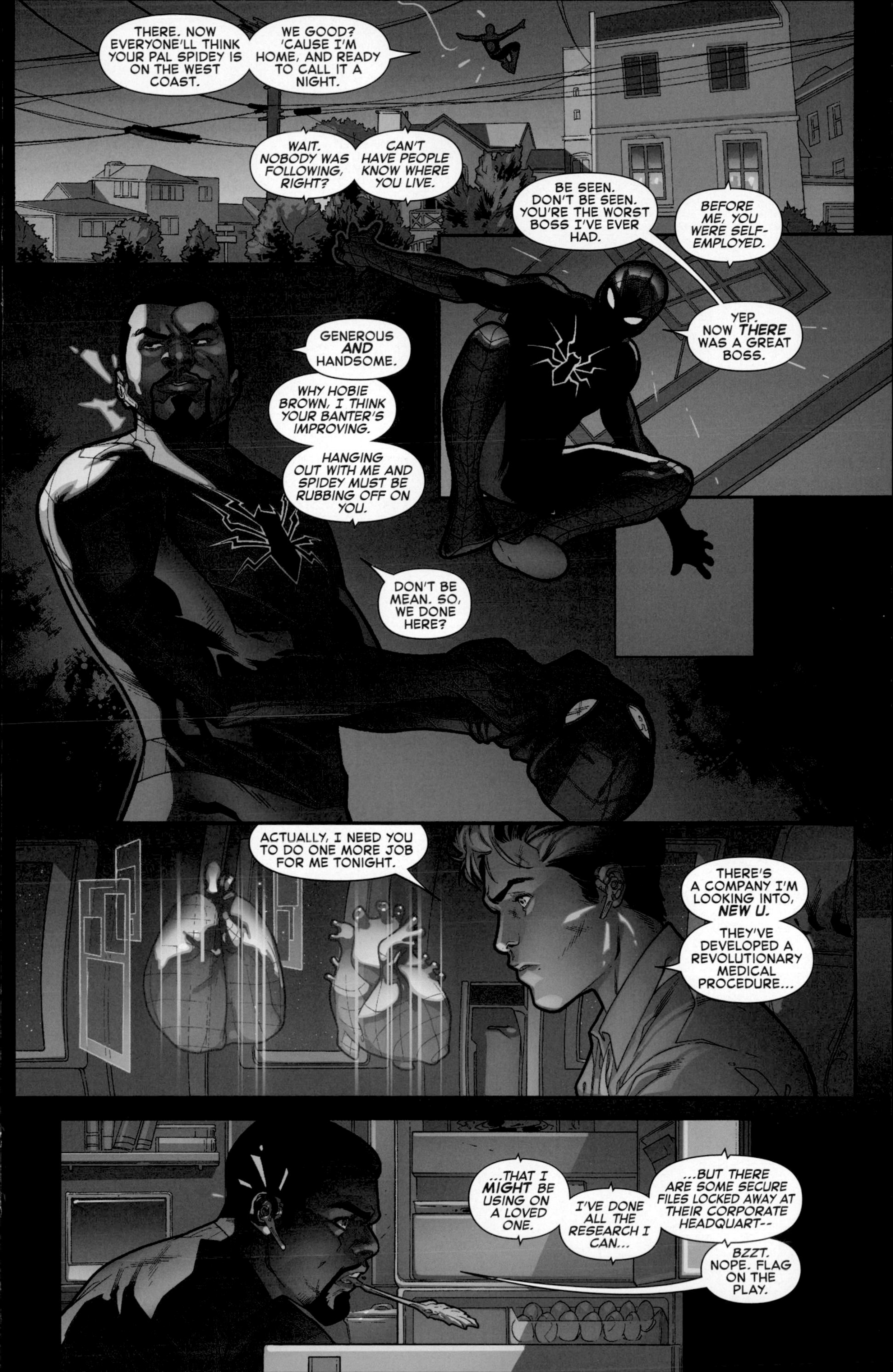
THERE. NOW EVERYONE'LL THINK YOUR PAL SPIDEY IS ON THE WEST COAST.
WE GOOD? 'CAUSE I'M HOME, AND READY TO CALL IT A NIGHT.
WAIT. NOBODY WAS FOLLOWING, RIGHT?
CAN'T HAVE PEOPLE KNOW WHERE YOU LIVE.
BE SEEN. DON'T BE SEEN. YOU'RE THE WORST BOSS I'VE EVER HAD.
BEFORE ME, YOU WERE SELF-EMPLOYED.
YEP. NOW THERE WAS A GREAT BOSS.
GENEROUS AND HANDSOME.
WHY HOBIE BROWN, I THINK YOUR BANTER'S IMPROVING.
HANGING OUT WITH ME AND SPIDEY MUST BE RUBBING OFF ON YOU.
DON'T BE MEAN. SO, WE DONE HERE?
ACTUALLY, I NEED YOU TO DO ONE MORE JOB FOR ME TONIGHT.
THERE'S A COMPANY I'M LOOKING INTO, NEW U.
THEY'VE DEVELOPED A REVOLUTIONARY MEDICAL PROCEDURE...
...THAT I MIGHT BE USING ON A LOVED ONE.
I'VE DONE ALL THE RESEARCH I CAN...
...BUT THERE ARE SOME SECURE FILES LOCKED AWAY AT THEIR CORPORATE HEADQUART--
BZZT. NOPE. FLAG ON THE PLAY.

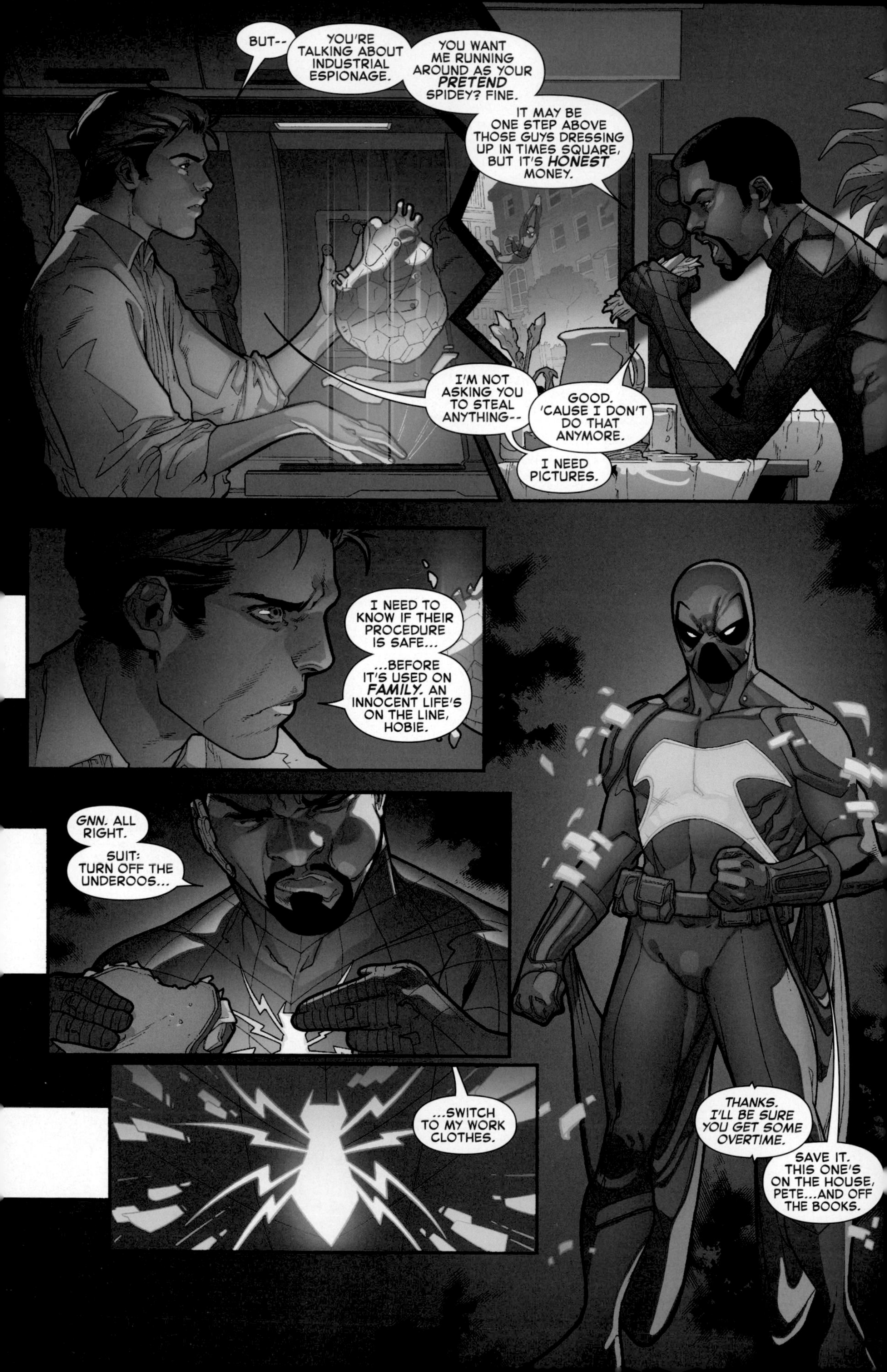
BUT--
YOU'RE TALKING ABOUT INDUSTRIAL ESPIONAGE.
YOU WANT ME RUNNING AROUND AS YOUR PRETEND SPIDEY? FINE.
IT MAY BE ONE STEP ABOVE THOSE GUYS DRESSING UP IN TIMES SQUARE, BUT IT'S HONEST MONEY.
I'M NOT ASKING YOU TO STEAL ANYTHING--
GOOD. 'CAUSE I DON'T DO THAT ANYMORE.
I NEED PICTURES.
I NEED TO KNOW IF THEIR PROCEDURE IS SAFE...
...BEFORE IT'S USED ON FAMILY. AN INNOCENT LIFE'S ON THE LINE, HOBIE.
GNN. ALL RIGHT.
SUIT: TURN OFF THE UNDEROOS...
...SWITCH TO MY WORK CLOTHES.
THANKS. I'LL BE SURE YOU GET SOME OVERTIME.
SAVE IT. THIS ONE'S ON THE HOUSE, PETE...AND OFF THE BOOKS.

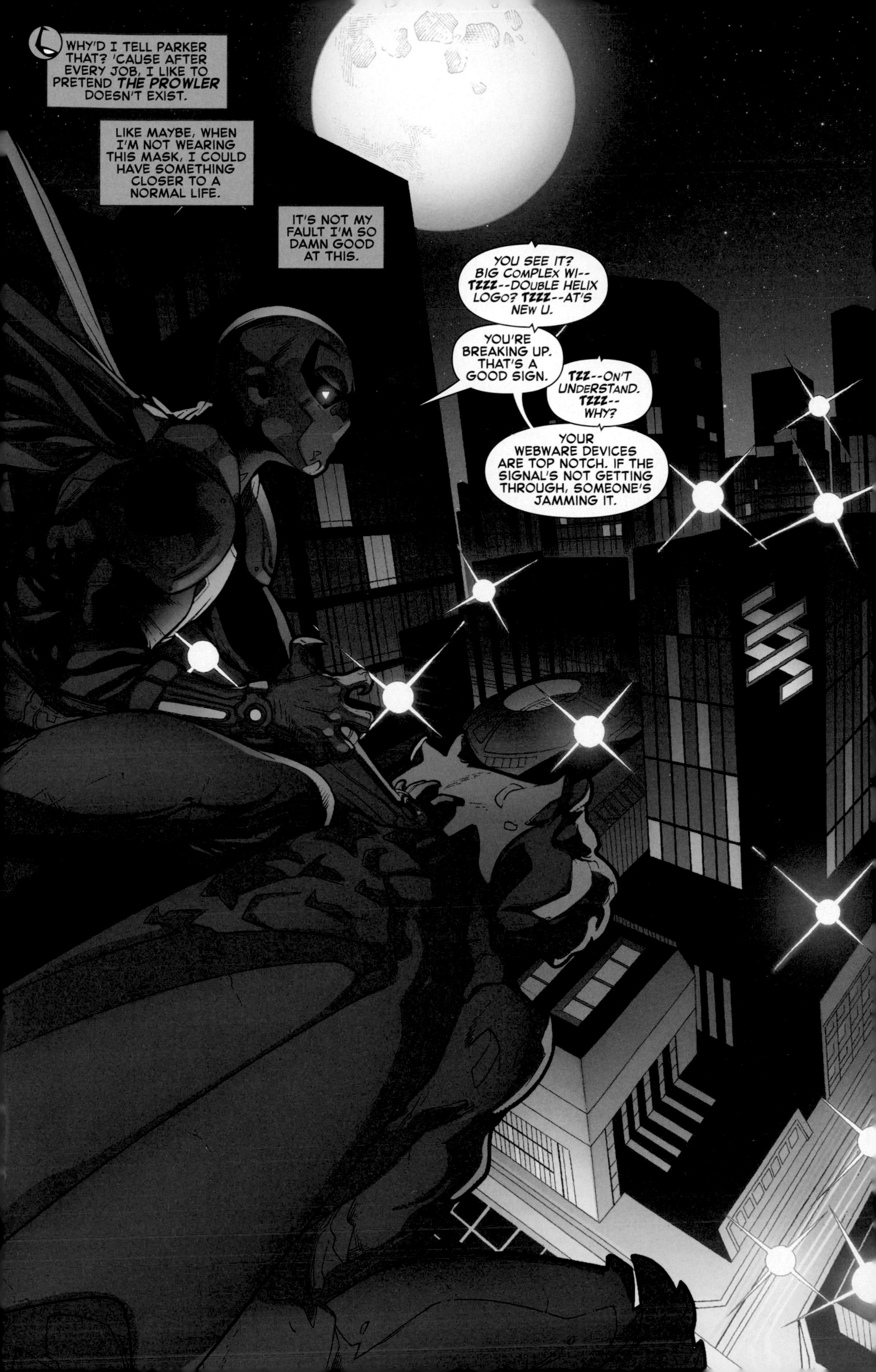
WHY'D I TELL PARKER THAT? 'CAUSE AFTER EVERY JOB, I LIKE TO PRETEND THE PROWLER DOESN'T EXIST.
LIKE MAYBE, WHEN I'M NOT WEARING THIS MASK, I COULD HAVE SOMETHING CLOSER TO A NORMAL LIFE.
IT'S NOT MY FAULT I'M SO DAMN GOOD AT THIS.
YOU SEE IT? BIG COMPLEX WI-- TZZZ--DOUBLE HELIX LOGO? TZZZ--AT'S NEW U.
YOU'RE BREAKING UP. THAT'S A GOOD SIGN.
TZZ--ON'T UNDERSTAND. TZZZ-- WHY?
YOUR WEBWARE DEVICES ARE TOP NOTCH. IF THE SIGNAL'S NOT GETTING THROUGH, SOMEONE'S JAMMING IT.

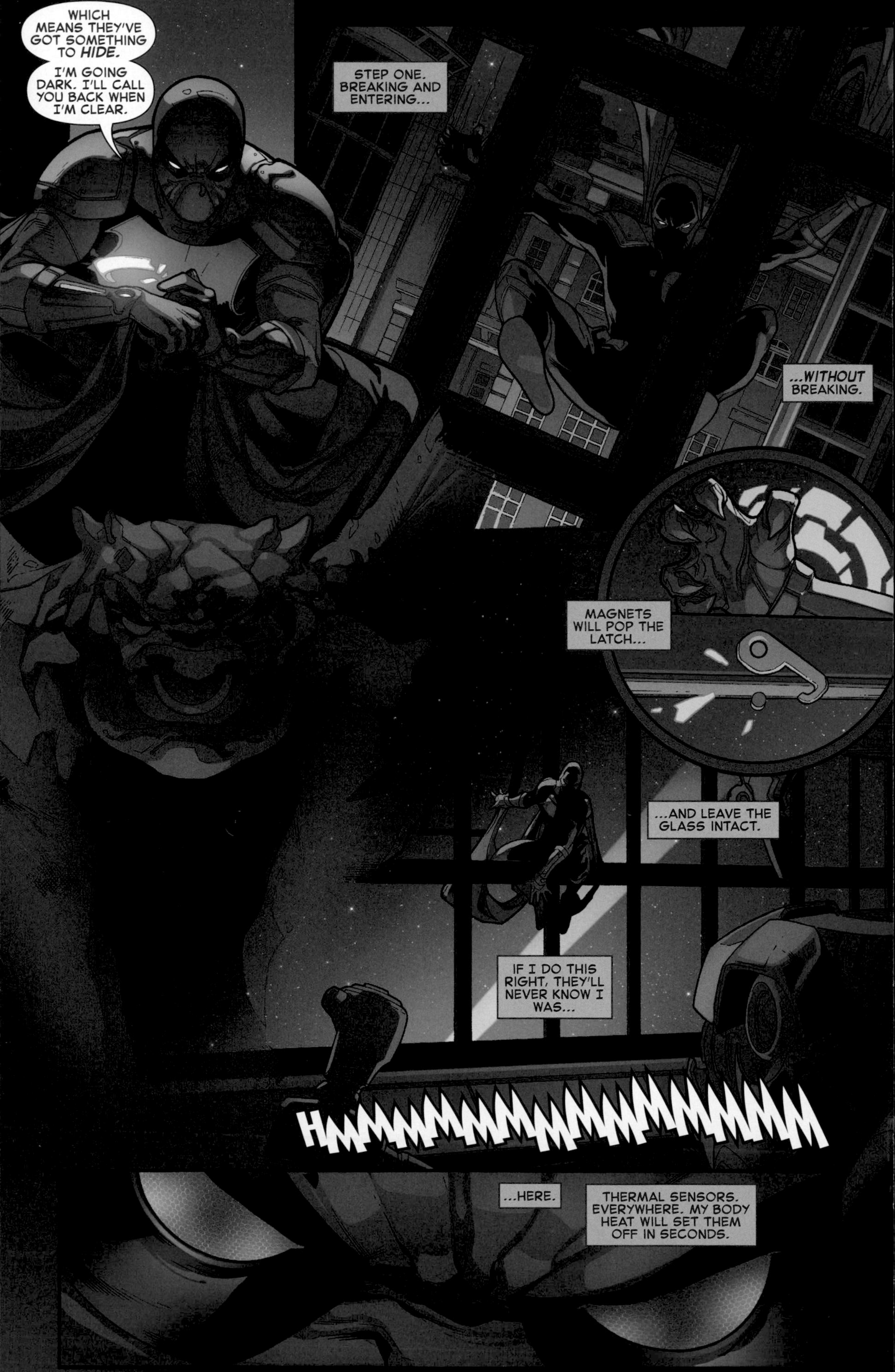
WHICH MEANS THEY'VE GOT SOMETHING TO *HIDE.*
I'M GOING DARK. I'LL CALL YOU BACK WHEN I'M CLEAR.
STEP ONE. BREAKING AND ENTERING...
...*WITHOUT* BREAKING.
MAGNETS WILL POP THE LATCH...
...AND LEAVE THE GLASS INTACT.
IF I DO THIS RIGHT, THEY'LL NEVER KNOW I WAS...
HMMMMMMMMMMMMMMMM
...HERE.
THERMAL SENSORS. EVERYWHERE. MY BODY HEAT WILL SET THEM OFF IN SECONDS.

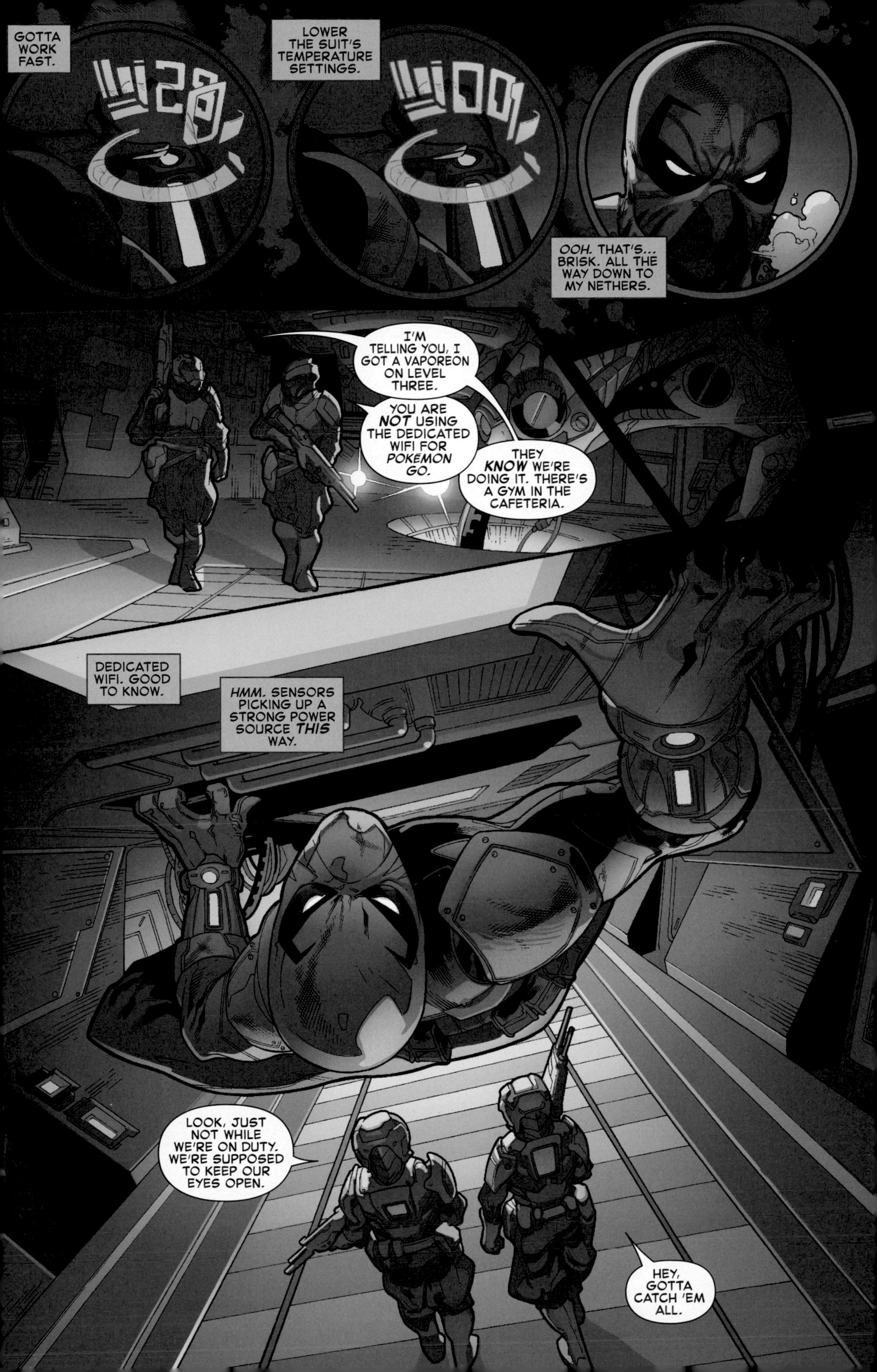
GOTTA WORK FAST.
LOWER THE SUIT'S TEMPERATURE SETTINGS.
OOH. THAT'S... BRISK. ALL THE WAY DOWN TO MY NETHERS.
I'M TELLING YOU, I GOT A VAPOREON ON LEVEL THREE.
YOU ARE NOT USING THE DEDICATED WIFI FOR POKÉMON GO.
THEY KNOW WE'RE DOING IT. THERE'S A GYM IN THE CAFETERIA.
DEDICATED WIFI. GOOD TO KNOW.
HMM. SENSORS PICKING UP A STRONG POWER SOURCE THIS WAY.
LOOK, JUST NOT WHILE WE'RE ON DUTY. WE'RE SUPPOSED TO KEEP OUR EYES OPEN.
HEY, GOTTA CATCH 'EM ALL.

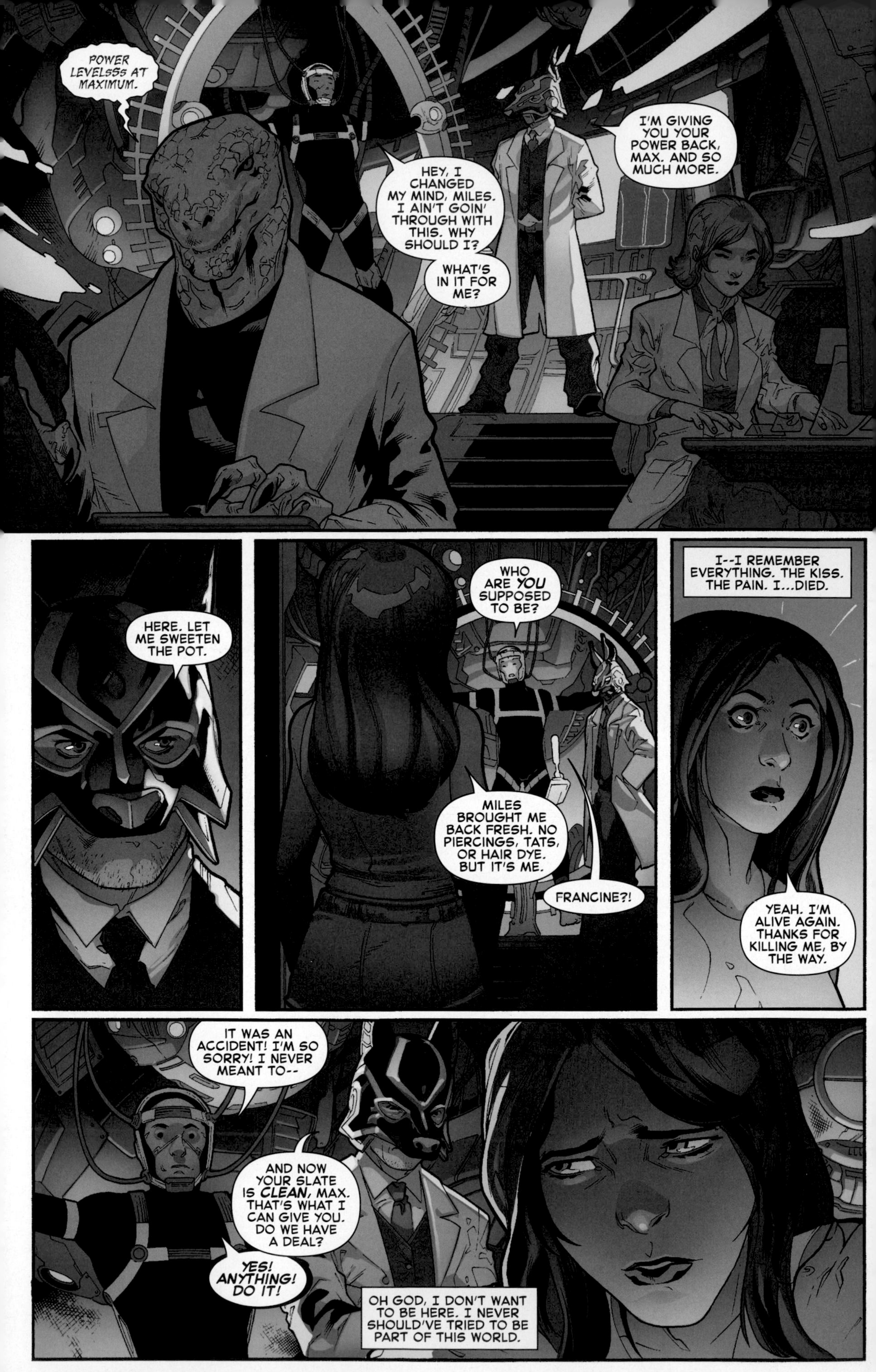
POWER LEVELSSS AT MAXIMUM.
HEY, I CHANGED MY MIND, MILES. I AIN'T GOIN' THROUGH WITH THIS. WHY SHOULD I?
WHAT'S IN IT FOR ME?
I'M GIVING YOU YOUR POWER BACK, MAX. AND SO MUCH MORE.
HERE. LET ME SWEETEN THE POT.
WHO ARE YOU SUPPOSED TO BE?
MILES BROUGHT ME BACK FRESH. NO PIERCINGS, TATS, OR HAIR DYE. BUT IT'S ME.
FRANCINE?!
I--I REMEMBER EVERYTHING. THE KISS. THE PAIN. I...DIED.
YEAH. I'M ALIVE AGAIN. THANKS FOR KILLING ME, BY THE WAY.
IT WAS AN ACCIDENT! I'M SO SORRY! I NEVER MEANT TO--
AND NOW YOUR SLATE IS CLEAN, MAX. THAT'S WHAT I CAN GIVE YOU. DO WE HAVE A DEAL?
YES! ANYTHING! DO IT!
OH GOD, I DON'T WANT TO BE HERE. I NEVER SHOULD'VE TRIED TO BE PART OF THIS WORLD.

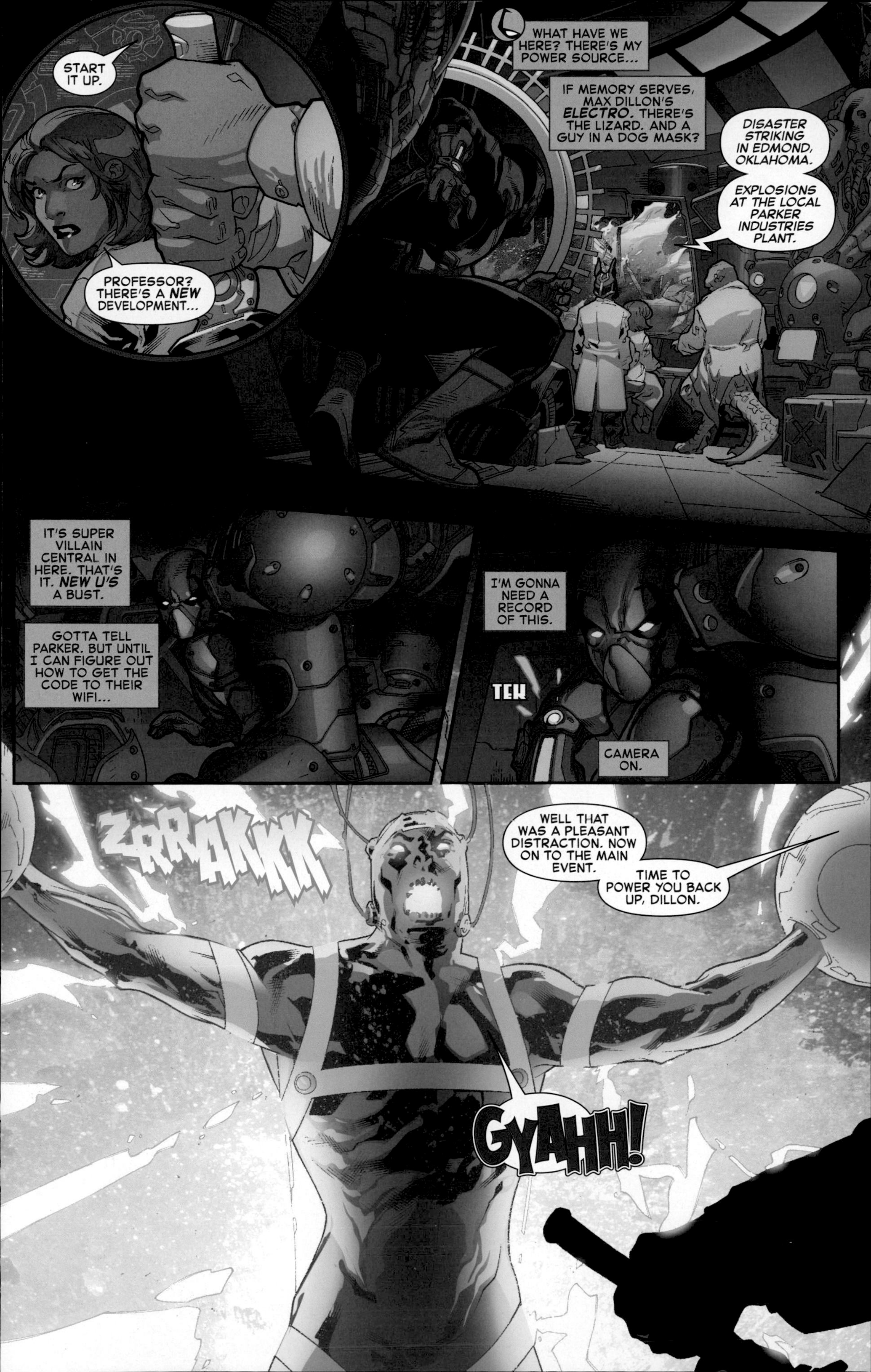
START IT UP.
PROFESSOR? THERE'S A NEW DEVELOPMENT...
WHAT HAVE WE HERE? THERE'S MY POWER SOURCE...
IF MEMORY SERVES, MAX DILLON'S ELECTRO. THERE'S THE LIZARD. AND A GUY IN A DOG MASK?
DISASTER STRIKING IN EDMOND, OKLAHOMA.
EXPLOSIONS AT THE LOCAL PARKER INDUSTRIES PLANT.
IT'S SUPER VILLAIN CENTRAL IN HERE. THAT'S IT. NEW U'S A BUST.
GOTTA TELL PARKER. BUT UNTIL I CAN FIGURE OUT HOW TO GET THE CODE TO THEIR WIFI...
I'M GONNA NEED A RECORD OF THIS.
TEK
CAMERA ON.
ZZRRAKKK
WELL THAT WAS A PLEASANT DISTRACTION. NOW ON TO THE MAIN EVENT.
TIME TO POWER YOU BACK UP, DILLON.
GYAHH!

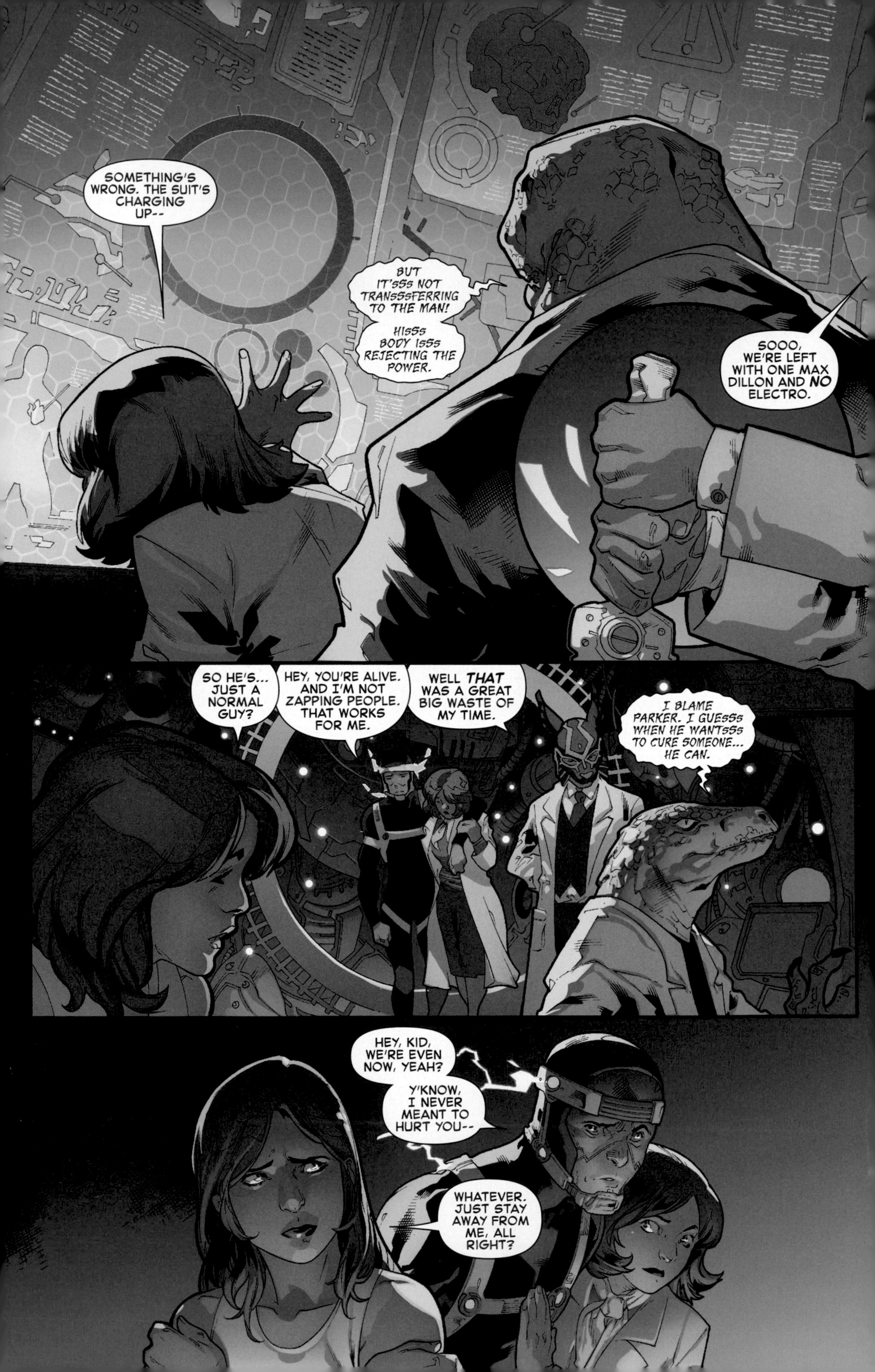
SOMETHING'S WRONG. THE SUIT'S CHARGING UP--
BUT IT'SSS NOT TRANSSSFERRING TO THE MAN!
HISSS BODY ISSS REJECTING THE POWER.
SOOO, WE'RE LEFT WITH ONE MAX DILLON AND NO ELECTRO.
SO HE'S... JUST A NORMAL GUY?
HEY, YOU'RE ALIVE. AND I'M NOT ZAPPING PEOPLE. THAT WORKS FOR ME.
WELL THAT WAS A GREAT BIG WASTE OF MY TIME.
I BLAME PARKER. I GUESSS WHEN HE WANTSSS TO CURE SOMEONE... HE CAN.
HEY, KID, WE'RE EVEN NOW, YEAH?
Y'KNOW, I NEVER MEANT TO HURT YOU--
WHATEVER. JUST STAY AWAY FROM ME, ALL RIGHT?

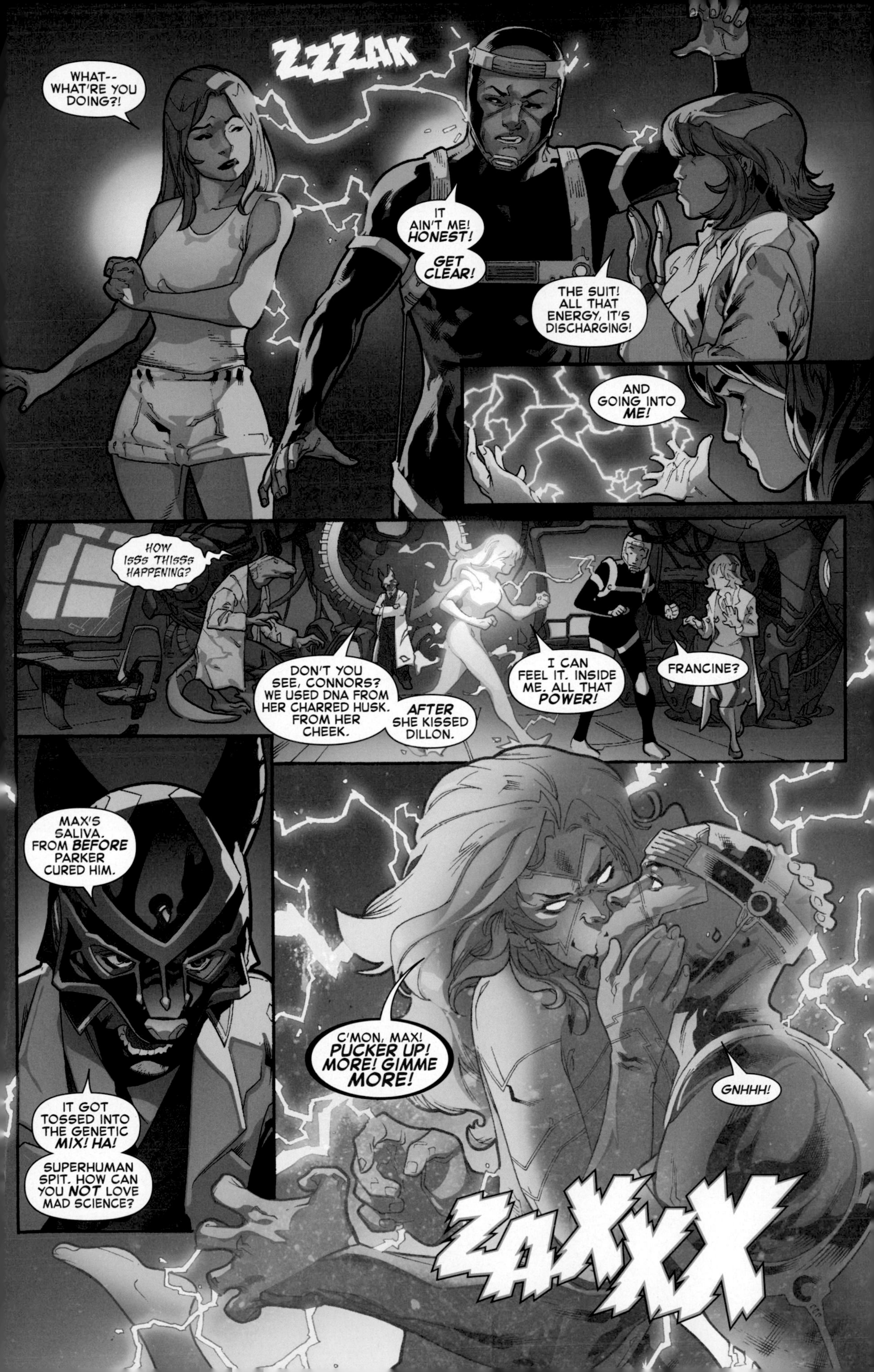
ZZZAK
WHAT-- WHAT'RE YOU DOING?!
IT AIN'T ME! HONEST!
GET CLEAR!
THE SUIT! ALL THAT ENERGY, IT'S DISCHARGING!
AND GOING INTO ME!
HOW ISSS THISSS HAPPENING?
DON'T YOU SEE, CONNORS? WE USED DNA FROM HER CHARRED HUSK. FROM HER CHEEK.
AFTER SHE KISSED DILLON.
I CAN FEEL IT. INSIDE ME. ALL THAT POWER!
FRANCINE?
MAX'S SALIVA. FROM BEFORE PARKER CURED HIM.
IT GOT TOSSED INTO THE GENETIC MIX! HA!
SUPERHUMAN SPIT. HOW CAN YOU NOT LOVE MAD SCIENCE?
C'MON, MAX! PUCKER UP! MORE! GIMME MORE!
GNHHH!
ZAXXX

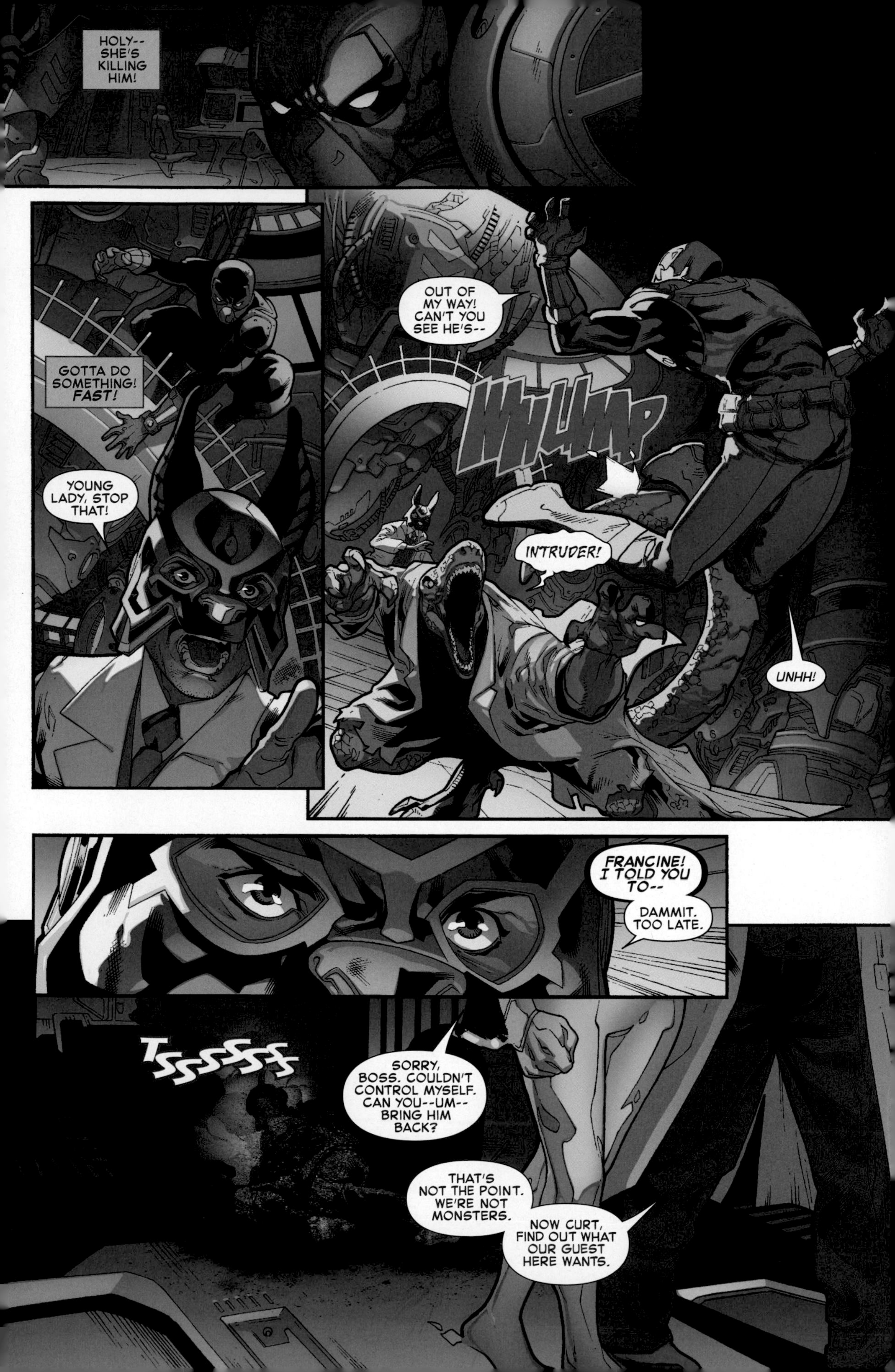
HOLY--
SHE'S
KILLING
HIM!
GOTTA DO
SOMETHING!
FAST!
YOUNG
LADY, STOP
THAT!
OUT OF
MY WAY!
CAN'T YOU
SEE HE'S--
WHUMP
INTRUDER!
UNHH!
FRANCINE!
I TOLD YOU
TO--
DAMMIT.
TOO LATE.
TSSSSSS
SORRY,
BOSS. COULDN'T
CONTROL MYSELF.
CAN YOU--UM--
BRING HIM
BACK?
THAT'S
NOT THE POINT.
WE'RE NOT
MONSTERS.
NOW CURT,
FIND OUT WHAT
OUR GUEST
HERE WANTS.

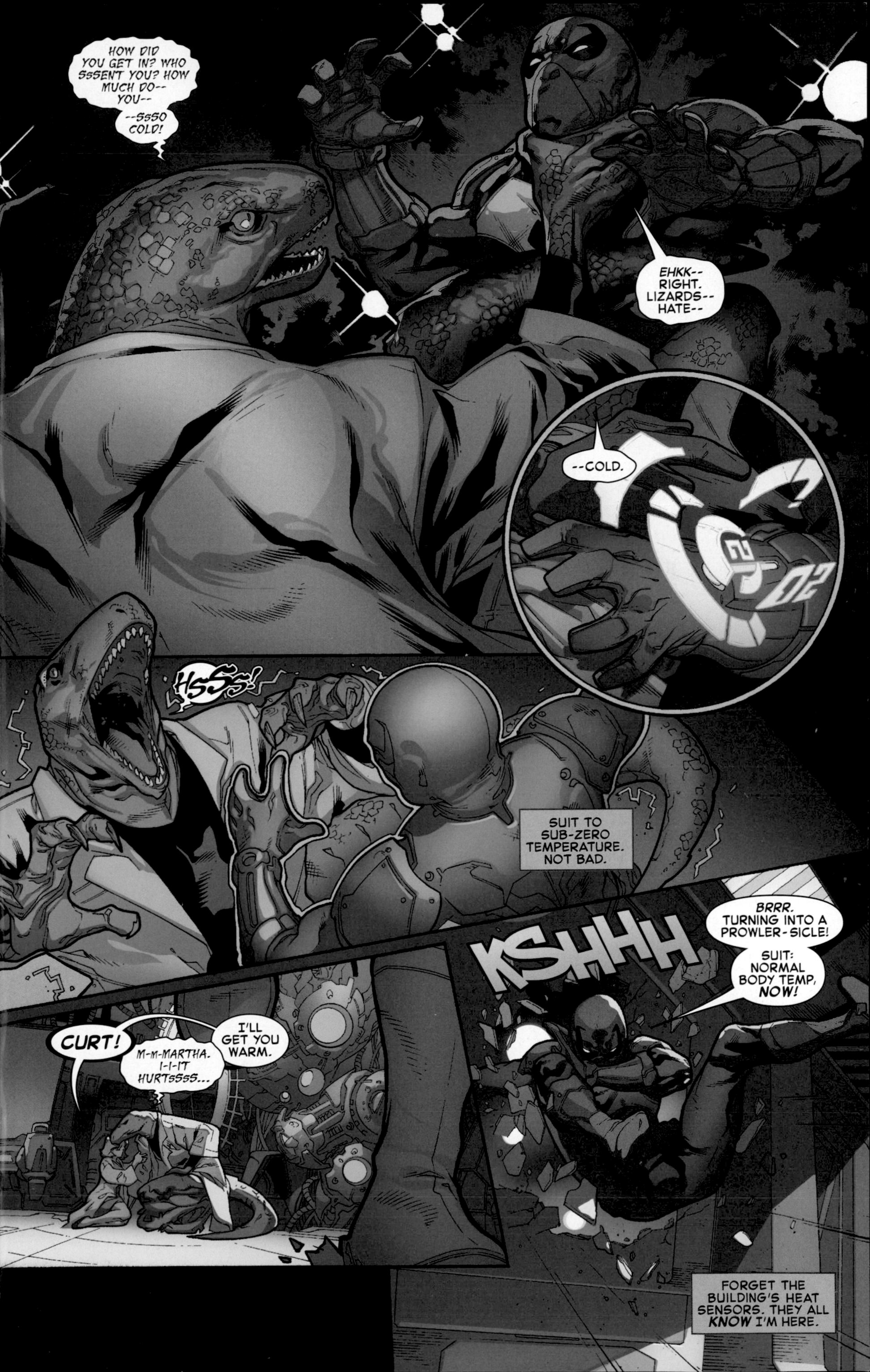

HOW DID YOU GET IN? WHO SsSENT YOU? HOW MUCH DO-- YOU--
--SsSO COLD!
EHKK-- RIGHT. LIZARDS-- HATE--
--COLD.
HSSS!
SUIT TO SUB-ZERO TEMPERATURE. NOT BAD.
KSHHH
BRRR. TURNING INTO A PROWLER-SICLE!
SUIT: NORMAL BODY TEMP, NOW!
CURT!
M-M-MARTHA. I-I-IT HURTSSSS...
I'LL GET YOU WARM.
FORGET THE BUILDING'S HEAT SENSORS. THEY ALL KNOW I'M HERE.

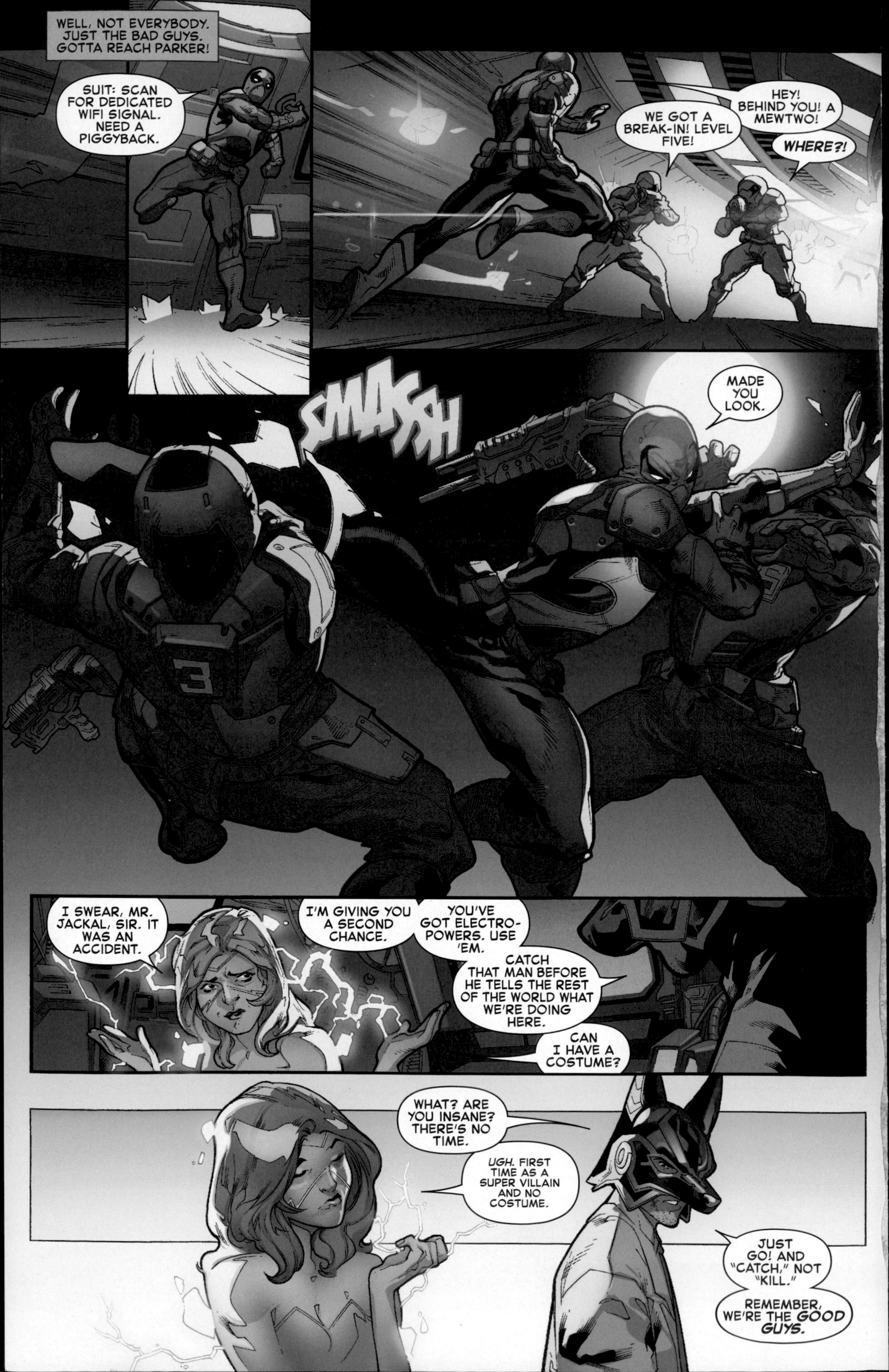

WELL, NOT EVERYBODY. JUST THE BAD GUYS. GOTTA REACH PARKER!
SUIT: SCAN FOR DEDICATED WIFI SIGNAL. NEED A PIGGYBACK.
WE GOT A BREAK-IN! LEVEL FIVE!
HEY! BEHIND YOU! A MEWTWO!
WHERE?!
SMASH
MADE YOU LOOK.
I SWEAR, MR. JACKAL, SIR. IT WAS AN ACCIDENT.
I'M GIVING YOU A SECOND CHANCE.
YOU'VE GOT ELECTRO-POWERS. USE 'EM.
CATCH THAT MAN BEFORE HE TELLS THE REST OF THE WORLD WHAT WE'RE DOING HERE.
CAN I HAVE A COSTUME?
WHAT? ARE YOU INSANE? THERE'S NO TIME.
UGH. FIRST TIME AS A SUPER VILLAIN AND NO COSTUME.
JUST GO! AND "CATCH," NOT "KILL."
REMEMBER, WE'RE THE GOOD GUYS.

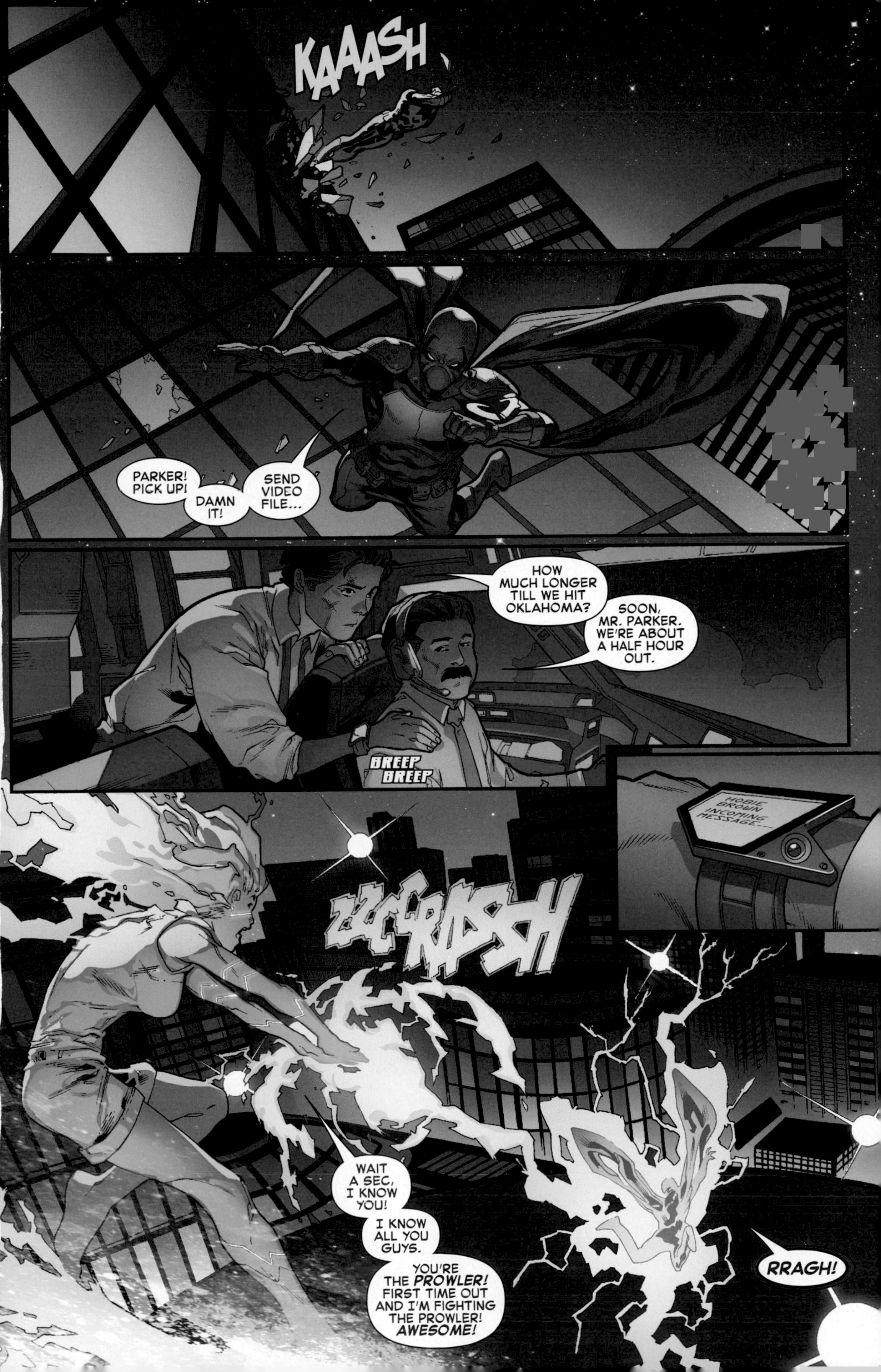
KAAASH
PARKER! PICK UP!
DAMN IT!
SEND VIDEO FILE...
HOW MUCH LONGER TILL WE HIT OKLAHOMA?
SOON, MR. PARKER. WE'RE ABOUT A HALF HOUR OUT.
BREEP BREEP
HOBIE BROWN INCOMING MESSAGE...
ZZZCRASSH
WAIT A SEC, I KNOW YOU!
I KNOW ALL YOU GUYS.
YOU'RE THE PROWLER! FIRST TIME OUT AND I'M FIGHTING THE PROWLER! AWESOME!
RRAGH!

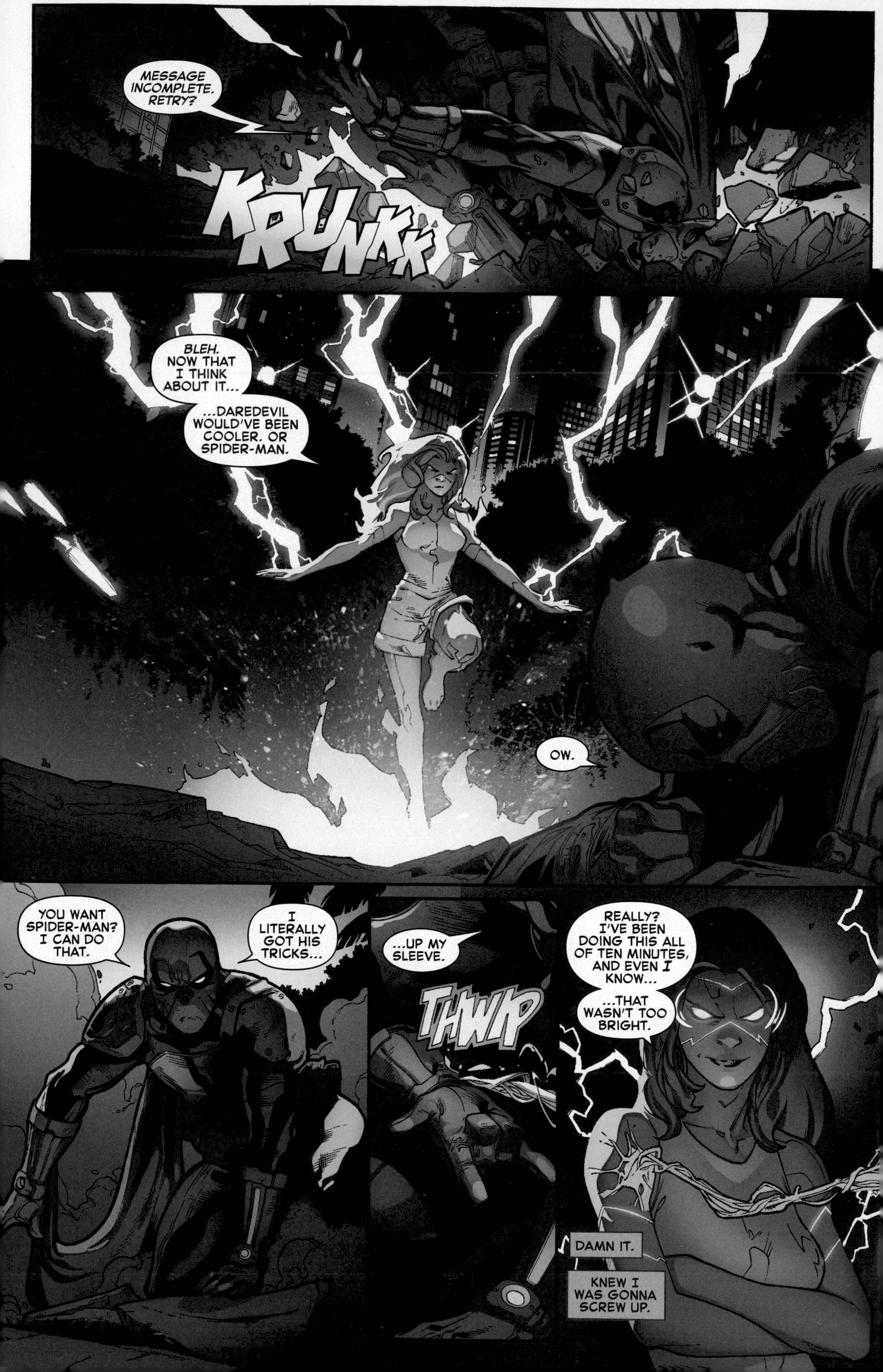
MESSAGE INCOMPLETE. RETRY?
KRUNKK
BLEH. NOW THAT I THINK ABOUT IT...
...DAREDEVIL WOULD'VE BEEN COOLER. OR SPIDER-MAN.
OW.
YOU WANT SPIDER-MAN? I CAN DO THAT.
I LITERALLY GOT HIS TRICKS...
...UP MY SLEEVE.
THWIP
REALLY? I'VE BEEN DOING THIS ALL OF TEN MINUTES, AND EVEN I KNOW...
...THAT WASN'T TOO BRIGHT.
DAMN IT.
KNEW I WAS GONNA SCREW UP.

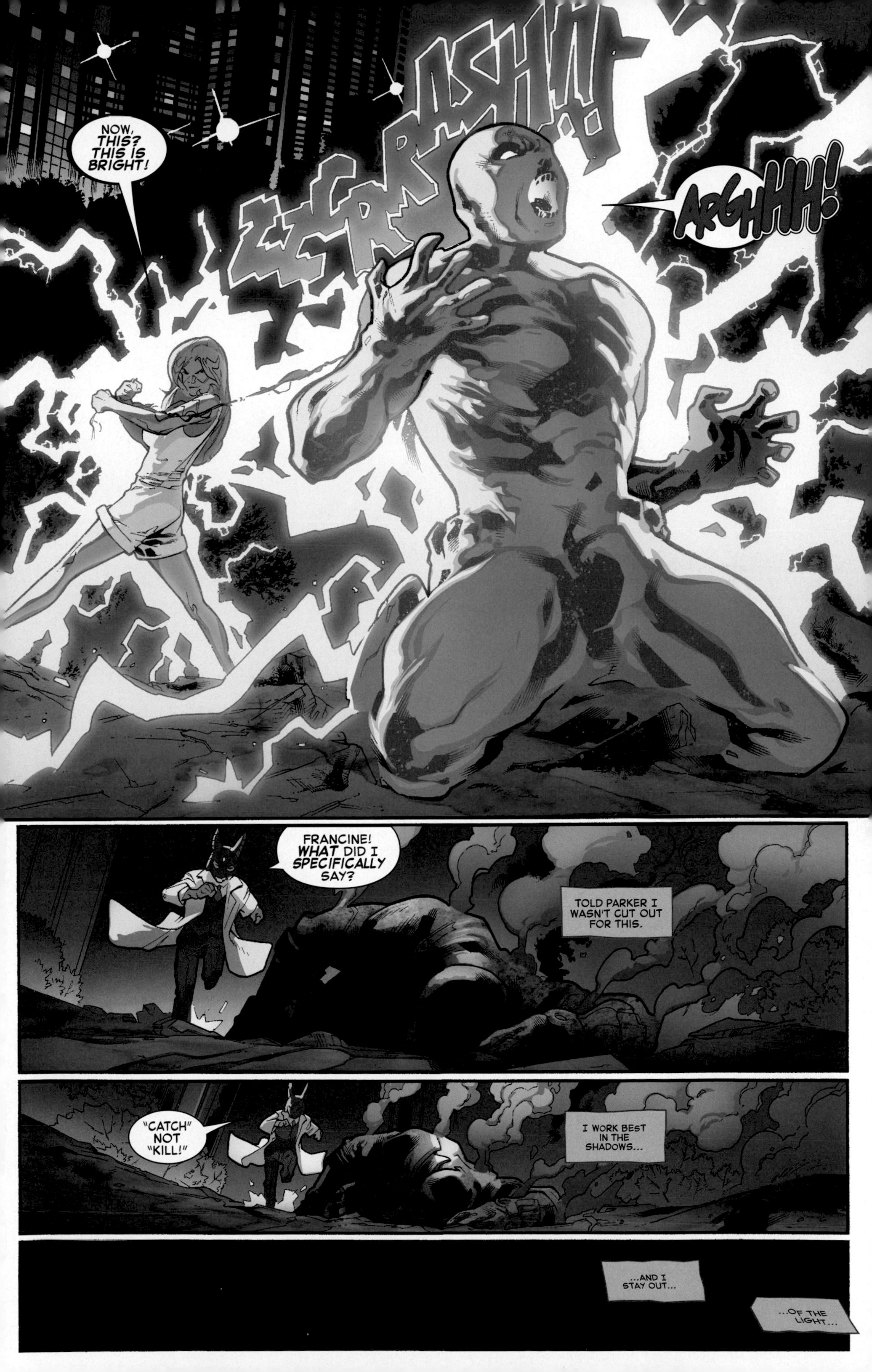
NOW, THIS? THIS IS BRIGHT!
ZZGRRRASHH!!
ARGHHH!
FRANCINE! WHAT DID I SPECIFICALLY SAY?
TOLD PARKER I WASN'T CUT OUT FOR THIS.
"CATCH" NOT "KILL!"
I WORK BEST IN THE SHADOWS...
...AND I STAY OUT...
...OF THE LIGHT...

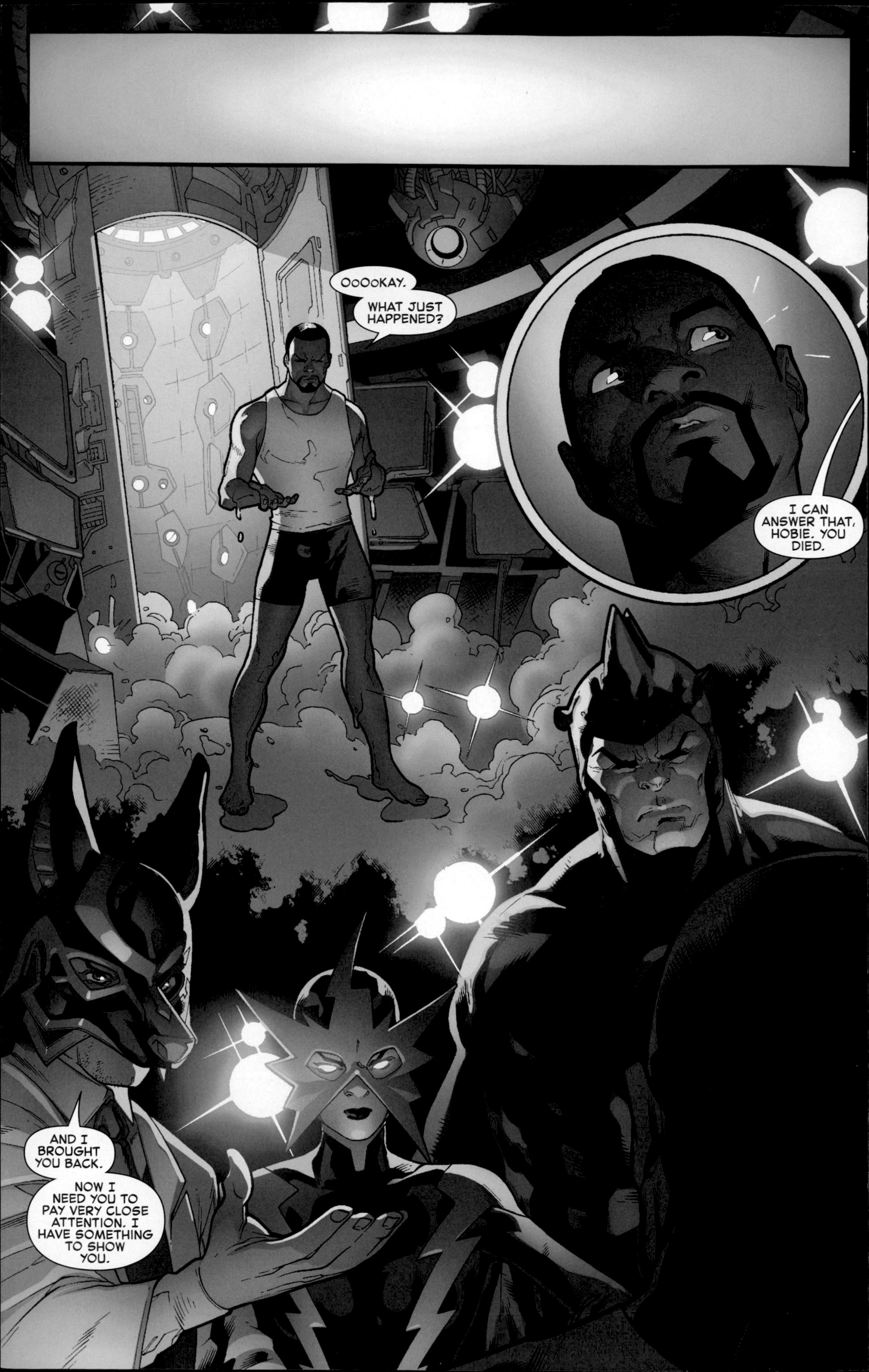
OOOOKAY.
WHAT JUST HAPPENED?
I CAN ANSWER THAT, HOBIE. YOU DIED.
AND I BROUGHT YOU BACK.
NOW I NEED YOU TO PAY VERY CLOSE ATTENTION. I HAVE SOMETHING TO SHOW YOU.

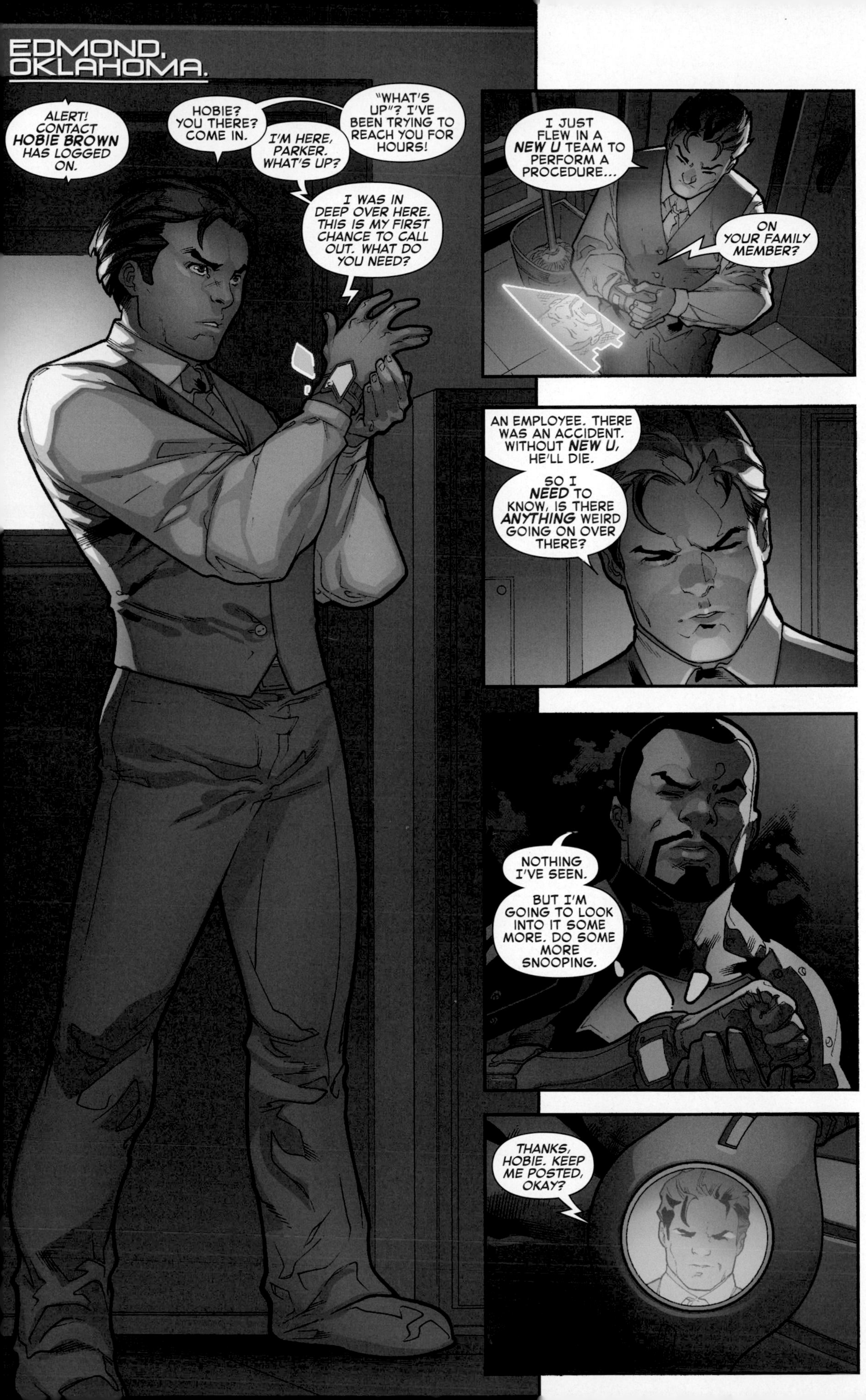
EDMOND, OKLAHOMA.
ALERT! CONTACT HOBIE BROWN HAS LOGGED ON.
HOBIE? YOU THERE? COME IN.
I'M HERE, PARKER. WHAT'S UP?
"WHAT'S UP"? I'VE BEEN TRYING TO REACH YOU FOR HOURS!
I WAS IN DEEP OVER HERE. THIS IS MY FIRST CHANCE TO CALL OUT. WHAT DO YOU NEED?
I JUST FLEW IN A NEW U TEAM TO PERFORM A PROCEDURE...
ON YOUR FAMILY MEMBER?
AN EMPLOYEE. THERE WAS AN ACCIDENT. WITHOUT NEW U, HE'LL DIE.
SO I NEED TO KNOW, IS THERE ANYTHING WEIRD GOING ON OVER THERE?
NOTHING I'VE SEEN.
BUT I'M GOING TO LOOK INTO IT SOME MORE. DO SOME MORE SNOOPING.
THANKS, HOBIE. KEEP ME POSTED, OKAY?

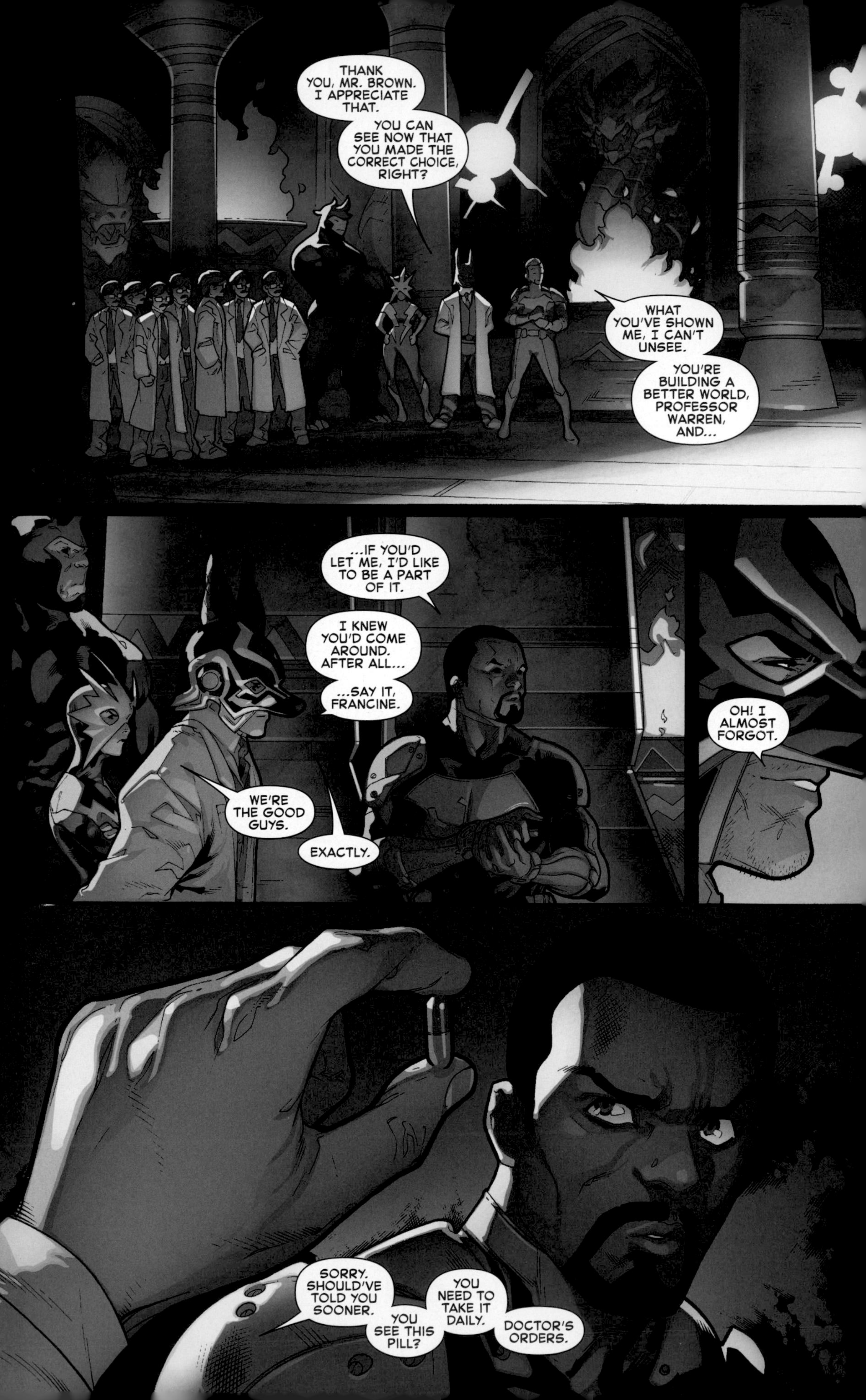
THANK YOU, MR. BROWN. I APPRECIATE THAT.
YOU CAN SEE NOW THAT YOU MADE THE CORRECT CHOICE, RIGHT?
WHAT YOU'VE SHOWN ME, I CAN'T UNSEE.
YOU'RE BUILDING A BETTER WORLD, PROFESSOR WARREN, AND...
...IF YOU'D LET ME, I'D LIKE TO BE A PART OF IT.
I KNEW YOU'D COME AROUND. AFTER ALL...
...SAY IT, FRANCINE.
WE'RE THE GOOD GUYS.
EXACTLY.
OH! I ALMOST FORGOT.
SORRY. SHOULD'VE TOLD YOU SOONER.
YOU SEE THIS PILL?
YOU NEED TO TAKE IT DAILY.
DOCTOR'S ORDERS.

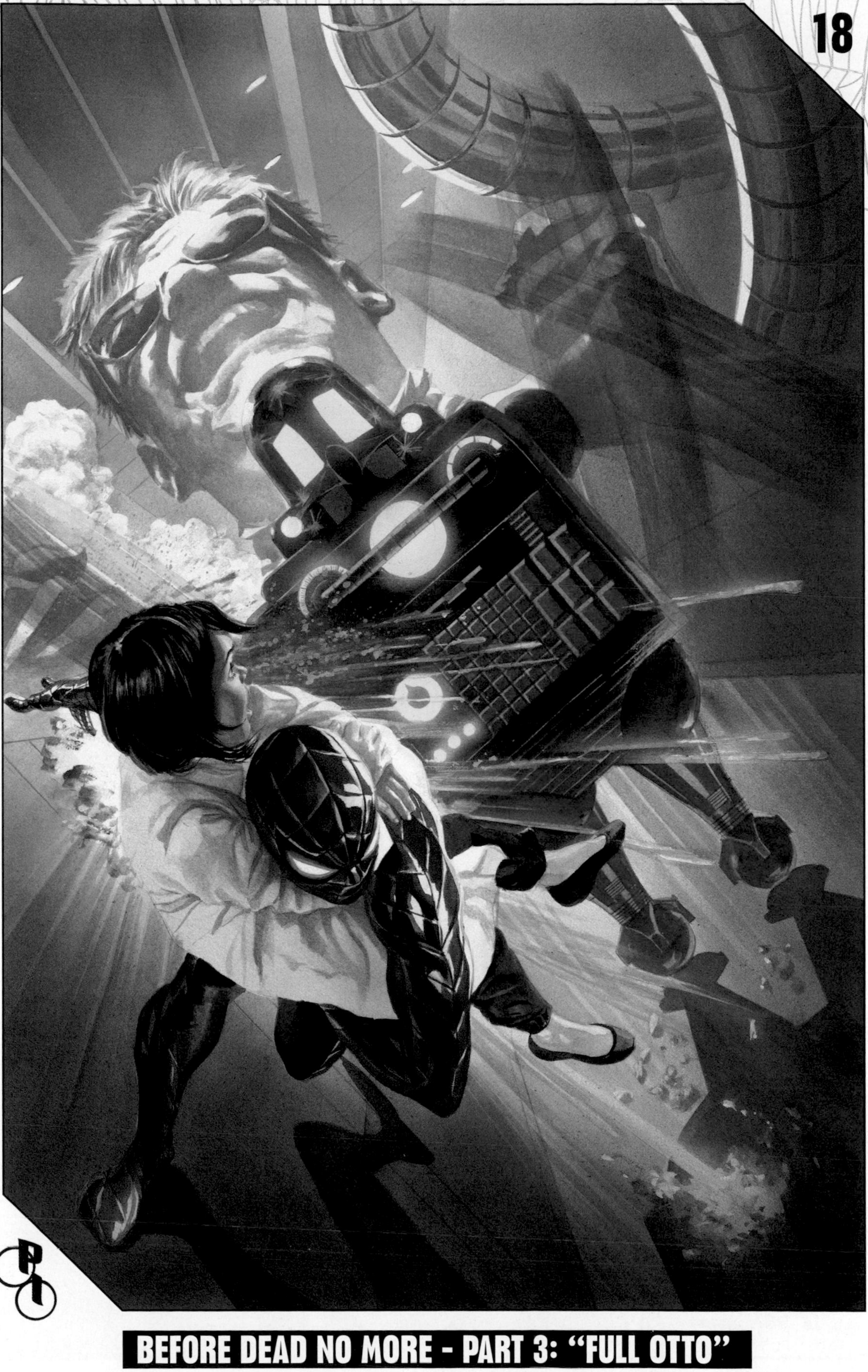

BEFORE DEAD NO MORE - PART 3: "FULL OTTO"

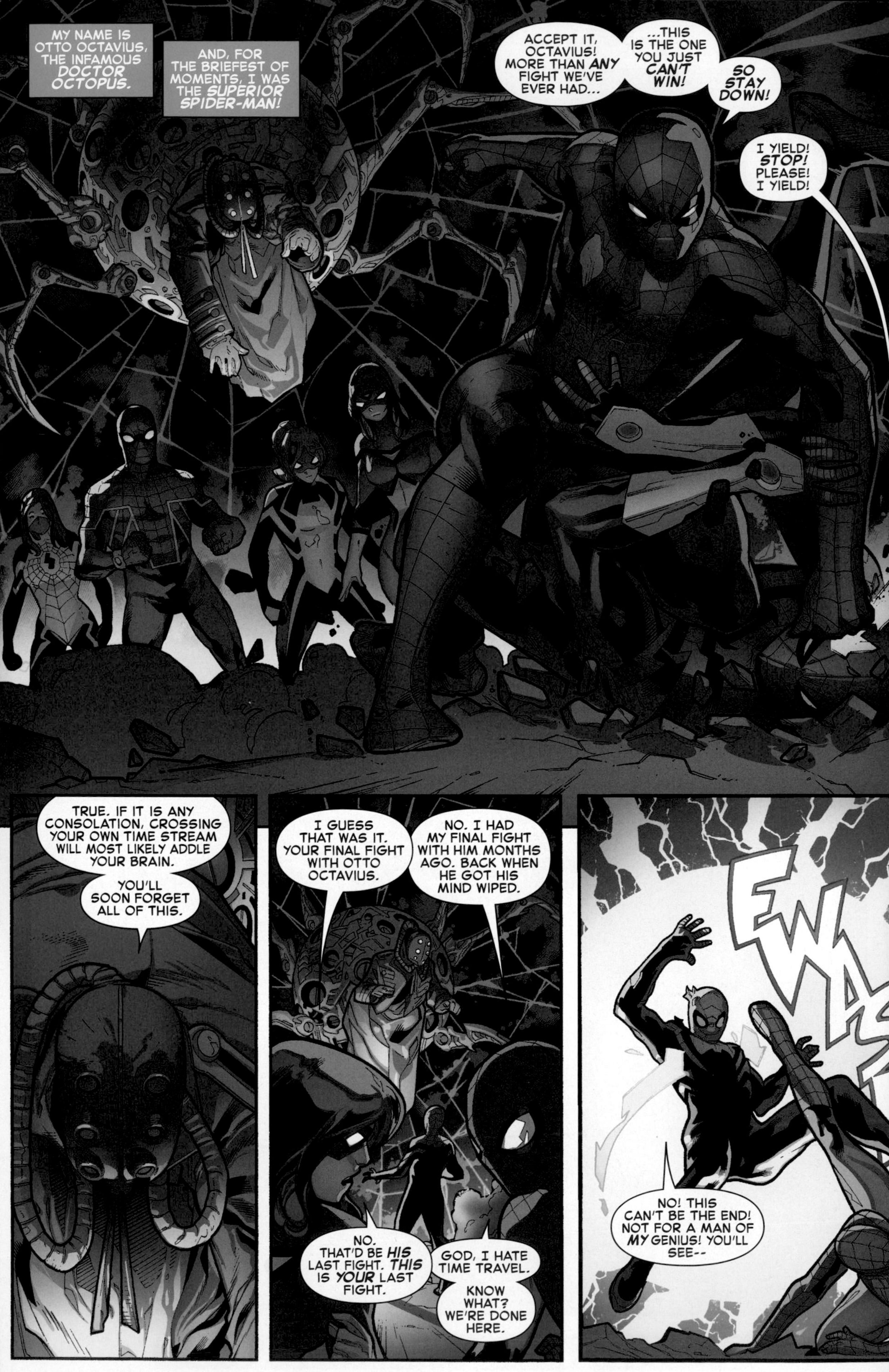
MY NAME IS OTTO OCTAVIUS, THE INFAMOUS DOCTOR OCTOPUS.
AND, FOR THE BRIEFEST OF MOMENTS, I WAS THE SUPERIOR SPIDER-MAN!
ACCEPT IT, OCTAVIUS! MORE THAN ANY FIGHT WE'VE EVER HAD...
...THIS IS THE ONE YOU JUST CAN'T WIN!
SO STAY DOWN!
I YIELD! STOP! PLEASE! I YIELD!
TRUE. IF IT IS ANY CONSOLATION, CROSSING YOUR OWN TIME STREAM WILL MOST LIKELY ADDLE YOUR BRAIN.
YOU'LL SOON FORGET ALL OF THIS.
I GUESS THAT WAS IT. YOUR FINAL FIGHT WITH OTTO OCTAVIUS.
NO. I HAD MY FINAL FIGHT WITH HIM MONTHS AGO. BACK WHEN HE GOT HIS MIND WIPED.
NO. THAT'D BE HIS LAST FIGHT. THIS IS YOUR LAST FIGHT.
GOD, I HATE TIME TRAVEL.
KNOW WHAT? WE'RE DONE HERE.
NO! THIS CAN'T BE THE END! NOT FOR A MAN OF MY GENIUS! YOU'LL SEE--

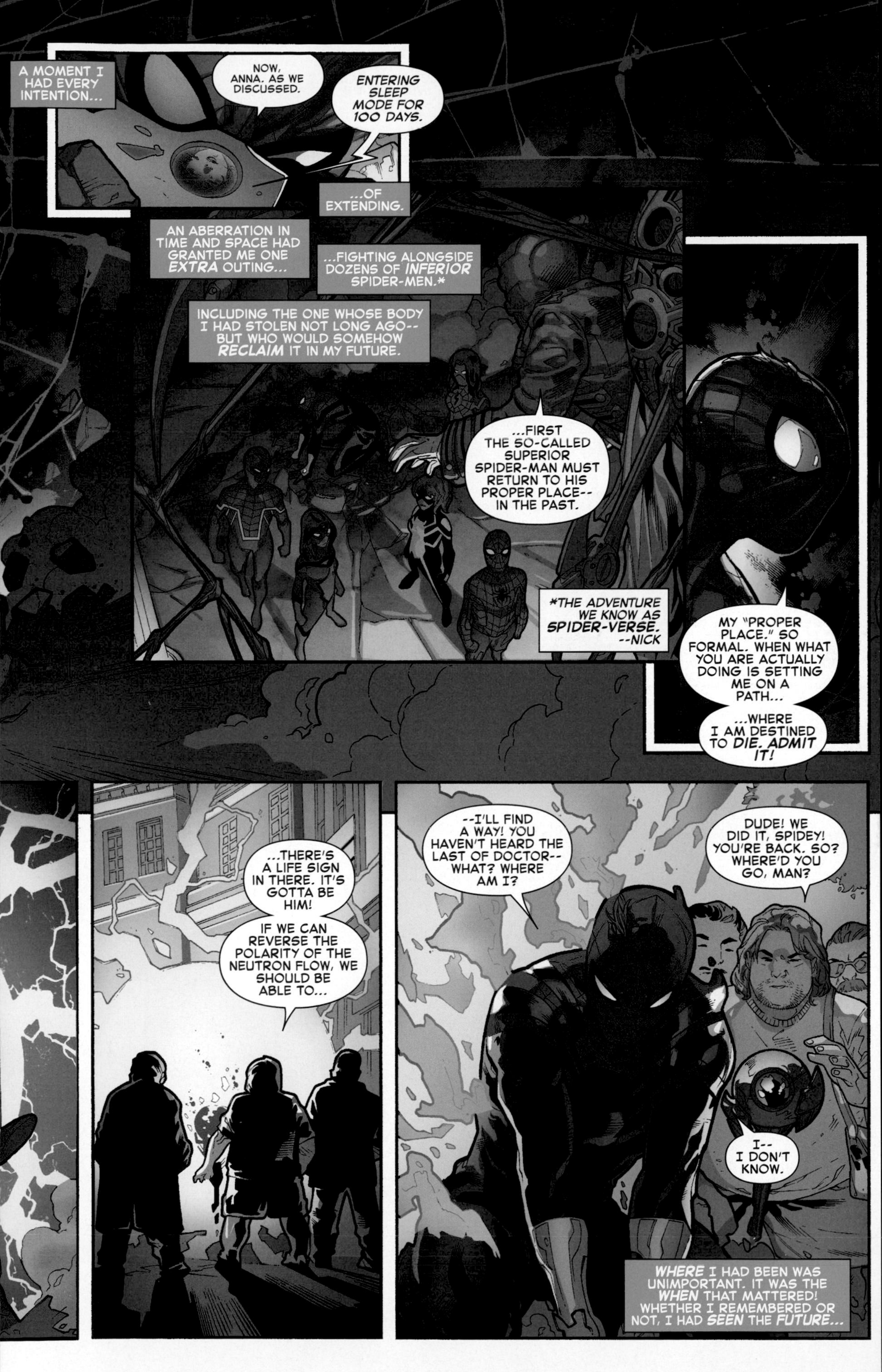
A MOMENT I HAD EVERY INTENTION...
NOW, ANNA. AS WE DISCUSSED.
ENTERING SLEEP MODE FOR 100 DAYS.
...OF EXTENDING.
AN ABERRATION IN TIME AND SPACE HAD GRANTED ME ONE EXTRA OUTING...
...FIGHTING ALONGSIDE DOZENS OF INFERIOR SPIDER-MEN.*
INCLUDING THE ONE WHOSE BODY I HAD STOLEN NOT LONG AGO--BUT WHO WOULD SOMEHOW RECLAIM IT IN MY FUTURE.
...FIRST THE SO-CALLED SUPERIOR SPIDER-MAN MUST RETURN TO HIS PROPER PLACE--IN THE PAST.
*THE ADVENTURE WE KNOW AS SPIDER-VERSE. --NICK
MY "PROPER PLACE." SO FORMAL. WHEN WHAT YOU ARE ACTUALLY DOING IS SETTING ME ON A PATH...
...WHERE I AM DESTINED TO DIE. ADMIT IT!
...THERE'S A LIFE SIGN IN THERE. IT'S GOTTA BE HIM!
IF WE CAN REVERSE THE POLARITY OF THE NEUTRON FLOW, WE SHOULD BE ABLE TO...
--I'LL FIND A WAY! YOU HAVEN'T HEARD THE LAST OF DOCTOR--WHAT? WHERE AM I?
DUDE! WE DID IT, SPIDEY! YOU'RE BACK. SO? WHERE'D YOU GO, MAN?
I--I DON'T KNOW.
WHERE I HAD BEEN WAS UNIMPORTANT. IT WAS THE WHEN THAT MATTERED! WHETHER I REMEMBERED OR NOT, I HAD SEEN THE FUTURE...

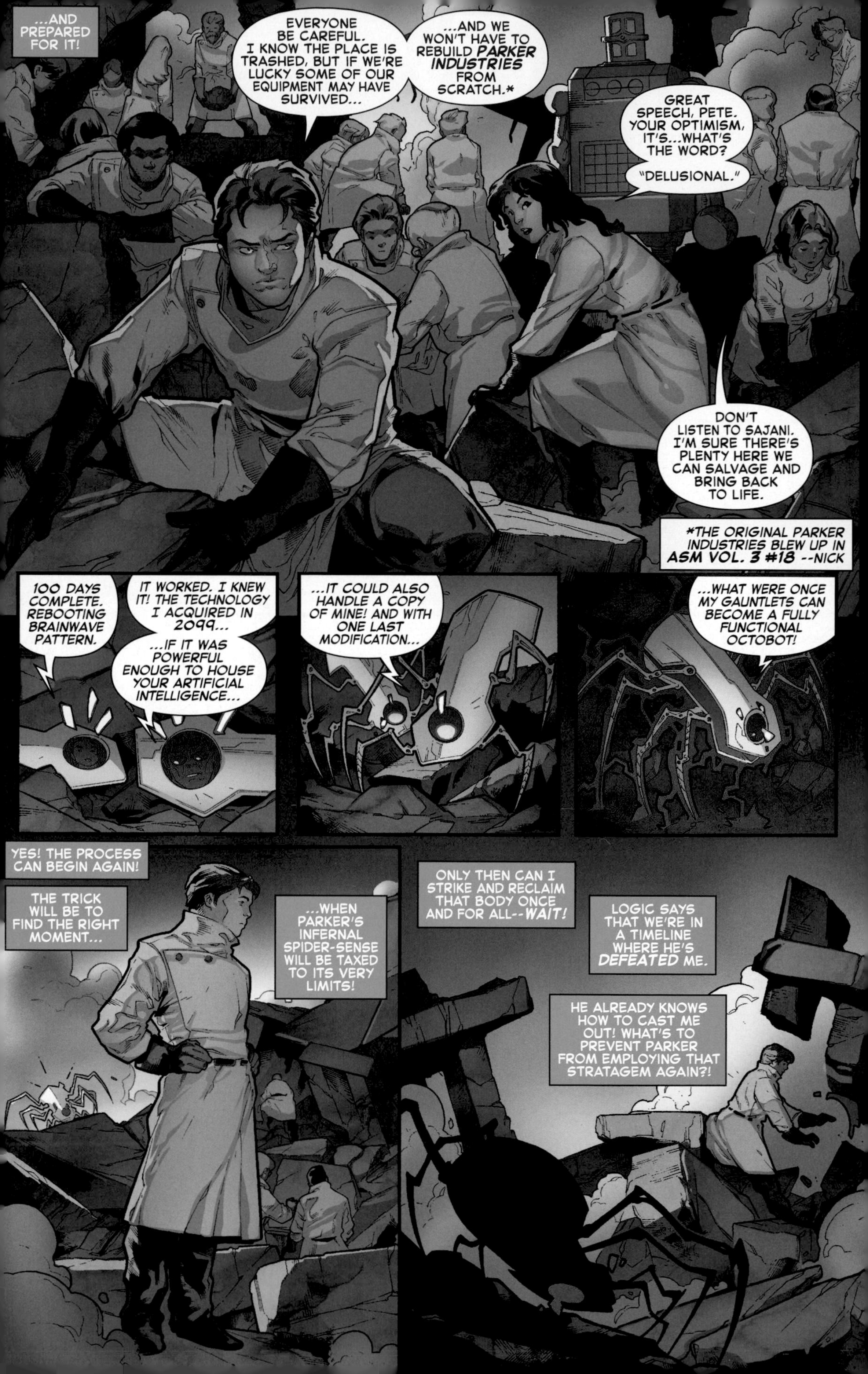
...AND PREPARED FOR IT!
EVERYONE BE CAREFUL. I KNOW THE PLACE IS TRASHED, BUT IF WE'RE LUCKY SOME OF OUR EQUIPMENT MAY HAVE SURVIVED...
...AND WE WON'T HAVE TO REBUILD PARKER INDUSTRIES FROM SCRATCH.*
GREAT SPEECH, PETE. YOUR OPTIMISM, IT'S...WHAT'S THE WORD?
"DELUSIONAL."
DON'T LISTEN TO SAJANI. I'M SURE THERE'S PLENTY HERE WE CAN SALVAGE AND BRING BACK TO LIFE.
*THE ORIGINAL PARKER INDUSTRIES BLEW UP IN ASM VOL. 3 #18 --NICK
100 DAYS COMPLETE. REBOOTING BRAINWAVE PATTERN.
IT WORKED. I KNEW IT! THE TECHNOLOGY I ACQUIRED IN 2099...
...IF IT WAS POWERFUL ENOUGH TO HOUSE YOUR ARTIFICIAL INTELLIGENCE...
...IT COULD ALSO HANDLE A COPY OF MINE! AND WITH ONE LAST MODIFICATION...
...WHAT WERE ONCE MY GAUNTLETS CAN BECOME A FULLY FUNCTIONAL OCTOBOT!
YES! THE PROCESS CAN BEGIN AGAIN!
THE TRICK WILL BE TO FIND THE RIGHT MOMENT...
...WHEN PARKER'S INFERNAL SPIDER-SENSE WILL BE TAXED TO ITS VERY LIMITS!
ONLY THEN CAN I STRIKE AND RECLAIM THAT BODY ONCE AND FOR ALL--WAIT!
LOGIC SAYS THAT WE'RE IN A TIMELINE WHERE HE'S DEFEATED ME.
HE ALREADY KNOWS HOW TO CAST ME OUT! WHAT'S TO PREVENT PARKER FROM EMPLOYING THAT STRATAGEM AGAIN?!

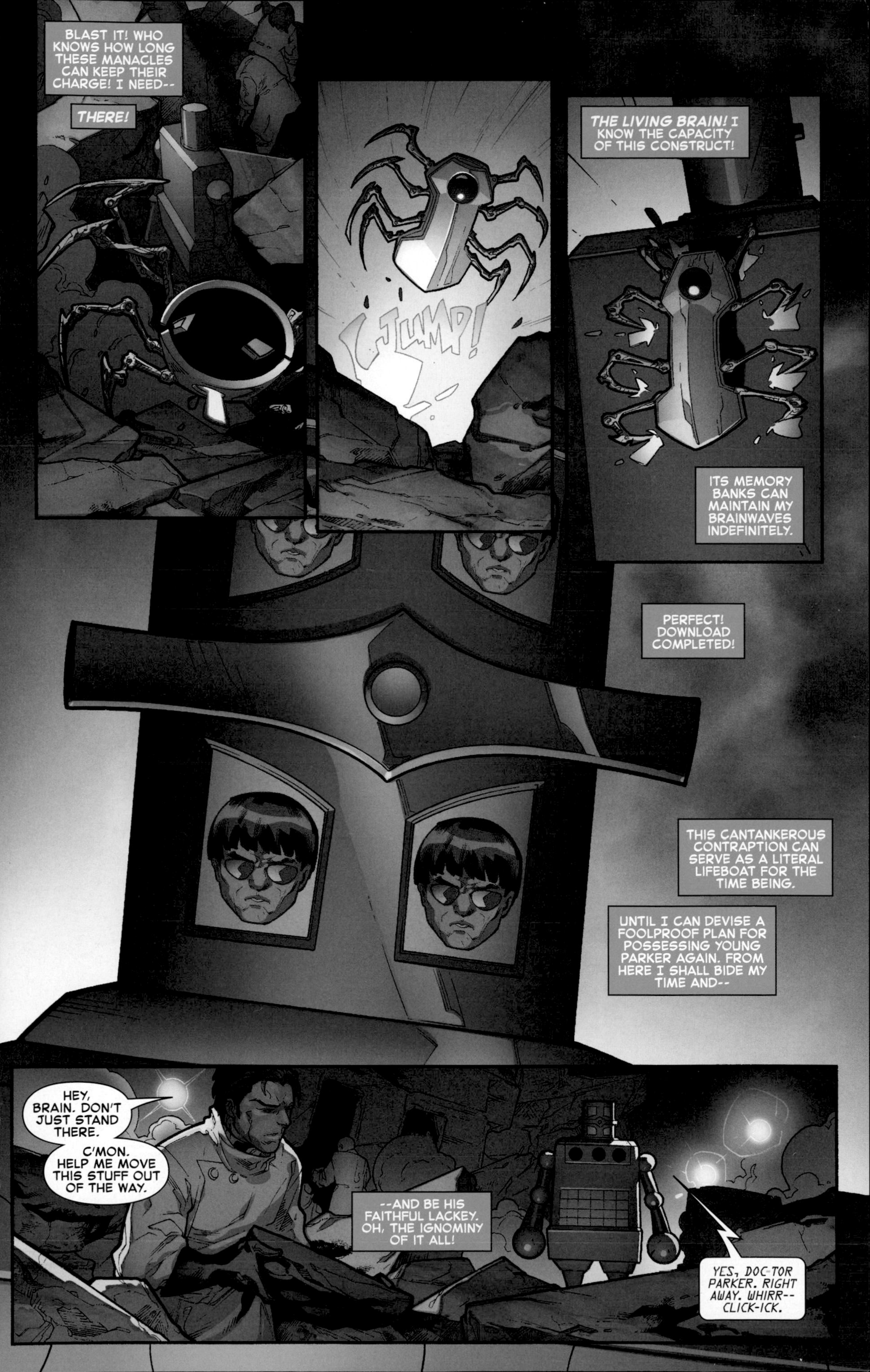
BLAST IT! WHO KNOWS HOW LONG THESE MANACLES CAN KEEP THEIR CHARGE! I NEED--
THERE!
CLUMP!
THE LIVING BRAIN! I KNOW THE CAPACITY OF THIS CONSTRUCT!
ITS MEMORY BANKS CAN MAINTAIN MY BRAINWAVES INDEFINITELY.
PERFECT! DOWNLOAD COMPLETED!
THIS CANTANKEROUS CONTRAPTION CAN SERVE AS A LITERAL LIFEBOAT FOR THE TIME BEING.
UNTIL I CAN DEVISE A FOOLPROOF PLAN FOR POSSESSING YOUNG PARKER AGAIN. FROM HERE I SHALL BIDE MY TIME AND--
HEY, BRAIN. DON'T JUST STAND THERE.
C'MON. HELP ME MOVE THIS STUFF OUT OF THE WAY.
--AND BE HIS FAITHFUL LACKEY. OH, THE IGNOMINY OF IT ALL!
YES, DOC-TOR PARKER. RIGHT AWAY. WHIRR-- CLICK-ICK.

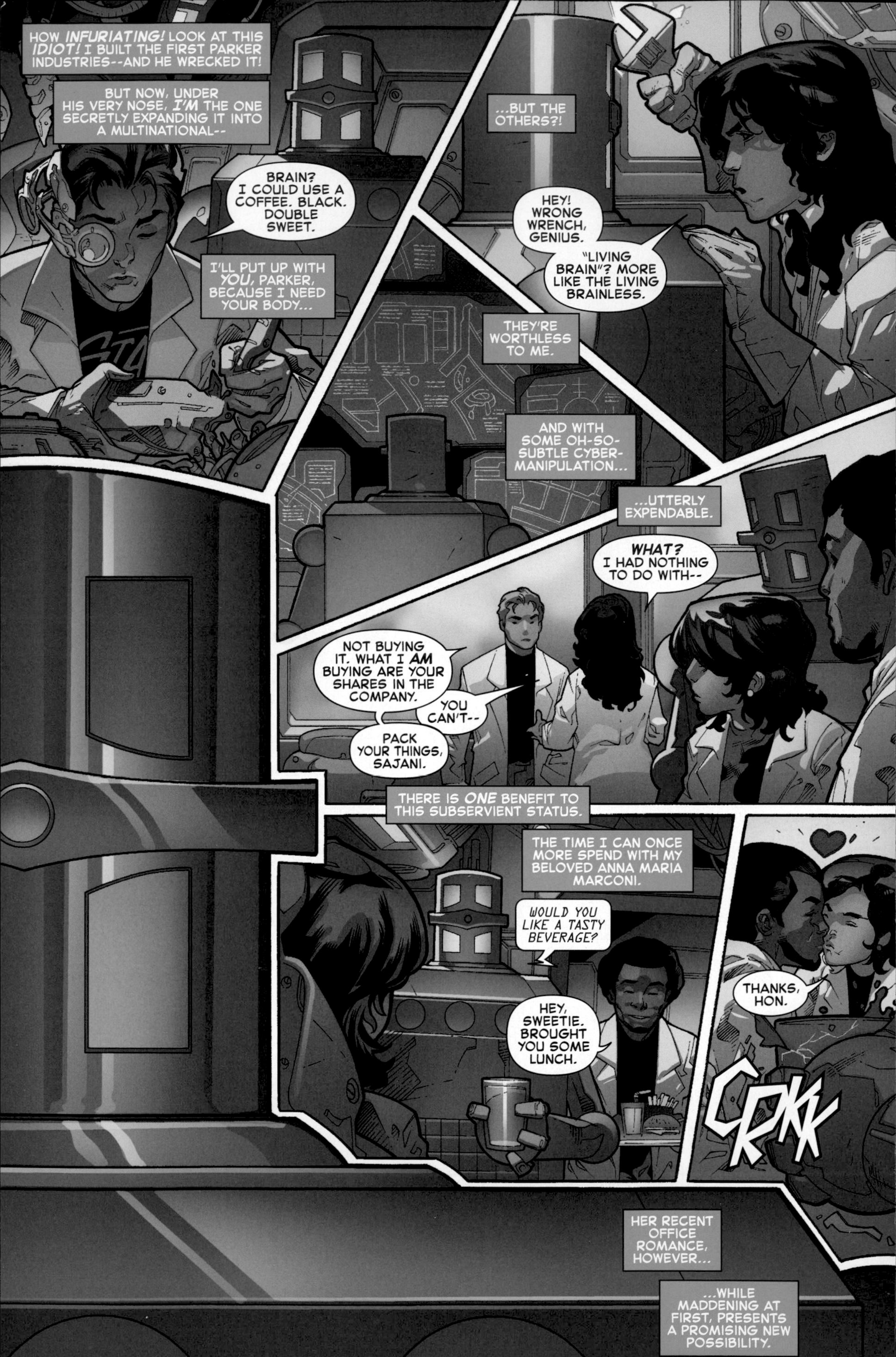
HOW INFURIATING! LOOK AT THIS IDIOT! I BUILT THE FIRST PARKER INDUSTRIES--AND HE WRECKED IT!
BUT NOW, UNDER HIS VERY NOSE, I'M THE ONE SECRETLY EXPANDING IT INTO A MULTINATIONAL--
BRAIN? I COULD USE A COFFEE. BLACK. DOUBLE SWEET.
I'LL PUT UP WITH YOU, PARKER, BECAUSE I NEED YOUR BODY...
...BUT THE OTHERS?!
HEY! WRONG WRENCH, GENIUS.
"LIVING BRAIN"? MORE LIKE THE LIVING BRAINLESS.
THEY'RE WORTHLESS TO ME.
AND WITH SOME OH-SO-SUBTLE CYBER-MANIPULATION...
...UTTERLY EXPENDABLE.
WHAT? I HAD NOTHING TO DO WITH--
NOT BUYING IT. WHAT I AM BUYING ARE YOUR SHARES IN THE COMPANY.
YOU CAN'T--
PACK YOUR THINGS, SAJANI.
THERE IS ONE BENEFIT TO THIS SUBSERVIENT STATUS.
THE TIME I CAN ONCE MORE SPEND WITH MY BELOVED ANNA MARIA MARCONI.
WOULD YOU LIKE A TASTY BEVERAGE?
HEY, SWEETIE. BROUGHT YOU SOME LUNCH.
THANKS, HON.
CRKK
HER RECENT OFFICE ROMANCE, HOWEVER...
...WHILE MADDENING AT FIRST, PRESENTS A PROMISING NEW POSSIBILITY.

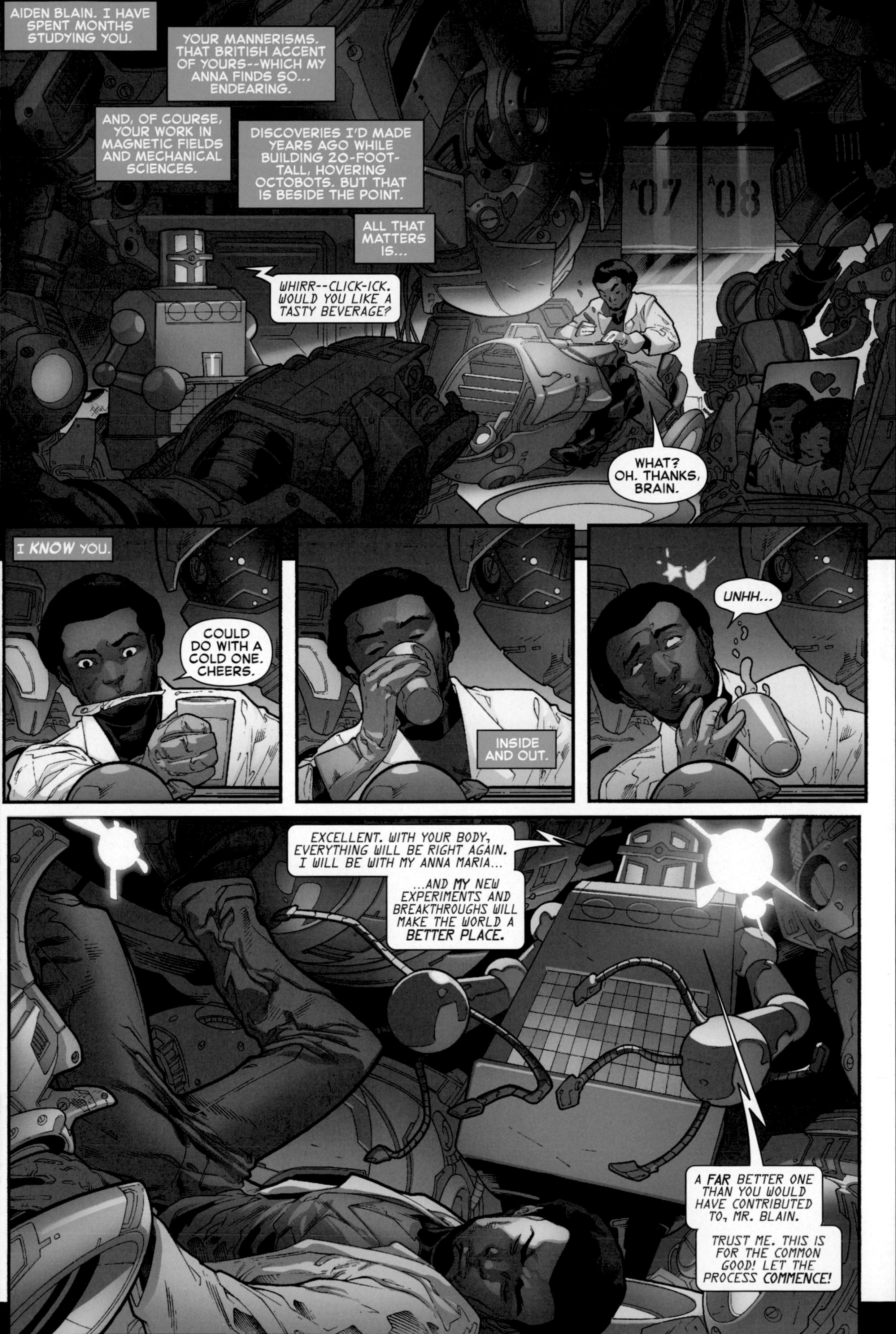

AIDEN BLAIN. I HAVE SPENT MONTHS STUDYING YOU.
YOUR MANNERISMS. THAT BRITISH ACCENT OF YOURS--WHICH MY ANNA FINDS SO... ENDEARING.
AND, OF COURSE, YOUR WORK IN MAGNETIC FIELDS AND MECHANICAL SCIENCES.
DISCOVERIES I'D MADE YEARS AGO WHILE BUILDING 20-FOOT-TALL, HOVERING OCTOBOTS. BUT THAT IS BESIDE THE POINT.
ALL THAT MATTERS IS...
WHIRR--CLICK-ICK. WOULD YOU LIKE A TASTY BEVERAGE?
A07
A08
WHAT? OH. THANKS, BRAIN.
I KNOW YOU.
COULD DO WITH A COLD ONE. CHEERS.
INSIDE AND OUT.
UNHH...
EXCELLENT. WITH YOUR BODY, EVERYTHING WILL BE RIGHT AGAIN. I WILL BE WITH MY ANNA MARIA...
...AND MY NEW EXPERIMENTS AND BREAKTHROUGHS WILL MAKE THE WORLD A BETTER PLACE.
A FAR BETTER ONE THAN YOU WOULD HAVE CONTRIBUTED TO, MR. BLAIN.
TRUST ME. THIS IS FOR THE COMMON GOOD! LET THE PROCESS COMMENCE!

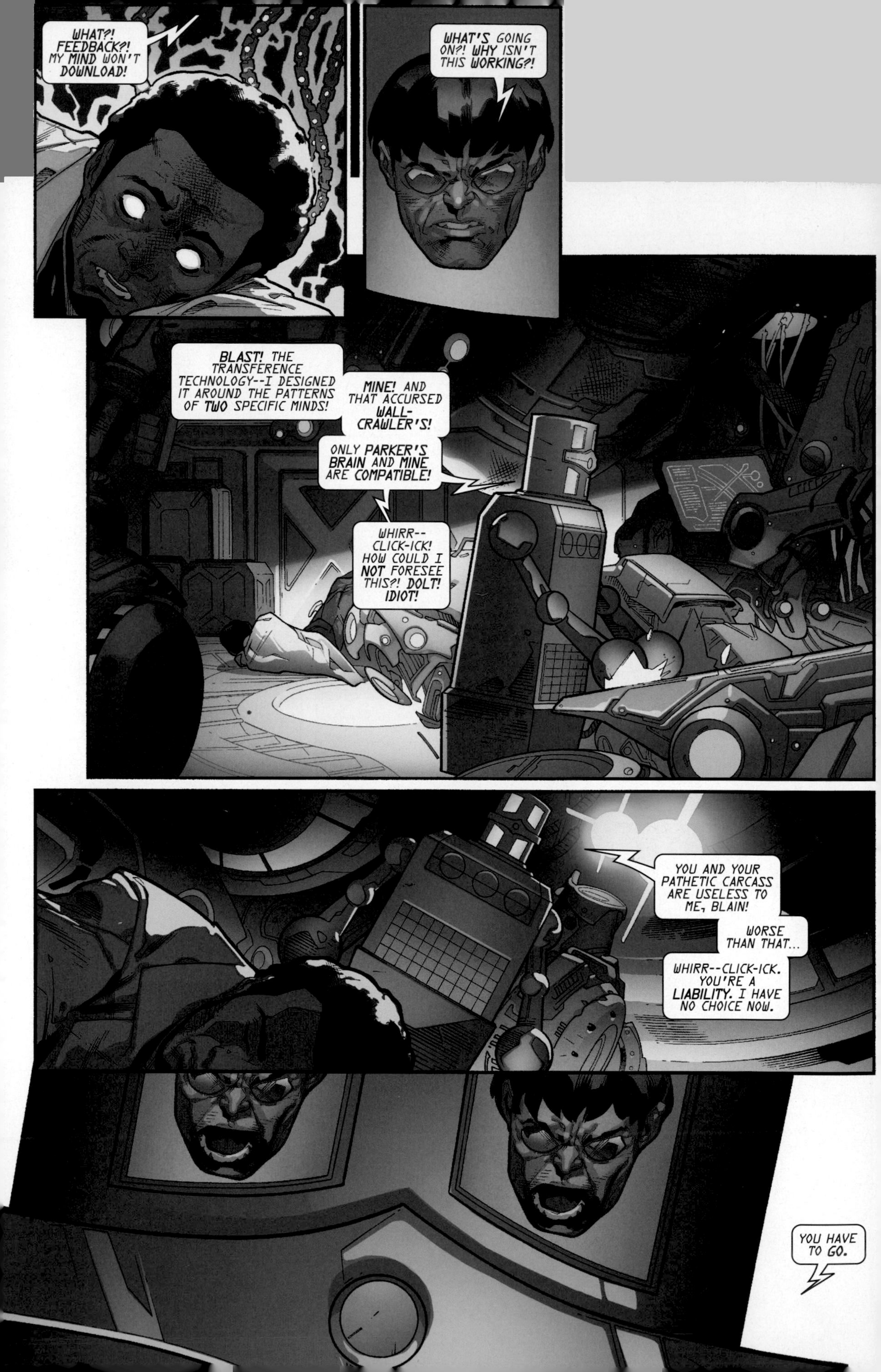
WHAT?! FEEDBACK?! MY MIND WON'T DOWNLOAD!
WHAT'S GOING ON?! WHY ISN'T THIS WORKING?!
BLAST! THE TRANSFERENCE TECHNOLOGY--I DESIGNED IT AROUND THE PATTERNS OF TWO SPECIFIC MINDS!
MINE! AND THAT ACCURSED WALL-CRAWLER'S!
ONLY PARKER'S BRAIN AND MINE ARE COMPATIBLE!
WHIRR--CLICK-ICK! HOW COULD I NOT FORESEE THIS?! DOLT! IDIOT!
YOU AND YOUR PATHETIC CARCASS ARE USELESS TO ME, BLAIN!
WORSE THAN THAT...
WHIRR--CLICK-ICK. YOU'RE A LIABILITY. I HAVE NO CHOICE NOW.
YOU HAVE TO GO.

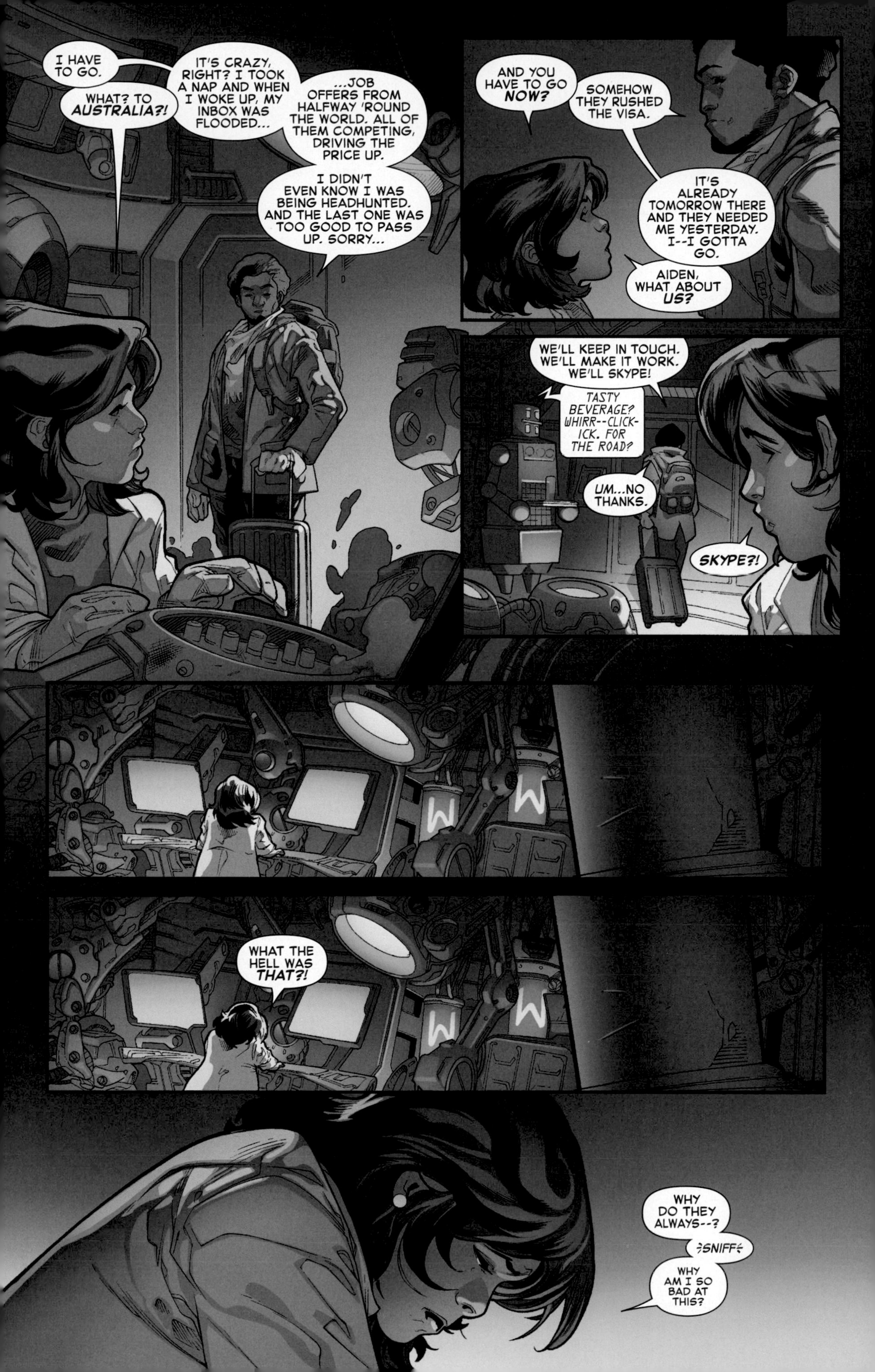
I HAVE TO GO.
WHAT? TO AUSTRALIA?!
IT'S CRAZY, RIGHT? I TOOK A NAP AND WHEN I WOKE UP, MY INBOX WAS FLOODED...
...JOB OFFERS FROM HALFWAY 'ROUND THE WORLD. ALL OF THEM COMPETING, DRIVING THE PRICE UP.
I DIDN'T EVEN KNOW I WAS BEING HEADHUNTED. AND THE LAST ONE WAS TOO GOOD TO PASS UP. SORRY...
AND YOU HAVE TO GO NOW?
SOMEHOW THEY RUSHED THE VISA.
IT'S ALREADY TOMORROW THERE AND THEY NEEDED ME YESTERDAY. I--I GOTTA GO.
AIDEN, WHAT ABOUT US?
WE'LL KEEP IN TOUCH. WE'LL MAKE IT WORK. WE'LL SKYPE!
TASTY BEVERAGE? WHIRR--CLICK-ICK. FOR THE ROAD?
UM...NO THANKS.
SKYPE?!
WHAT THE HELL WAS THAT?!
WHY DO THEY ALWAYS--?
SNIFF
WHY AM I SO BAD AT THIS?

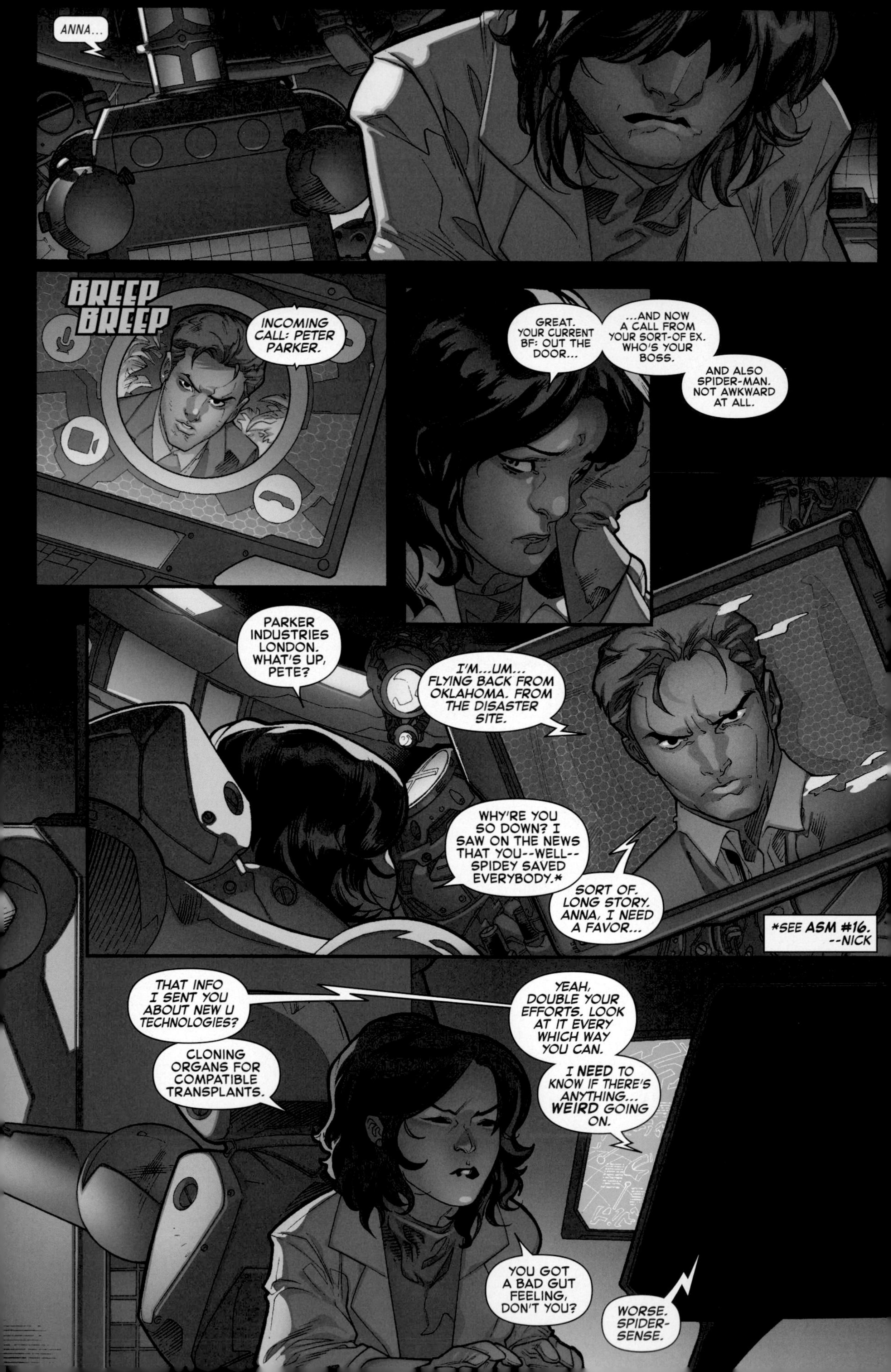
ANNA...
BREEP BREEP
INCOMING CALL: PETER PARKER.
GREAT. YOUR CURRENT BF: OUT THE DOOR...
...AND NOW A CALL FROM YOUR SORT-OF EX. WHO'S YOUR BOSS.
AND ALSO SPIDER-MAN. NOT AWKWARD AT ALL.
PARKER INDUSTRIES LONDON. WHAT'S UP, PETE?
I'M...UM... FLYING BACK FROM OKLAHOMA. FROM THE DISASTER SITE.
WHY'RE YOU SO DOWN? I SAW ON THE NEWS THAT YOU--WELL-- SPIDEY SAVED EVERYBODY.*
SORT OF. LONG STORY. ANNA, I NEED A FAVOR...
*SEE ASM #16. --NICK
THAT INFO I SENT YOU ABOUT NEW U TECHNOLOGIES?
CLONING ORGANS FOR COMPATIBLE TRANSPLANTS.
YEAH, DOUBLE YOUR EFFORTS. LOOK AT IT EVERY WHICH WAY YOU CAN.
I NEED TO KNOW IF THERE'S ANYTHING... WEIRD GOING ON.
YOU GOT A BAD GUT FEELING, DON'T YOU?
WORSE. SPIDER-SENSE.

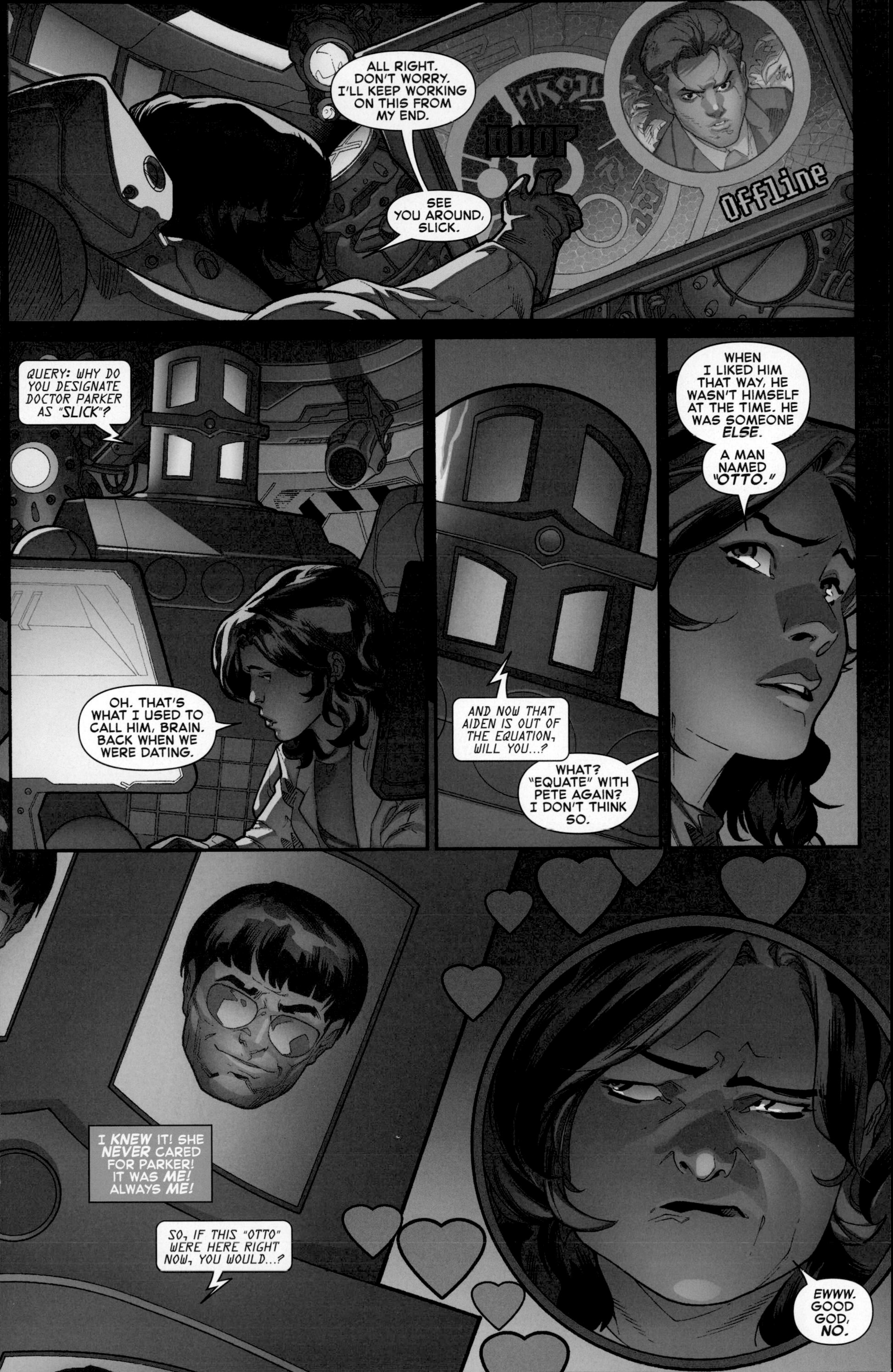
ALL RIGHT. DON'T WORRY. I'LL KEEP WORKING ON THIS FROM MY END.
SEE YOU AROUND, SLICK.
Offline
QUERY: WHY DO YOU DESIGNATE DOCTOR PARKER AS "SLICK"?
OH. THAT'S WHAT I USED TO CALL HIM, BRAIN. BACK WHEN WE WERE DATING.
AND NOW THAT AIDEN IS OUT OF THE EQUATION, WILL YOU...?
WHAT? "EQUATE" WITH PETE AGAIN? I DON'T THINK SO.
WHEN I LIKED HIM THAT WAY, HE WASN'T HIMSELF AT THE TIME. HE WAS SOMEONE ELSE.
A MAN NAMED "OTTO."
I KNEW IT! SHE NEVER CARED FOR PARKER! IT WAS ME! ALWAYS ME!
SO, IF THIS "OTTO" WERE HERE RIGHT NOW, YOU WOULD...?
EWWW. GOOD GOD, NO.

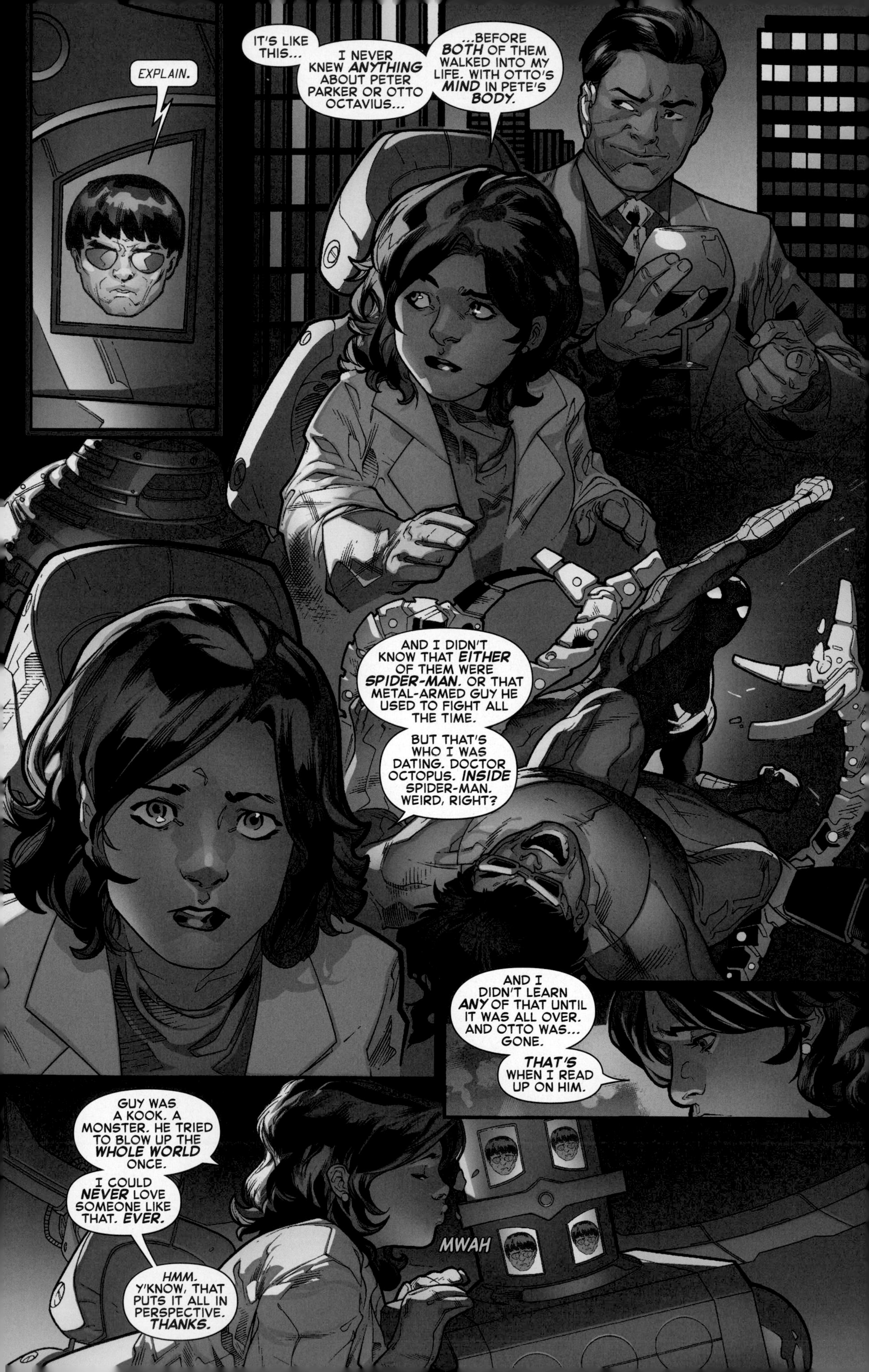
EXPLAIN.
IT'S LIKE THIS...
I NEVER KNEW ANYTHING ABOUT PETER PARKER OR OTTO OCTAVIUS...
...BEFORE BOTH OF THEM WALKED INTO MY LIFE. WITH OTTO'S MIND IN PETE'S BODY.
AND I DIDN'T KNOW THAT EITHER OF THEM WERE SPIDER-MAN. OR THAT METAL-ARMED GUY HE USED TO FIGHT ALL THE TIME.
BUT THAT'S WHO I WAS DATING. DOCTOR OCTOPUS. INSIDE SPIDER-MAN. WEIRD, RIGHT?
AND I DIDN'T LEARN ANY OF THAT UNTIL IT WAS ALL OVER. AND OTTO WAS... GONE.
THAT'S WHEN I READ UP ON HIM.
GUY WAS A KOOK. A MONSTER. HE TRIED TO BLOW UP THE WHOLE WORLD ONCE.
I COULD NEVER LOVE SOMEONE LIKE THAT. EVER.
HMM. Y'KNOW, THAT PUTS IT ALL IN PERSPECTIVE. THANKS.
MWAH

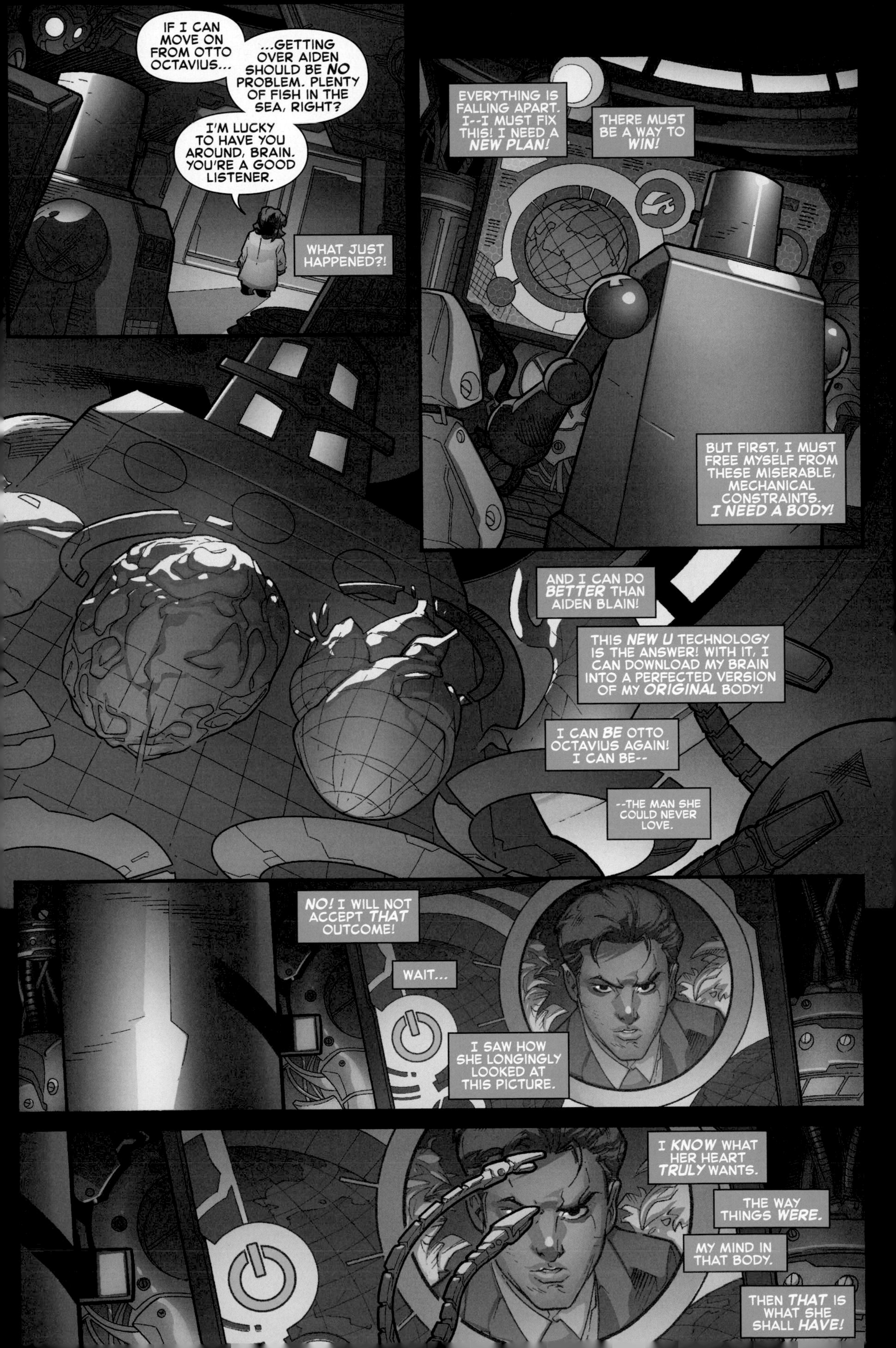
IF I CAN MOVE ON FROM OTTO OCTAVIUS...
...GETTING OVER AIDEN SHOULD BE NO PROBLEM. PLENTY OF FISH IN THE SEA, RIGHT?
I'M LUCKY TO HAVE YOU AROUND, BRAIN. YOU'RE A GOOD LISTENER.
WHAT JUST HAPPENED?!
EVERYTHING IS FALLING APART. I--I MUST FIX THIS! I NEED A NEW PLAN!
THERE MUST BE A WAY TO WIN!
BUT FIRST, I MUST FREE MYSELF FROM THESE MISERABLE, MECHANICAL CONSTRAINTS. I NEED A BODY!
AND I CAN DO BETTER THAN AIDEN BLAIN!
THIS NEW U TECHNOLOGY IS THE ANSWER! WITH IT, I CAN DOWNLOAD MY BRAIN INTO A PERFECTED VERSION OF MY ORIGINAL BODY!
I CAN BE OTTO OCTAVIUS AGAIN! I CAN BE--
--THE MAN SHE COULD NEVER LOVE.
NO! I WILL NOT ACCEPT THAT OUTCOME!
WAIT...
I SAW HOW SHE LONGINGLY LOOKED AT THIS PICTURE.
I KNOW WHAT HER HEART TRULY WANTS.
THE WAY THINGS WERE.
MY MIND IN THAT BODY.
THEN THAT IS WHAT SHE SHALL HAVE!

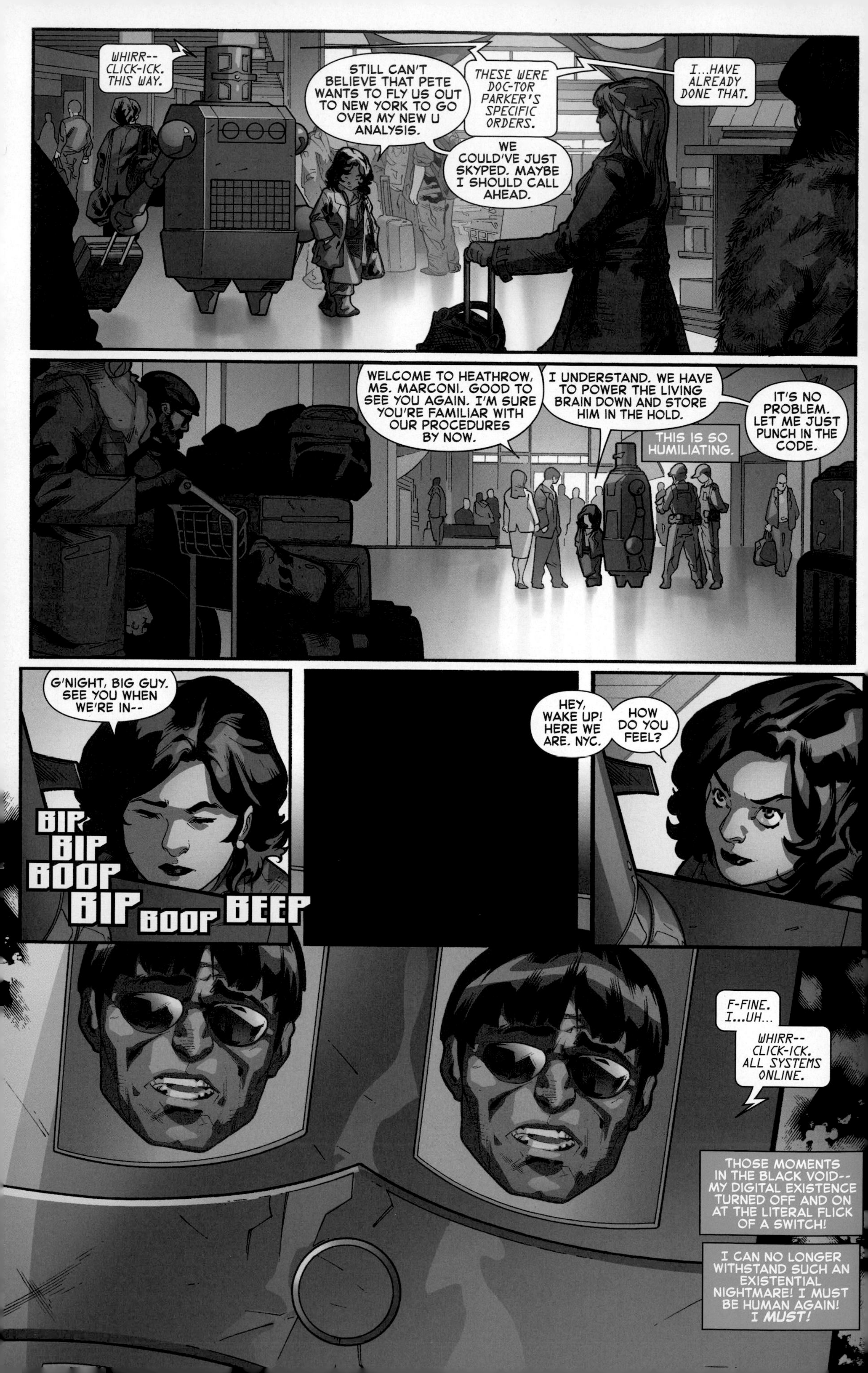
WHIRR-- CLICK-ICK. THIS WAY.
STILL CAN'T BELIEVE THAT PETE WANTS TO FLY US OUT TO NEW YORK TO GO OVER MY NEW U ANALYSIS.
THESE WERE DOC-TOR PARKER'S SPECIFIC ORDERS.
WE COULD'VE JUST SKYPED. MAYBE I SHOULD CALL AHEAD.
I...HAVE ALREADY DONE THAT.
WELCOME TO HEATHROW, MS. MARCONI. GOOD TO SEE YOU AGAIN. I'M SURE YOU'RE FAMILIAR WITH OUR PROCEDURES BY NOW.
I UNDERSTAND. WE HAVE TO POWER THE LIVING BRAIN DOWN AND STORE HIM IN THE HOLD.
THIS IS SO HUMILIATING.
IT'S NO PROBLEM. LET ME JUST PUNCH IN THE CODE.
G'NIGHT, BIG GUY. SEE YOU WHEN WE'RE IN--
BIP BIP BOOP BIP BOOP BEEP
HEY, WAKE UP! HERE WE ARE. NYC.
HOW DO YOU FEEL?
F-FINE. I...UH...
WHIRR-- CLICK-ICK. ALL SYSTEMS ONLINE.
THOSE MOMENTS IN THE BLACK VOID-- MY DIGITAL EXISTENCE TURNED OFF AND ON AT THE LITERAL FLICK OF A SWITCH!
I CAN NO LONGER WITHSTAND SUCH AN EXISTENTIAL NIGHTMARE! I MUST BE HUMAN AGAIN! I MUST!

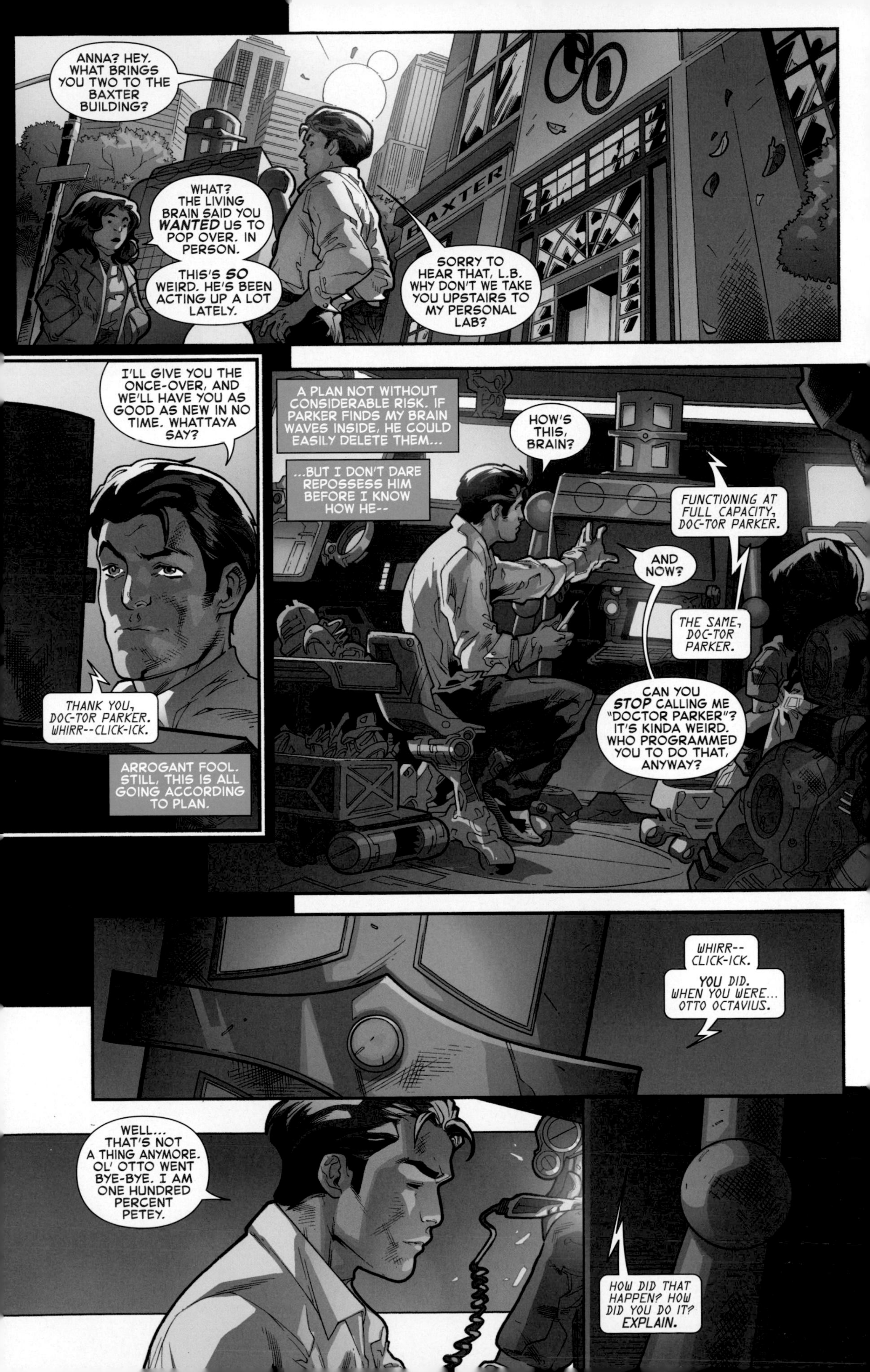
ANNA? HEY. WHAT BRINGS YOU TWO TO THE BAXTER BUILDING?
WHAT? THE LIVING BRAIN SAID YOU WANTED US TO POP OVER. IN PERSON.
THIS'S SO WEIRD. HE'S BEEN ACTING UP A LOT LATELY.
SORRY TO HEAR THAT, L.B. WHY DON'T WE TAKE YOU UPSTAIRS TO MY PERSONAL LAB?
BAXTER
I'LL GIVE YOU THE ONCE-OVER, AND WE'LL HAVE YOU AS GOOD AS NEW IN NO TIME. WHATTAYA SAY?
THANK YOU, DOC-TOR PARKER. WHIRR--CLICK-ICK.
ARROGANT FOOL. STILL, THIS IS ALL GOING ACCORDING TO PLAN.
A PLAN NOT WITHOUT CONSIDERABLE RISK. IF PARKER FINDS MY BRAIN WAVES INSIDE, HE COULD EASILY DELETE THEM...
...BUT I DON'T DARE REPOSSESS HIM BEFORE I KNOW HOW HE--
HOW'S THIS, BRAIN?
FUNCTIONING AT FULL CAPACITY, DOC-TOR PARKER.
AND NOW?
THE SAME, DOC-TOR PARKER.
CAN YOU STOP CALLING ME "DOCTOR PARKER"? IT'S KINDA WEIRD. WHO PROGRAMMED YOU TO DO THAT, ANYWAY?
WHIRR-- CLICK-ICK.
YOU DID. WHEN YOU WERE... OTTO OCTAVIUS.
WELL... THAT'S NOT A THING ANYMORE. OL' OTTO WENT BYE-BYE. I AM ONE HUNDRED PERCENT PETEY.
HOW DID THAT HAPPEN? HOW DID YOU DO IT? EXPLAIN.

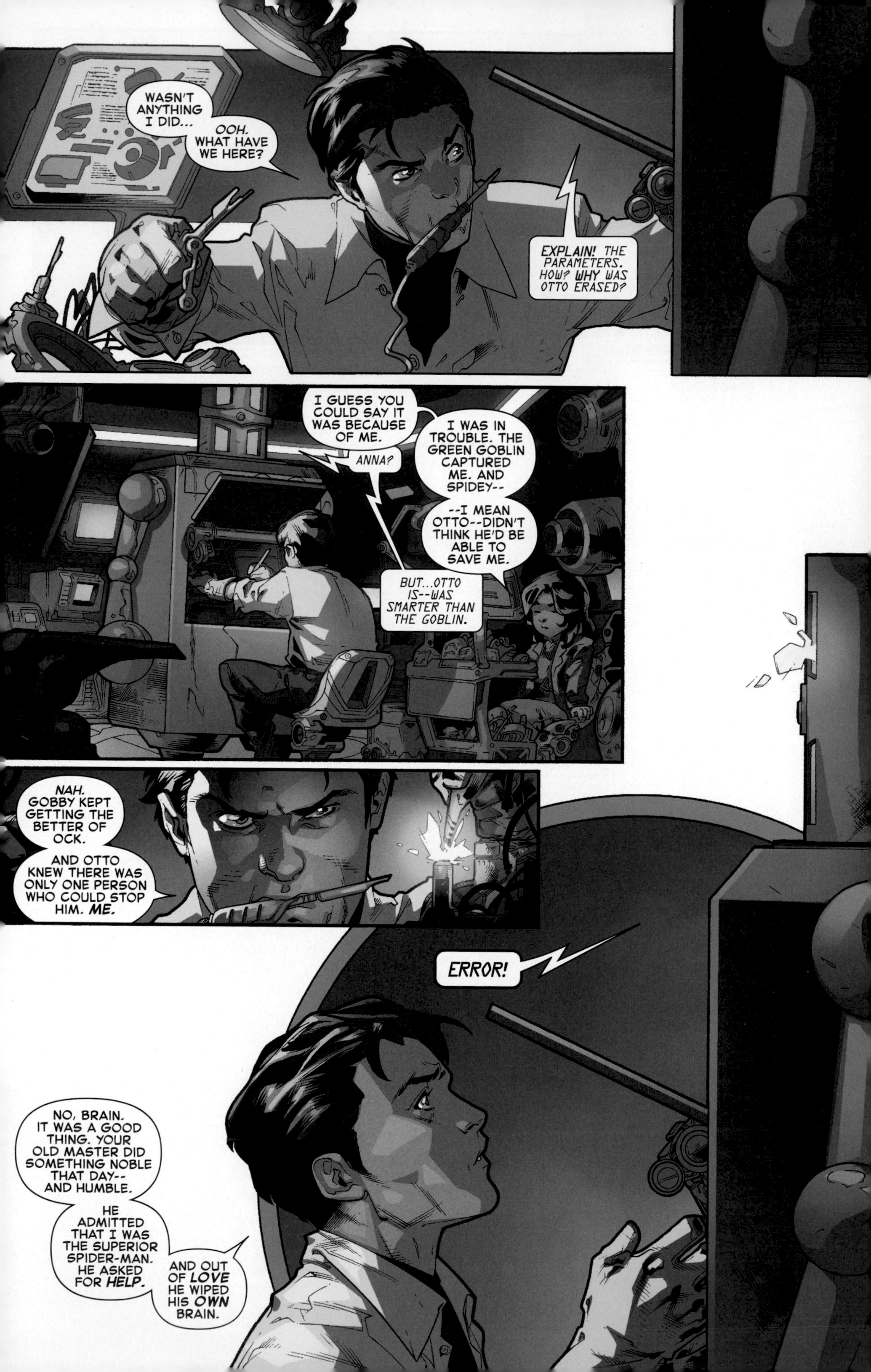
WASN'T ANYTHING I DID...
OOH. WHAT HAVE WE HERE?
EXPLAIN! THE PARAMETERS. HOW? WHY WAS OTTO ERASED?
I GUESS YOU COULD SAY IT WAS BECAUSE OF ME.
ANNA?
I WAS IN TROUBLE. THE GREEN GOBLIN CAPTURED ME. AND SPIDEY--
--I MEAN OTTO--DIDN'T THINK HE'D BE ABLE TO SAVE ME.
BUT...OTTO IS--WAS SMARTER THAN THE GOBLIN.
NAH. GOBBY KEPT GETTING THE BETTER OF OCK.
AND OTTO KNEW THERE WAS ONLY ONE PERSON WHO COULD STOP HIM. ME.
ERROR!
NO, BRAIN. IT WAS A GOOD THING. YOUR OLD MASTER DID SOMETHING NOBLE THAT DAY-- AND HUMBLE.
HE ADMITTED THAT I WAS THE SUPERIOR SPIDER-MAN. HE ASKED FOR HELP.
AND OUT OF LOVE HE WIPED HIS OWN BRAIN.

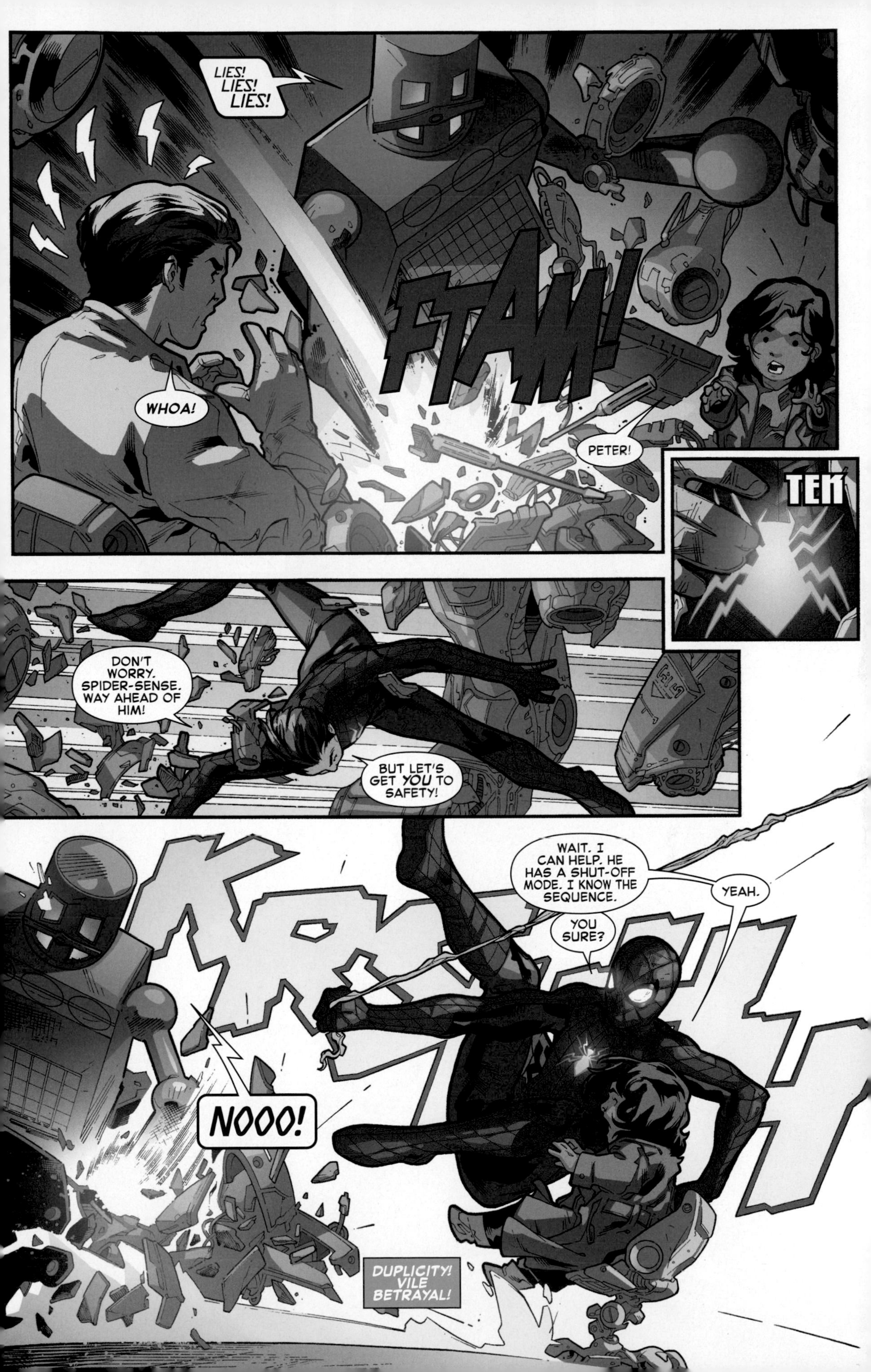
LIES! LIES! LIES!
WHOA!
FTAM!
PETER!
TEN
DON'T WORRY. SPIDER-SENSE. WAY AHEAD OF HIM!
BUT LET'S GET YOU TO SAFETY!
WAIT. I CAN HELP. HE HAS A SHUT-OFF MODE. I KNOW THE SEQUENCE.
YOU SURE?
YEAH.
NOOO!
DUPLICITY! VILE BETRAYAL!

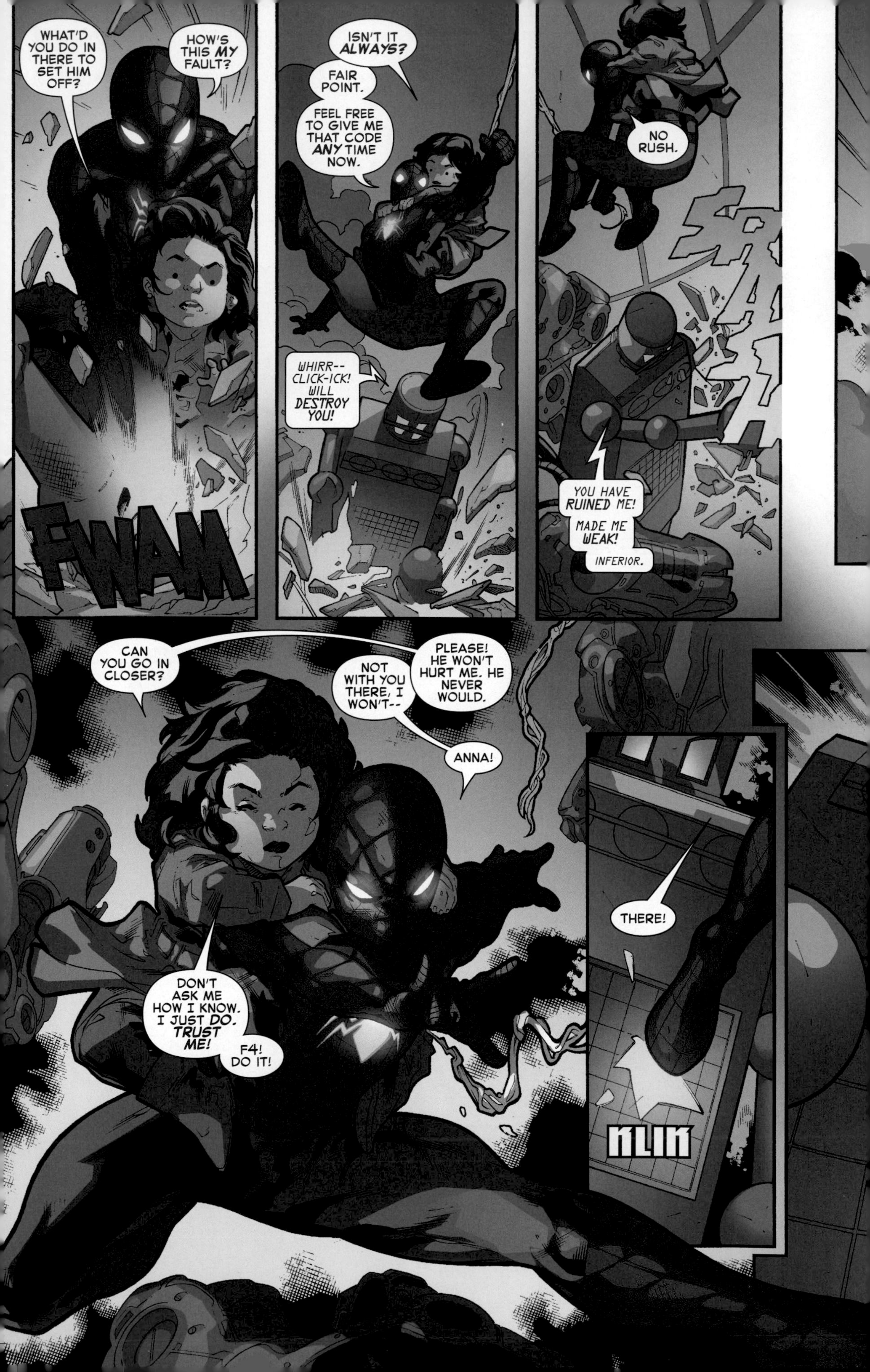
WHAT'D YOU DO IN THERE TO SET HIM OFF?
HOW'S THIS MY FAULT?
FWAM
ISN'T IT ALWAYS?
FAIR POINT.
FEEL FREE TO GIVE ME THAT CODE ANY TIME NOW.
WHIRR-- CLICK-ICK! WILL DESTROY YOU!
NO RUSH.
YOU HAVE RUINED ME!
MADE ME WEAK!
INFERIOR.
CAN YOU GO IN CLOSER?
PLEASE! HE WON'T HURT ME. HE NEVER WOULD.
NOT WITH YOU THERE, I WON'T--
ANNA!
DON'T ASK ME HOW I KNOW. I JUST DO. TRUST ME!
F4! DO IT!
THERE!
KLIK

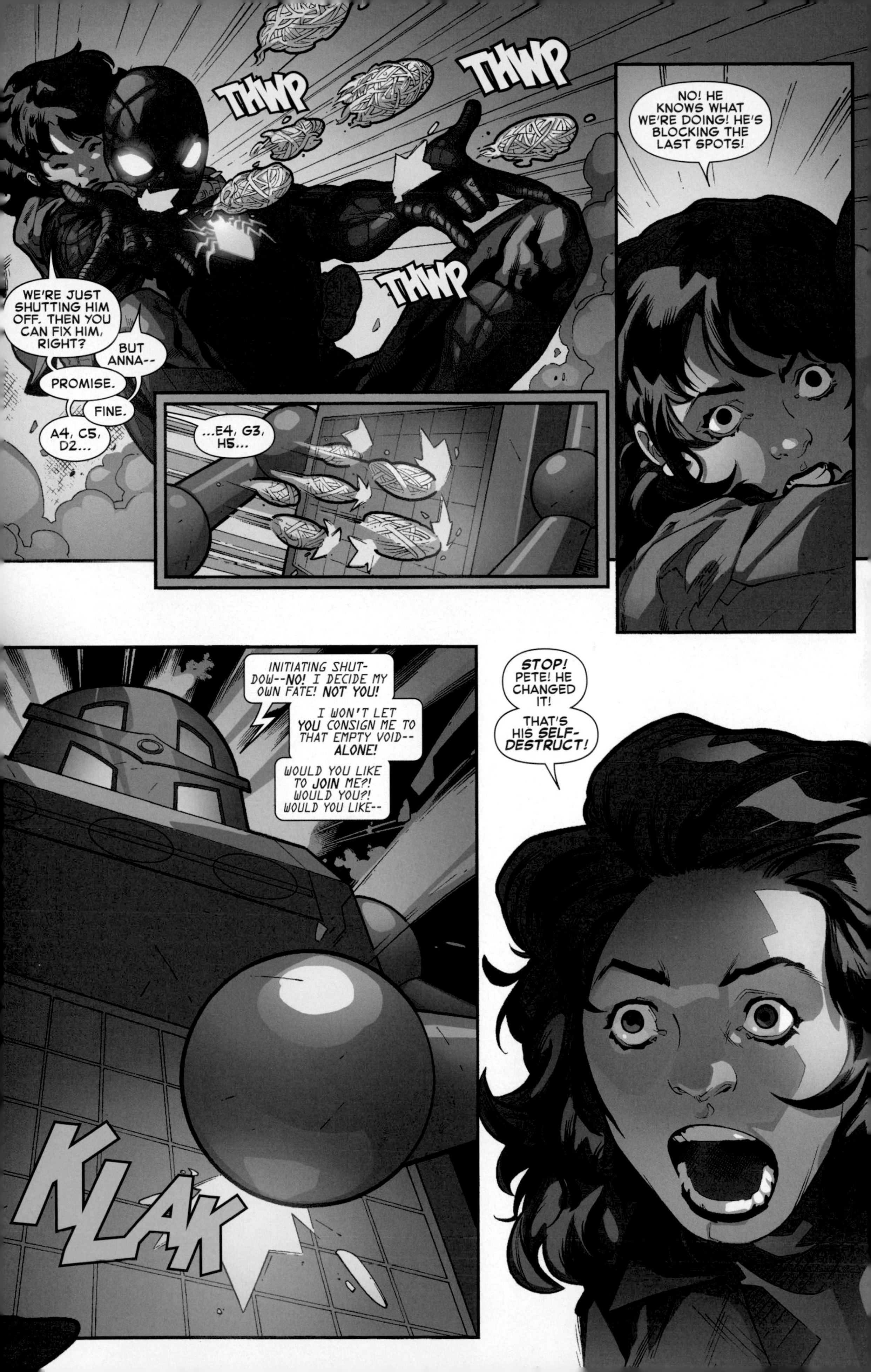
THWP
THWP
NO! HE KNOWS WHAT WE'RE DOING! HE'S BLOCKING THE LAST SPOTS!
WE'RE JUST SHUTTING HIM OFF. THEN YOU CAN FIX HIM, RIGHT?
BUT ANNA--
PROMISE.
FINE.
THWP
A4, C5, D2...
...E4, G3, H5...
INITIATING SHUT-DOW--NO! I DECIDE MY OWN FATE! NOT YOU!
I WON'T LET YOU CONSIGN ME TO THAT EMPTY VOID--ALONE!
WOULD YOU LIKE TO JOIN ME?! WOULD YOU?! WOULD YOU LIKE--
STOP! PETE! HE CHANGED IT!
THAT'S HIS SELF-DESTRUCT!
KLAK

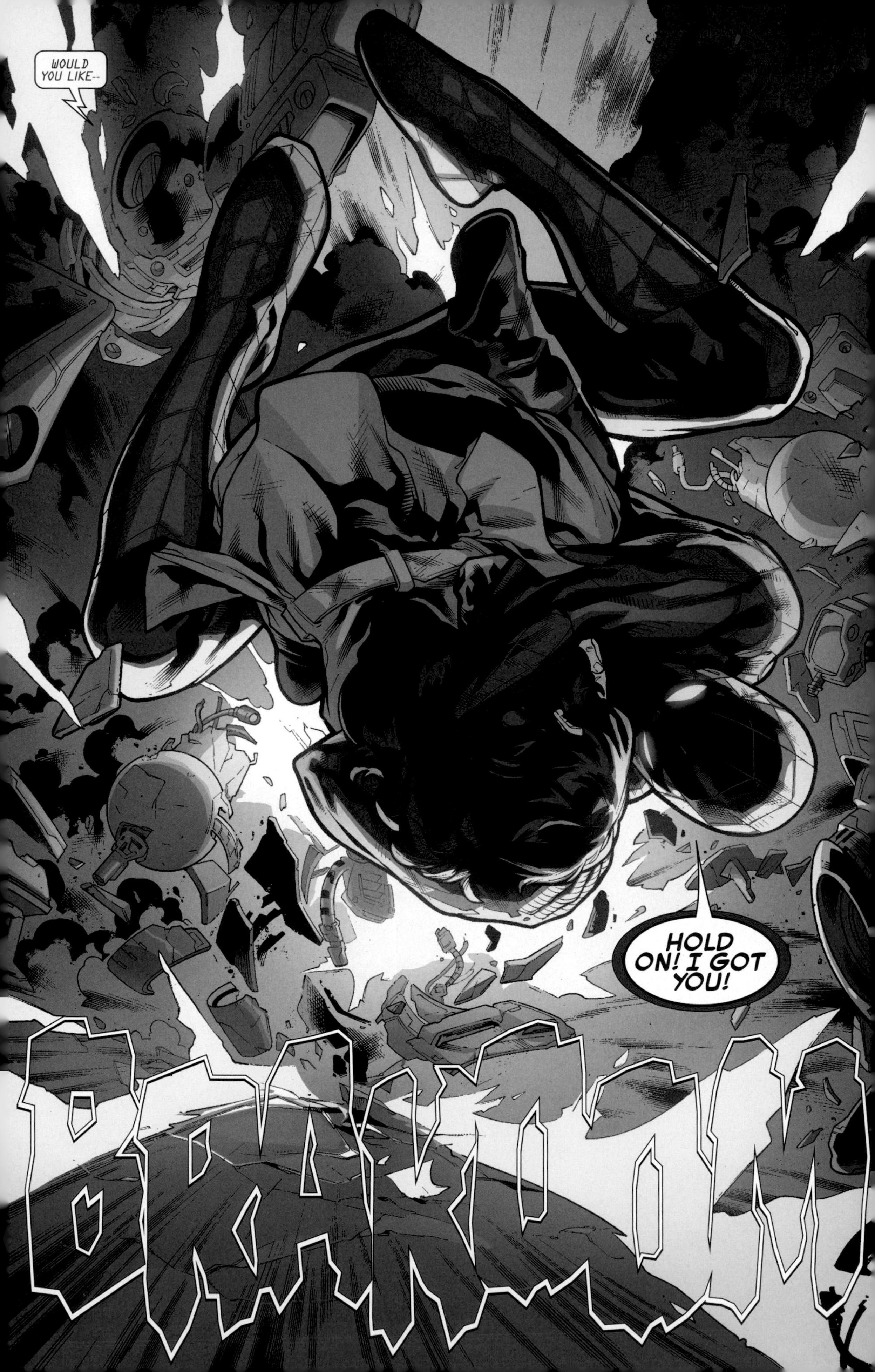
WOULD YOU LIKE--
HOLD ON! I GOT YOU!

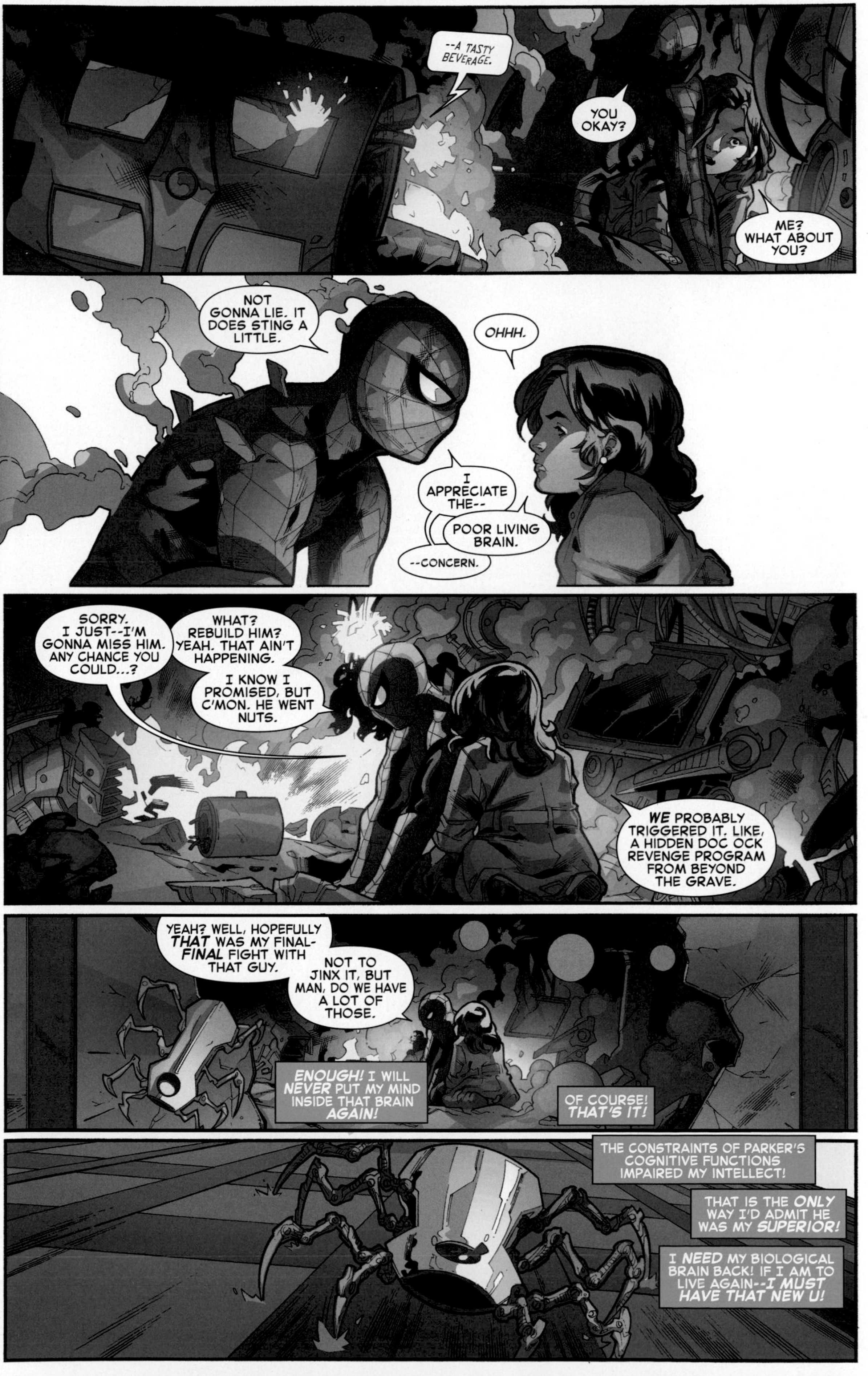
--A TASTY BEVERAGE.
YOU OKAY?
ME? WHAT ABOUT YOU?
NOT GONNA LIE. IT DOES STING A LITTLE.
OHHH.
I APPRECIATE THE--
POOR LIVING BRAIN.
--CONCERN.
SORRY. I JUST--I'M GONNA MISS HIM. ANY CHANCE YOU COULD...?
WHAT? REBUILD HIM? YEAH. THAT AIN'T HAPPENING.
I KNOW I PROMISED, BUT C'MON. HE WENT NUTS.
WE PROBABLY TRIGGERED IT. LIKE, A HIDDEN DOC OCK REVENGE PROGRAM FROM BEYOND THE GRAVE.
YEAH? WELL, HOPEFULLY THAT WAS MY FINAL-FINAL FIGHT WITH THAT GUY.
NOT TO JINX IT, BUT MAN, DO WE HAVE A LOT OF THOSE.
ENOUGH! I WILL NEVER PUT MY MIND INSIDE THAT BRAIN AGAIN!
OF COURSE! THAT'S IT!
THE CONSTRAINTS OF PARKER'S COGNITIVE FUNCTIONS IMPAIRED MY INTELLECT!
THAT IS THE ONLY WAY I'D ADMIT HE WAS MY SUPERIOR!
I NEED MY BIOLOGICAL BRAIN BACK! IF I AM TO LIVE AGAIN--I MUST HAVE THAT NEW U!

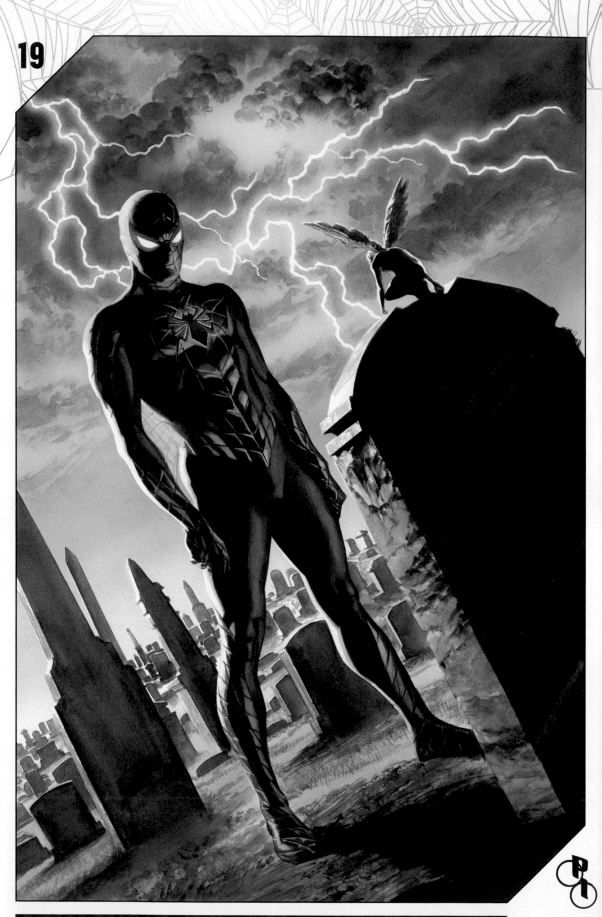

BEFORE DEAD NO MORE -- PART 4: "CHANGE OF HEART"

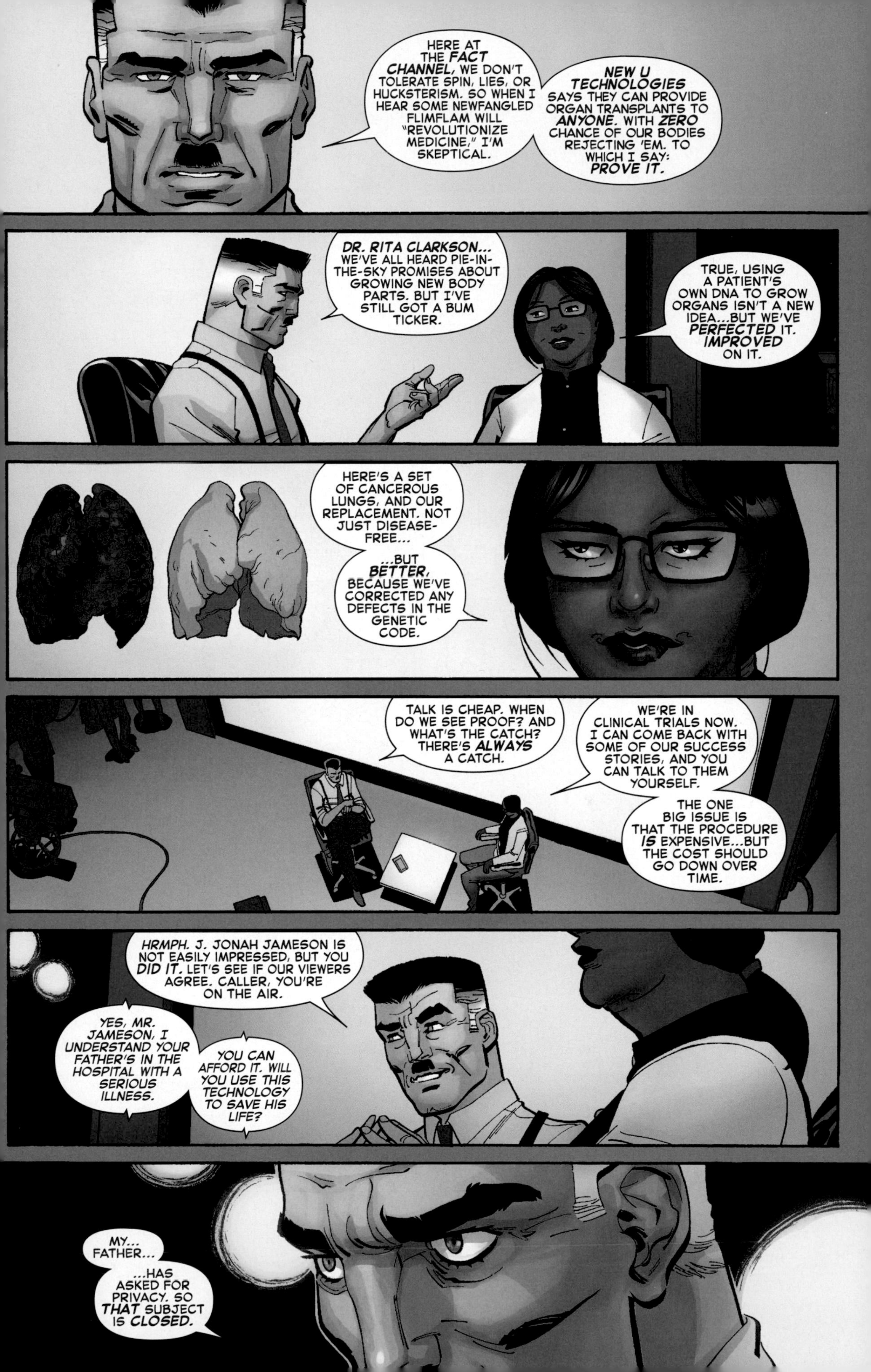
HERE AT THE FACT CHANNEL, WE DON'T TOLERATE SPIN, LIES, OR HUCKSTERISM. SO WHEN I HEAR SOME NEWFANGLED FLIMFLAM WILL "REVOLUTIONIZE MEDICINE," I'M SKEPTICAL.
NEW U TECHNOLOGIES SAYS THEY CAN PROVIDE ORGAN TRANSPLANTS TO ANYONE. WITH ZERO CHANCE OF OUR BODIES REJECTING 'EM. TO WHICH I SAY: PROVE IT.
DR. RITA CLARKSON... WE'VE ALL HEARD PIE-IN-THE-SKY PROMISES ABOUT GROWING NEW BODY PARTS. BUT I'VE STILL GOT A BUM TICKER.
TRUE, USING A PATIENT'S OWN DNA TO GROW ORGANS ISN'T A NEW IDEA...BUT WE'VE PERFECTED IT. IMPROVED ON IT.
HERE'S A SET OF CANCEROUS LUNGS, AND OUR REPLACEMENT. NOT JUST DISEASE-FREE...
...BUT BETTER, BECAUSE WE'VE CORRECTED ANY DEFECTS IN THE GENETIC CODE.
TALK IS CHEAP. WHEN DO WE SEE PROOF? AND WHAT'S THE CATCH? THERE'S ALWAYS A CATCH.
WE'RE IN CLINICAL TRIALS NOW. I CAN COME BACK WITH SOME OF OUR SUCCESS STORIES, AND YOU CAN TALK TO THEM YOURSELF.
THE ONE BIG ISSUE IS THAT THE PROCEDURE IS EXPENSIVE...BUT THE COST SHOULD GO DOWN OVER TIME.
HRMPH. J. JONAH JAMESON IS NOT EASILY IMPRESSED, BUT YOU DID IT. LET'S SEE IF OUR VIEWERS AGREE. CALLER, YOU'RE ON THE AIR.
YES, MR. JAMESON, I UNDERSTAND YOUR FATHER'S IN THE HOSPITAL WITH A SERIOUS ILLNESS.
YOU CAN AFFORD IT. WILL YOU USE THIS TECHNOLOGY TO SAVE HIS LIFE?
MY... FATHER...
...HAS ASKED FOR PRIVACY. SO THAT SUBJECT IS CLOSED.

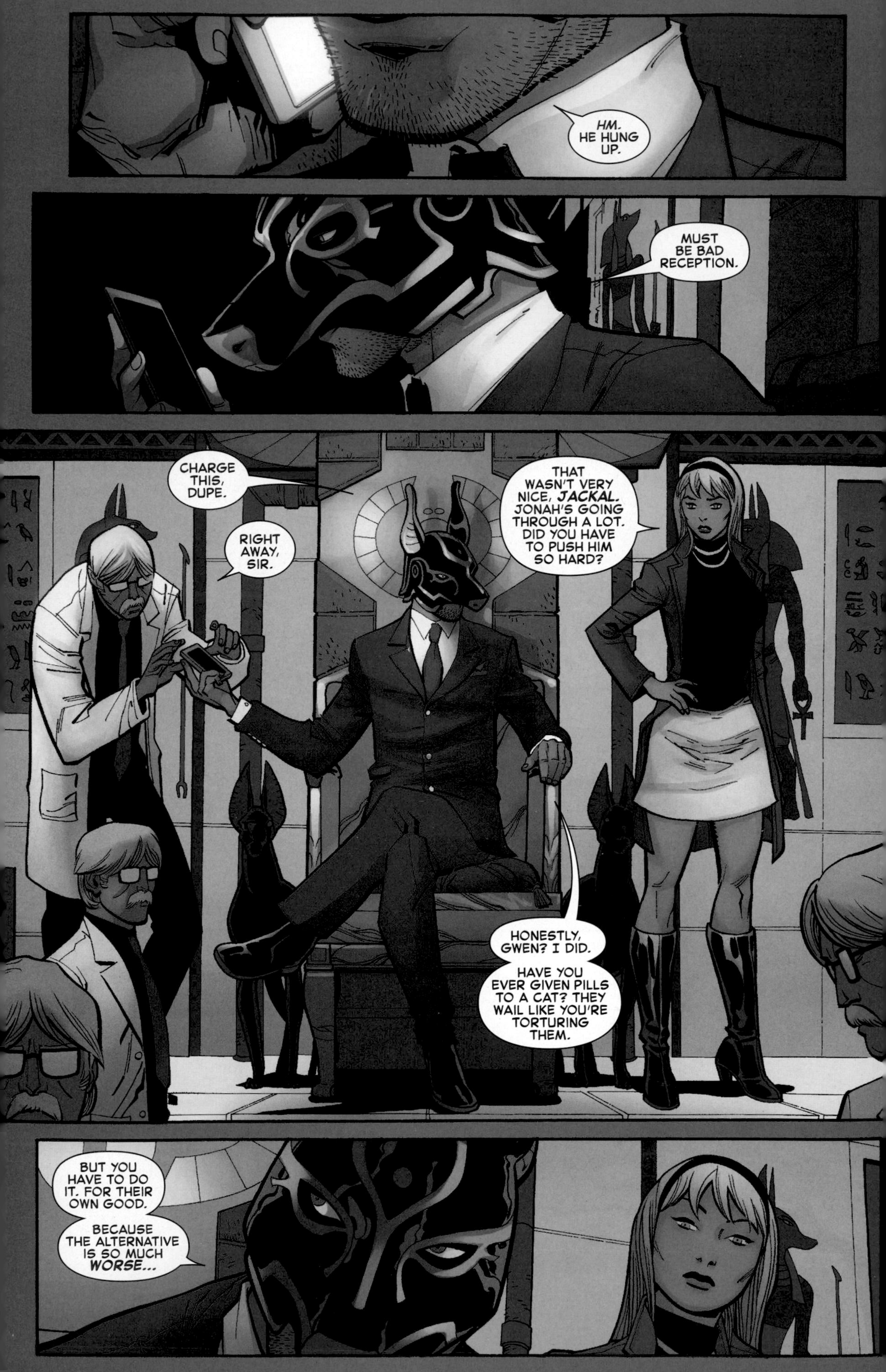
HM. HE HUNG UP.
MUST BE BAD RECEPTION.
CHARGE THIS, DUPE.
RIGHT AWAY, SIR.
THAT WASN'T VERY NICE, ***JACKAL.*** JONAH'S GOING THROUGH A LOT. DID YOU HAVE TO PUSH HIM SO HARD?
HONESTLY, GWEN? I DID.
HAVE YOU EVER GIVEN PILLS TO A CAT? THEY WAIL LIKE YOU'RE TORTURING THEM.
BUT YOU HAVE TO DO IT. FOR THEIR OWN GOOD.
BECAUSE THE ALTERNATIVE IS SO MUCH ***WORSE...***

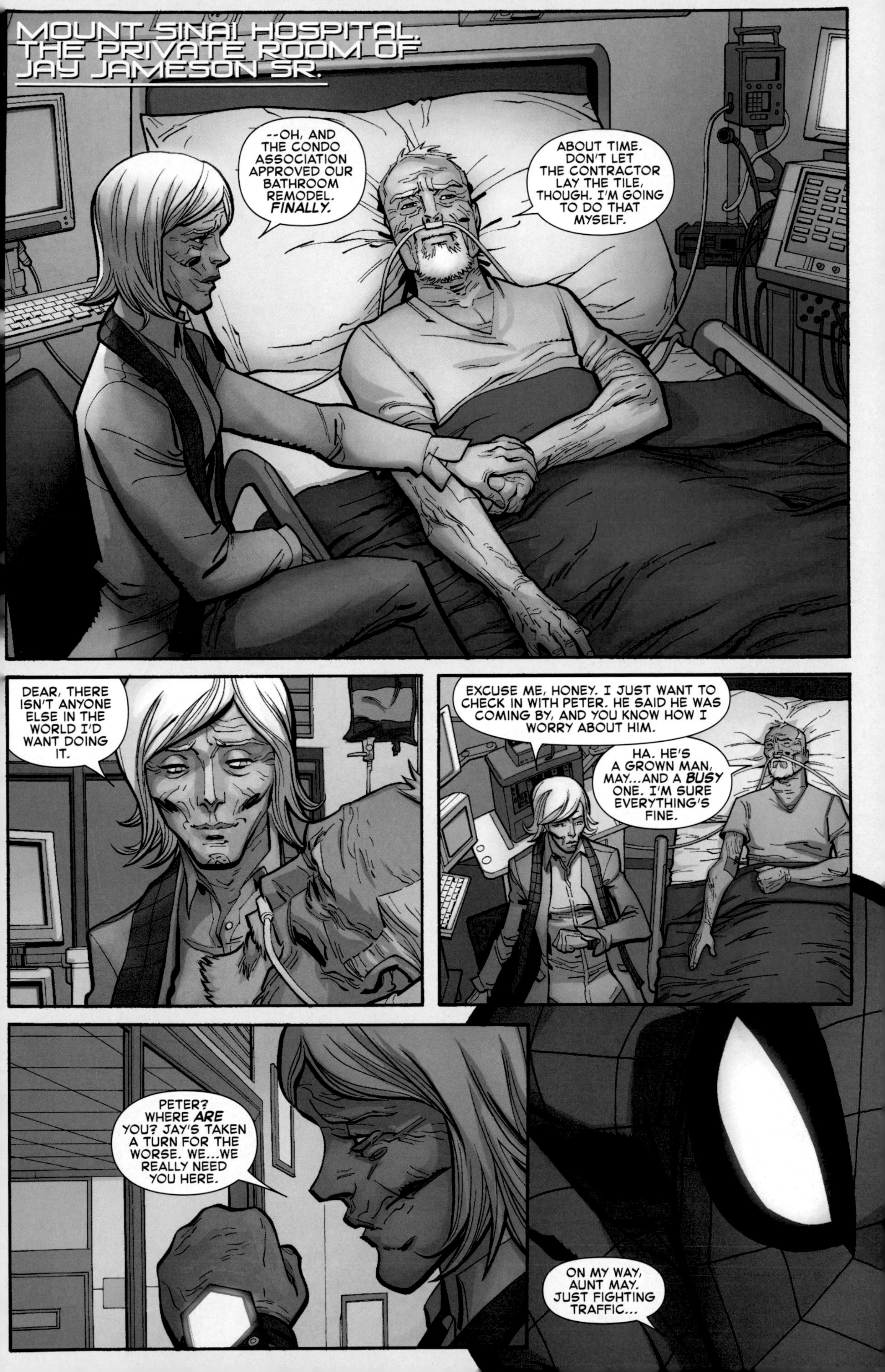
MOUNT SINAI HOSPITAL. THE PRIVATE ROOM OF JAY JAMESON SR.
--OH, AND THE CONDO ASSOCIATION APPROVED OUR BATHROOM REMODEL. FINALLY.
ABOUT TIME. DON'T LET THE CONTRACTOR LAY THE TILE, THOUGH. I'M GOING TO DO THAT MYSELF.
DEAR, THERE ISN'T ANYONE ELSE IN THE WORLD I'D WANT DOING IT.
EXCUSE ME, HONEY. I JUST WANT TO CHECK IN WITH PETER. HE SAID HE WAS COMING BY, AND YOU KNOW HOW I WORRY ABOUT HIM.
HA. HE'S A GROWN MAN, MAY...AND A BUSY ONE. I'M SURE EVERYTHING'S FINE.
PETER? WHERE ARE YOU? JAY'S TAKEN A TURN FOR THE WORSE. WE...WE REALLY NEED YOU HERE.
ON MY WAY, AUNT MAY. JUST FIGHTING TRAFFIC...

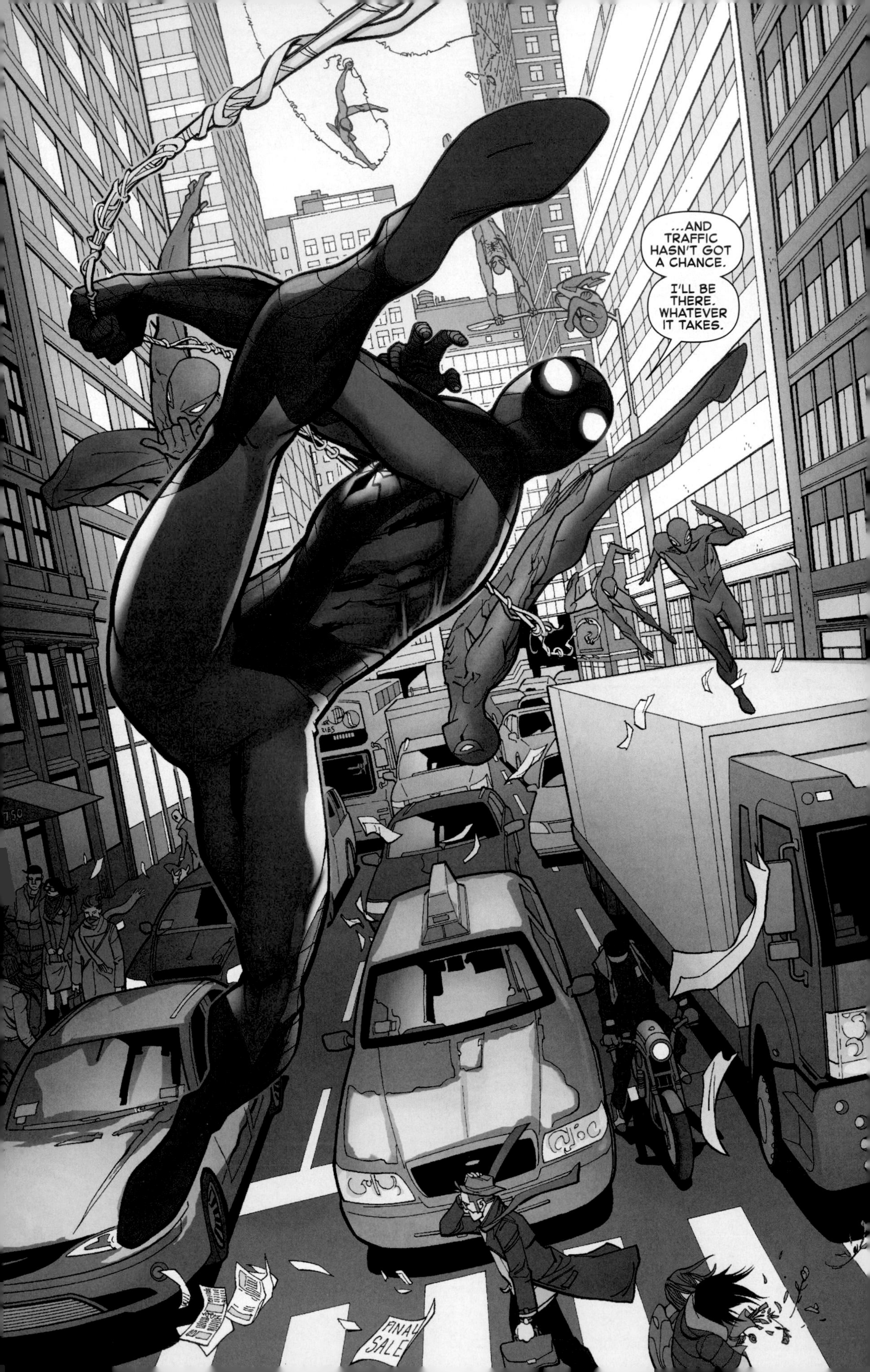

...AND TRAFFIC HASN'T GOT A CHANCE.
I'LL BE THERE. WHATEVER IT TAKES.
750
FINAL SALE

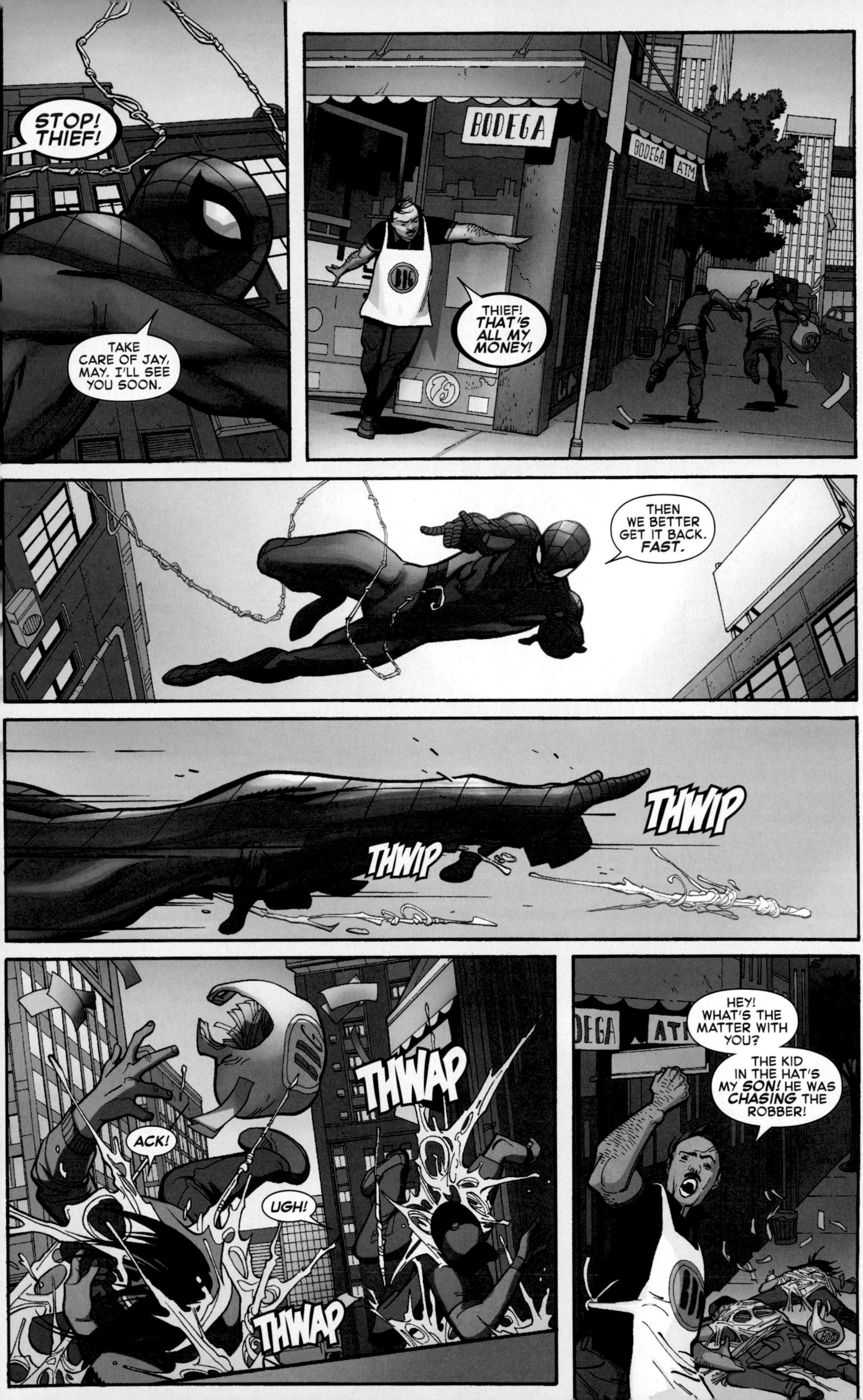
STOP! THIEF!
TAKE CARE OF JAY, MAY. I'LL SEE YOU SOON.
BODEGA
BODEGA
ATM
THIEF! THAT'S ALL MY MONEY!
THEN WE BETTER GET IT BACK. FAST.
THWIP
THWIP
THWAP
ACK!
UGH!
THWAP
DEGA
ATM
HEY! WHAT'S THE MATTER WITH YOU?
THE KID IN THE HAT'S MY SON! HE WAS CHASING THE ROBBER!

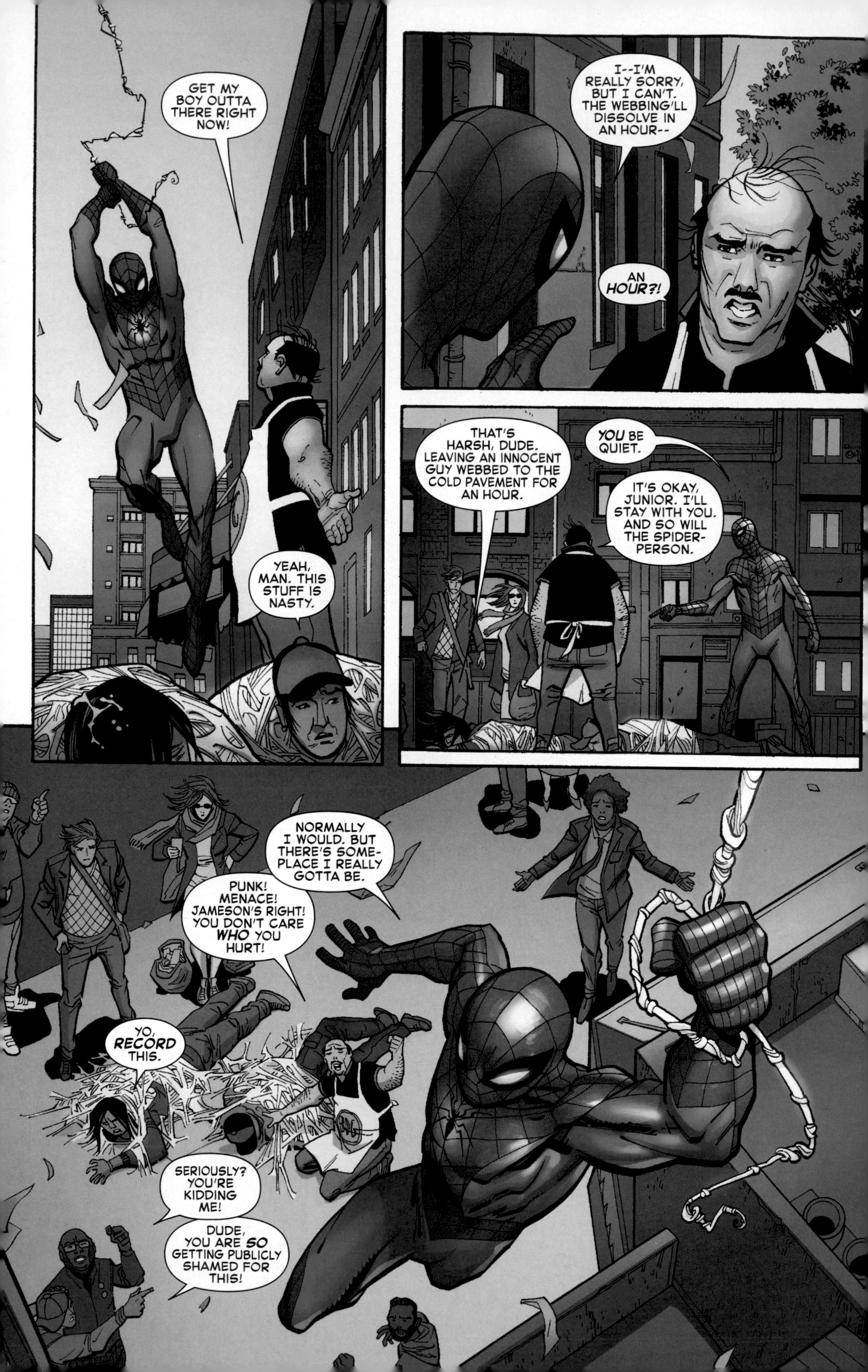
GET MY BOY OUTTA THERE RIGHT NOW!
YEAH, MAN. THIS STUFF IS NASTY.
I--I'M REALLY SORRY, BUT I CAN'T. THE WEBBING'LL DISSOLVE IN AN HOUR--
AN HOUR?!
THAT'S HARSH, DUDE. LEAVING AN INNOCENT GUY WEBBED TO THE COLD PAVEMENT FOR AN HOUR.
YOU BE QUIET.
IT'S OKAY, JUNIOR. I'LL STAY WITH YOU. AND SO WILL THE SPIDER-PERSON.
NORMALLY I WOULD. BUT THERE'S SOME-PLACE I REALLY GOTTA BE.
PUNK! MENACE! JAMESON'S RIGHT! YOU DON'T CARE WHO YOU HURT!
YO, RECORD THIS.
SERIOUSLY? YOU'RE KIDDING ME!
DUDE, YOU ARE SO GETTING PUBLICLY SHAMED FOR THIS!

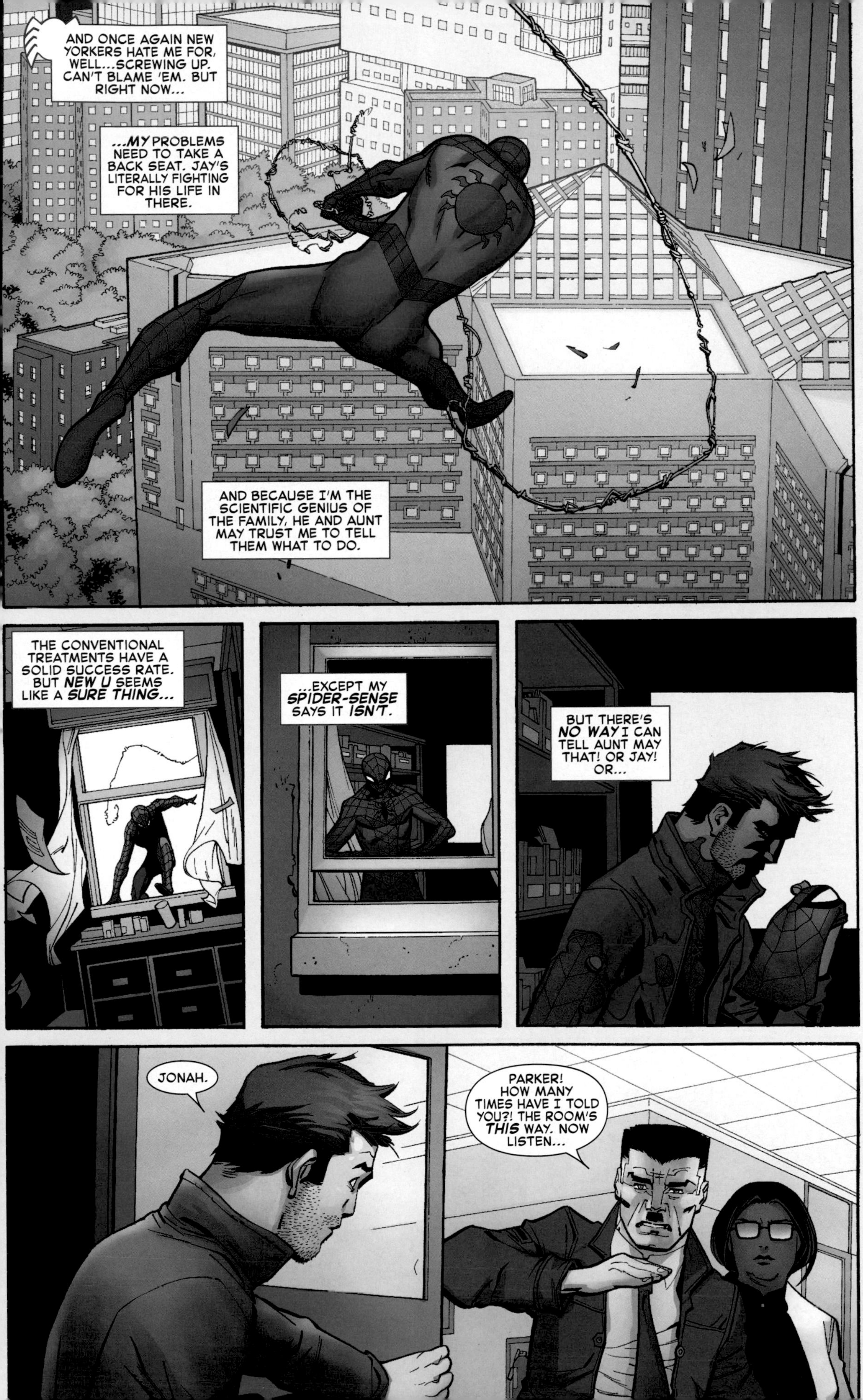
AND ONCE AGAIN NEW YORKERS HATE ME FOR, WELL...SCREWING UP. CAN'T BLAME 'EM. BUT RIGHT NOW...
...MY PROBLEMS NEED TO TAKE A BACK SEAT. JAY'S LITERALLY FIGHTING FOR HIS LIFE IN THERE.
AND BECAUSE I'M THE SCIENTIFIC GENIUS OF THE FAMILY, HE AND AUNT MAY TRUST ME TO TELL THEM WHAT TO DO.
THE CONVENTIONAL TREATMENTS HAVE A SOLID SUCCESS RATE. BUT NEW U SEEMS LIKE A SURE THING...
...EXCEPT MY SPIDER-SENSE SAYS IT ISN'T.
BUT THERE'S NO WAY I CAN TELL AUNT MAY THAT! OR JAY! OR...
JONAH.
PARKER! HOW MANY TIMES HAVE I TOLD YOU?! THE ROOM'S THIS WAY. NOW LISTEN...

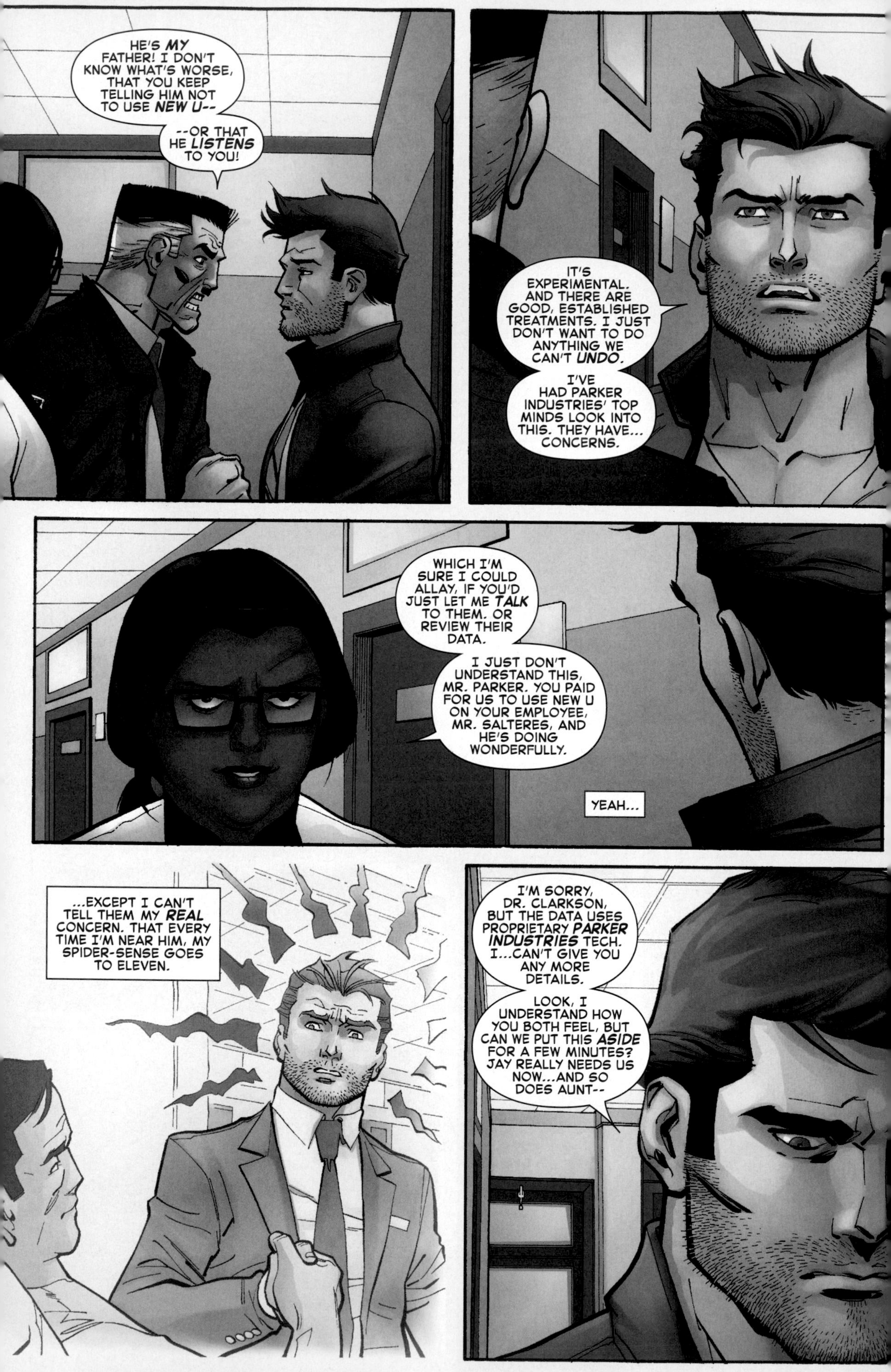
HE'S MY FATHER! I DON'T KNOW WHAT'S WORSE, THAT YOU KEEP TELLING HIM NOT TO USE NEW U--
--OR THAT HE LISTENS TO YOU!
IT'S EXPERIMENTAL. AND THERE ARE GOOD, ESTABLISHED TREATMENTS. I JUST DON'T WANT TO DO ANYTHING WE CAN'T UNDO.
I'VE HAD PARKER INDUSTRIES' TOP MINDS LOOK INTO THIS. THEY HAVE... CONCERNS.
WHICH I'M SURE I COULD ALLAY, IF YOU'D JUST LET ME TALK TO THEM. OR REVIEW THEIR DATA.
I JUST DON'T UNDERSTAND THIS, MR. PARKER. YOU PAID FOR US TO USE NEW U ON YOUR EMPLOYEE, MR. SALTERES, AND HE'S DOING WONDERFULLY.
YEAH...
...EXCEPT I CAN'T TELL THEM MY REAL CONCERN. THAT EVERY TIME I'M NEAR HIM, MY SPIDER-SENSE GOES TO ELEVEN.
I'M SORRY, DR. CLARKSON, BUT THE DATA USES PROPRIETARY PARKER INDUSTRIES TECH. I...CAN'T GIVE YOU ANY MORE DETAILS.
LOOK, I UNDERSTAND HOW YOU BOTH FEEL, BUT CAN WE PUT THIS ASIDE FOR A FEW MINUTES? JAY REALLY NEEDS US NOW...AND SO DOES AUNT--

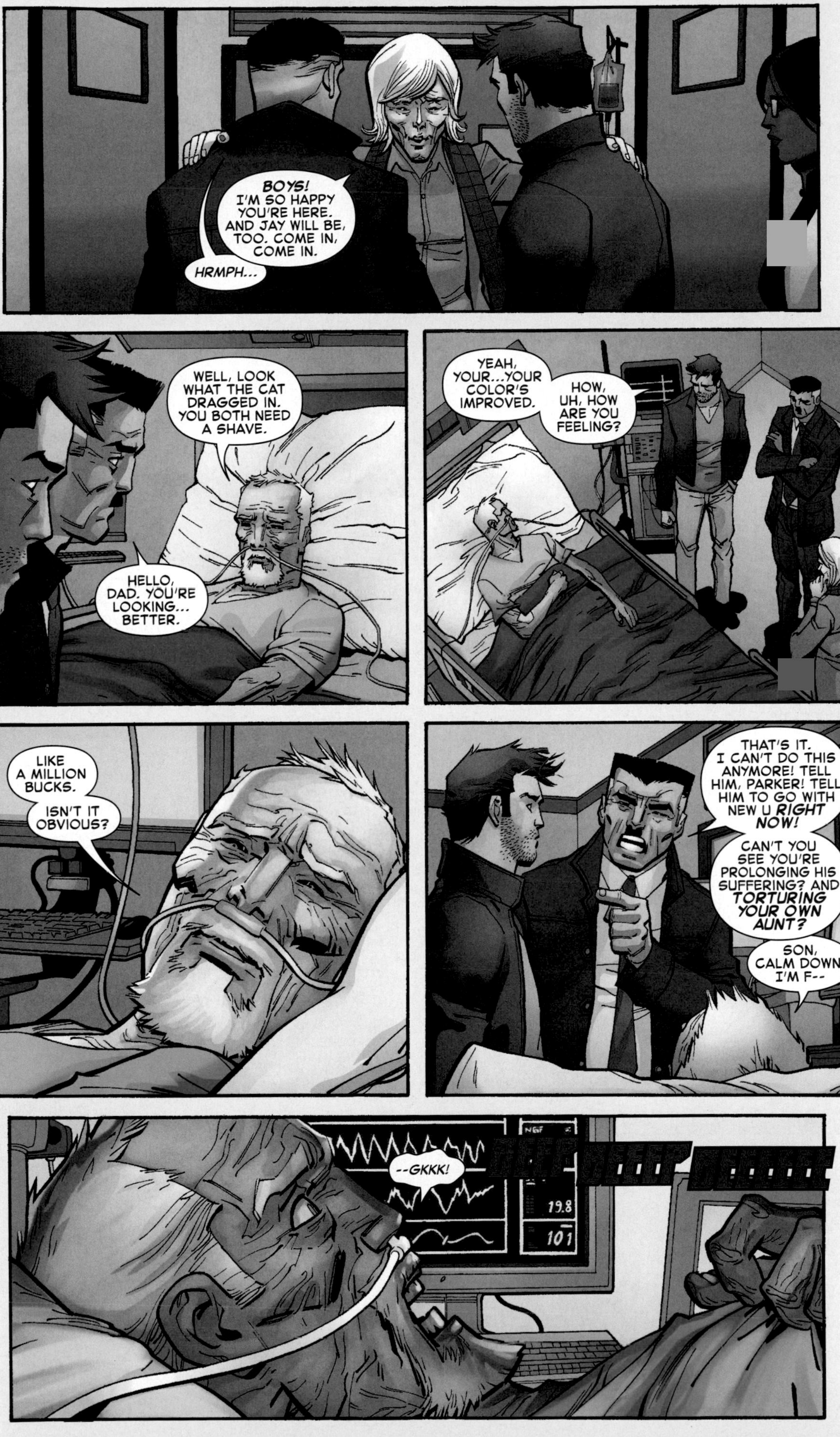
BOYS! I'M SO HAPPY YOU'RE HERE. AND JAY WILL BE, TOO. COME IN, COME IN.
HRMPH...
WELL, LOOK WHAT THE CAT DRAGGED IN. YOU BOTH NEED A SHAVE.
HELLO, DAD. YOU'RE LOOKING... BETTER.
YEAH, YOUR...YOUR COLOR'S IMPROVED.
HOW, UH, HOW ARE YOU FEELING?
LIKE A MILLION BUCKS.
ISN'T IT OBVIOUS?
THAT'S IT. I CAN'T DO THIS ANYMORE! TELL HIM, PARKER! TELL HIM TO GO WITH NEW U RIGHT NOW!
CAN'T YOU SEE YOU'RE PROLONGING HIS SUFFERING? AND TORTURING YOUR OWN AUNT?
SON, CALM DOWN! I'M F--
--GKKK!
19.8
101

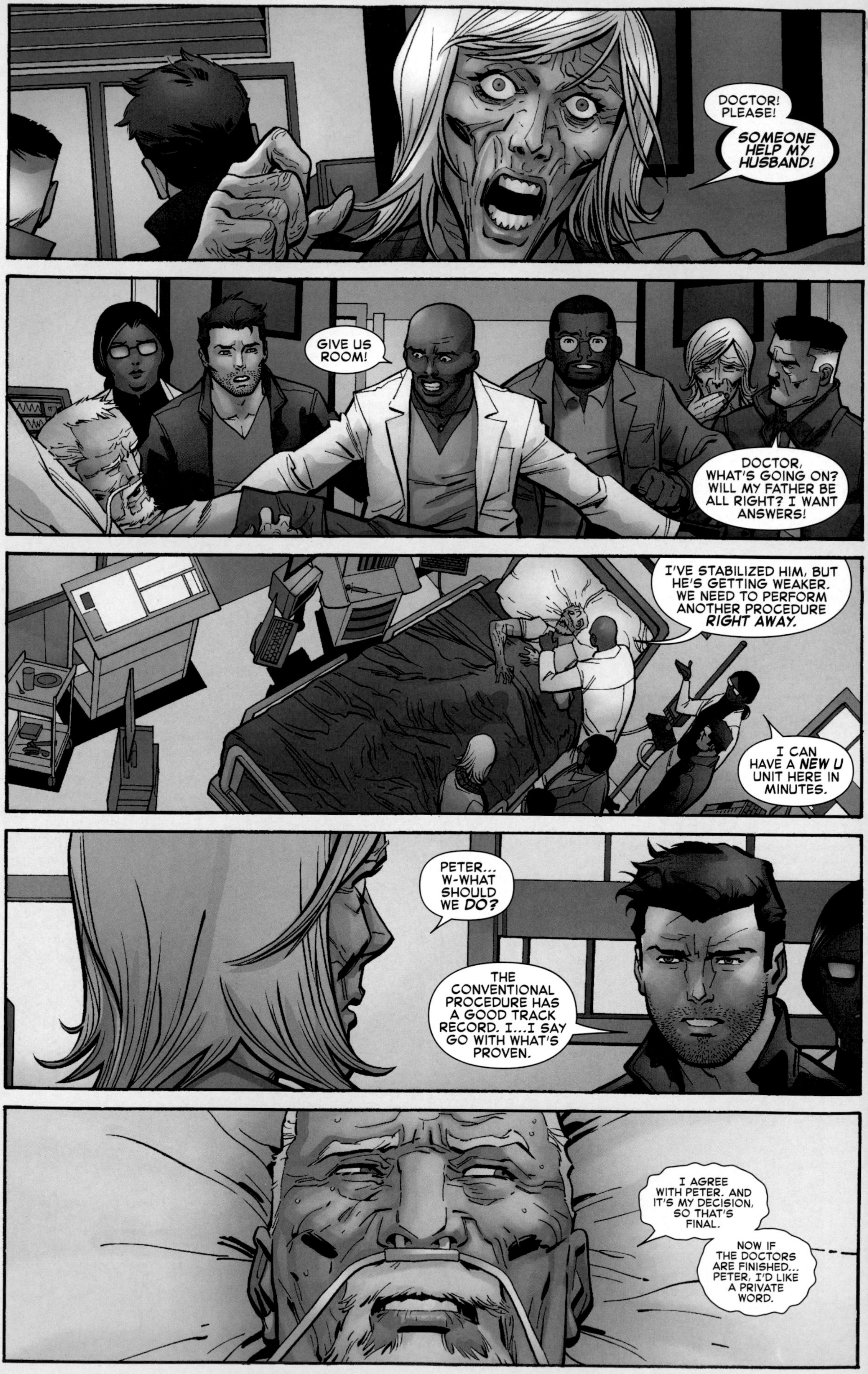
DOCTOR! PLEASE!
SOMEONE HELP MY HUSBAND!
GIVE US ROOM!
DOCTOR, WHAT'S GOING ON? WILL MY FATHER BE ALL RIGHT? I WANT ANSWERS!
I'VE STABILIZED HIM, BUT HE'S GETTING WEAKER. WE NEED TO PERFORM ANOTHER PROCEDURE RIGHT AWAY.
I CAN HAVE A NEW U UNIT HERE IN MINUTES.
PETER... W-WHAT SHOULD WE DO?
THE CONVENTIONAL PROCEDURE HAS A GOOD TRACK RECORD. I...I SAY GO WITH WHAT'S PROVEN.
I AGREE WITH PETER. AND IT'S MY DECISION, SO THAT'S FINAL.
NOW IF THE DOCTORS ARE FINISHED... PETER, I'D LIKE A PRIVATE WORD.

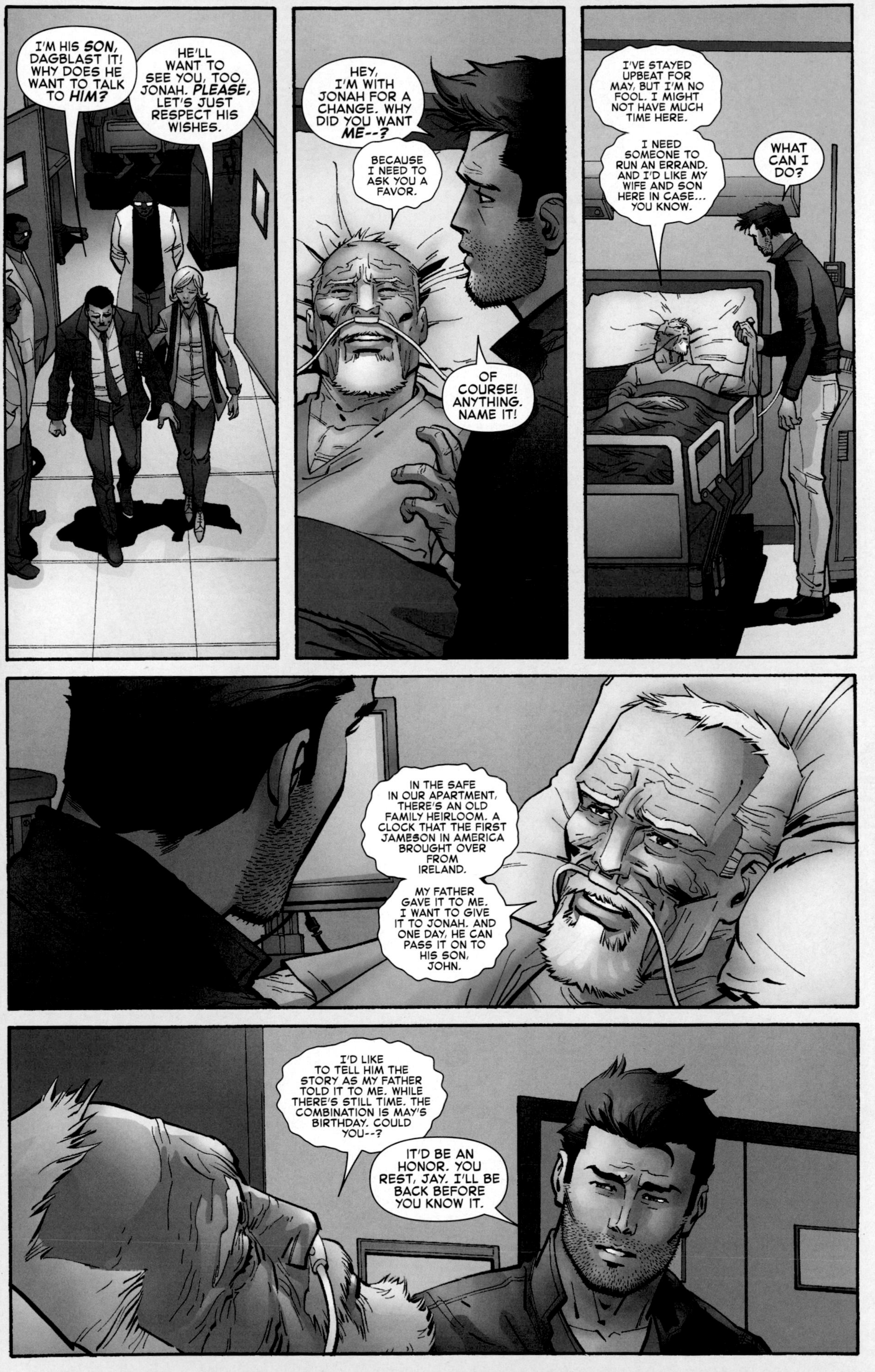

I'M HIS SON, DAGBLAST IT! WHY DOES HE WANT TO TALK TO HIM?
HE'LL WANT TO SEE YOU, TOO, JONAH. PLEASE, LET'S JUST RESPECT HIS WISHES.
HEY, I'M WITH JONAH FOR A CHANGE. WHY DID YOU WANT ME--?
BECAUSE I NEED TO ASK YOU A FAVOR.
OF COURSE! ANYTHING. NAME IT!
I'VE STAYED UPBEAT FOR MAY, BUT I'M NO FOOL. I MIGHT NOT HAVE MUCH TIME HERE.
I NEED SOMEONE TO RUN AN ERRAND. AND I'D LIKE MY WIFE AND SON HERE IN CASE... YOU KNOW.
WHAT CAN I DO?
IN THE SAFE IN OUR APARTMENT, THERE'S AN OLD FAMILY HEIRLOOM. A CLOCK THAT THE FIRST JAMESON IN AMERICA BROUGHT OVER FROM IRELAND.
MY FATHER GAVE IT TO ME. I WANT TO GIVE IT TO JONAH. AND ONE DAY, HE CAN PASS IT ON TO HIS SON, JOHN.
I'D LIKE TO TELL HIM THE STORY AS MY FATHER TOLD IT TO ME. WHILE THERE'S STILL TIME. THE COMBINATION IS MAY'S BIRTHDAY. COULD YOU--?
IT'D BE AN HONOR. YOU REST, JAY. I'LL BE BACK BEFORE YOU KNOW IT.

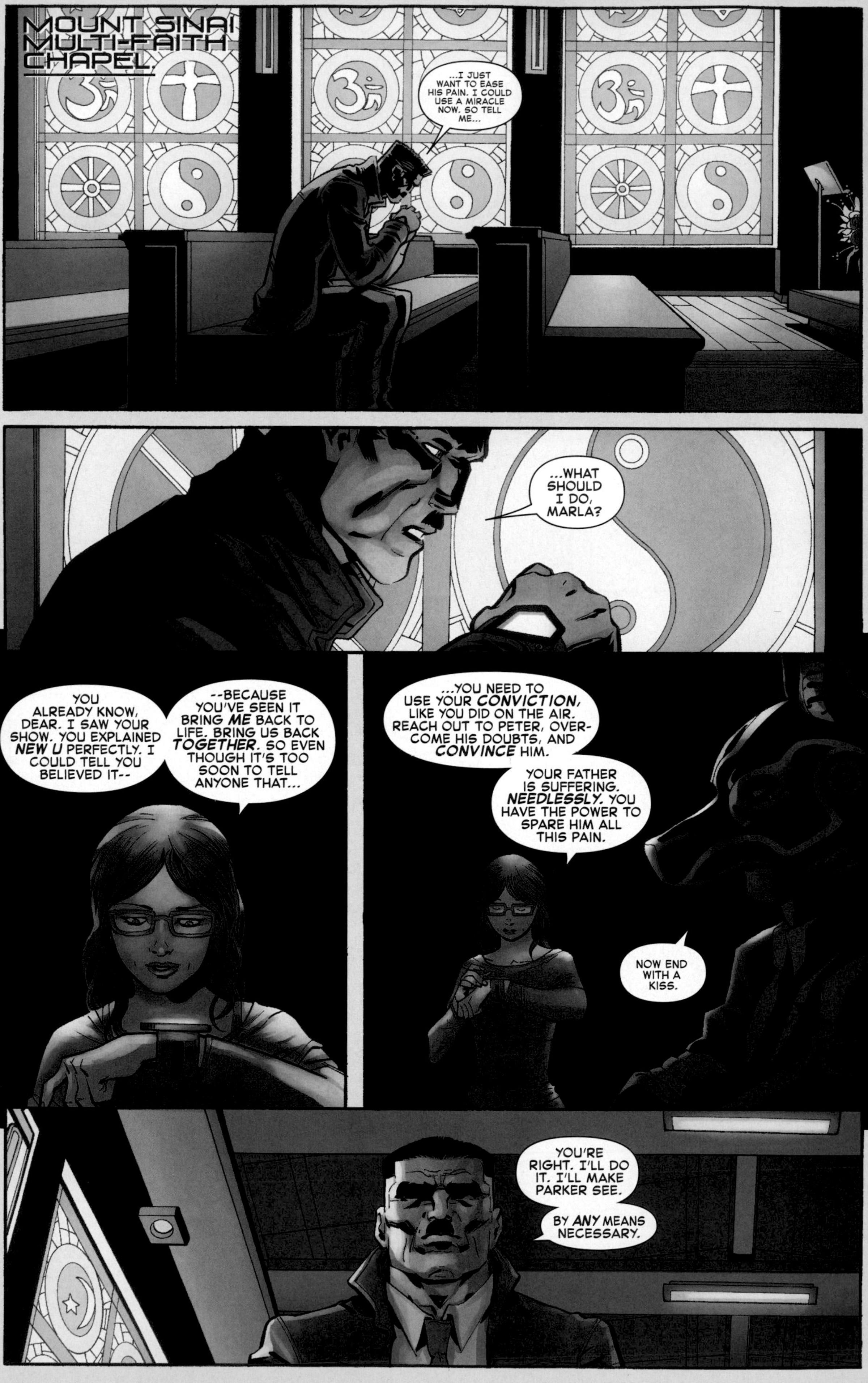
MOUNT SINAI MULTI-FAITH CHAPEL.
...I JUST WANT TO EASE HIS PAIN. I COULD USE A MIRACLE NOW. SO TELL ME...
...WHAT SHOULD I DO, MARLA?
YOU ALREADY KNOW, DEAR. I SAW YOUR SHOW. YOU EXPLAINED NEW U PERFECTLY. I COULD TELL YOU BELIEVED IT--
--BECAUSE YOU'VE SEEN IT BRING ME BACK TO LIFE. BRING US BACK TOGETHER. SO EVEN THOUGH IT'S TOO SOON TO TELL ANYONE THAT...
...YOU NEED TO USE YOUR CONVICTION, LIKE YOU DID ON THE AIR. REACH OUT TO PETER, OVER-COME HIS DOUBTS, AND CONVINCE HIM.
YOUR FATHER IS SUFFERING. NEEDLESSLY. YOU HAVE THE POWER TO SPARE HIM ALL THIS PAIN.
NOW END WITH A KISS.
YOU'RE RIGHT. I'LL DO IT. I'LL MAKE PARKER SEE.
BY ANY MEANS NECESSARY.

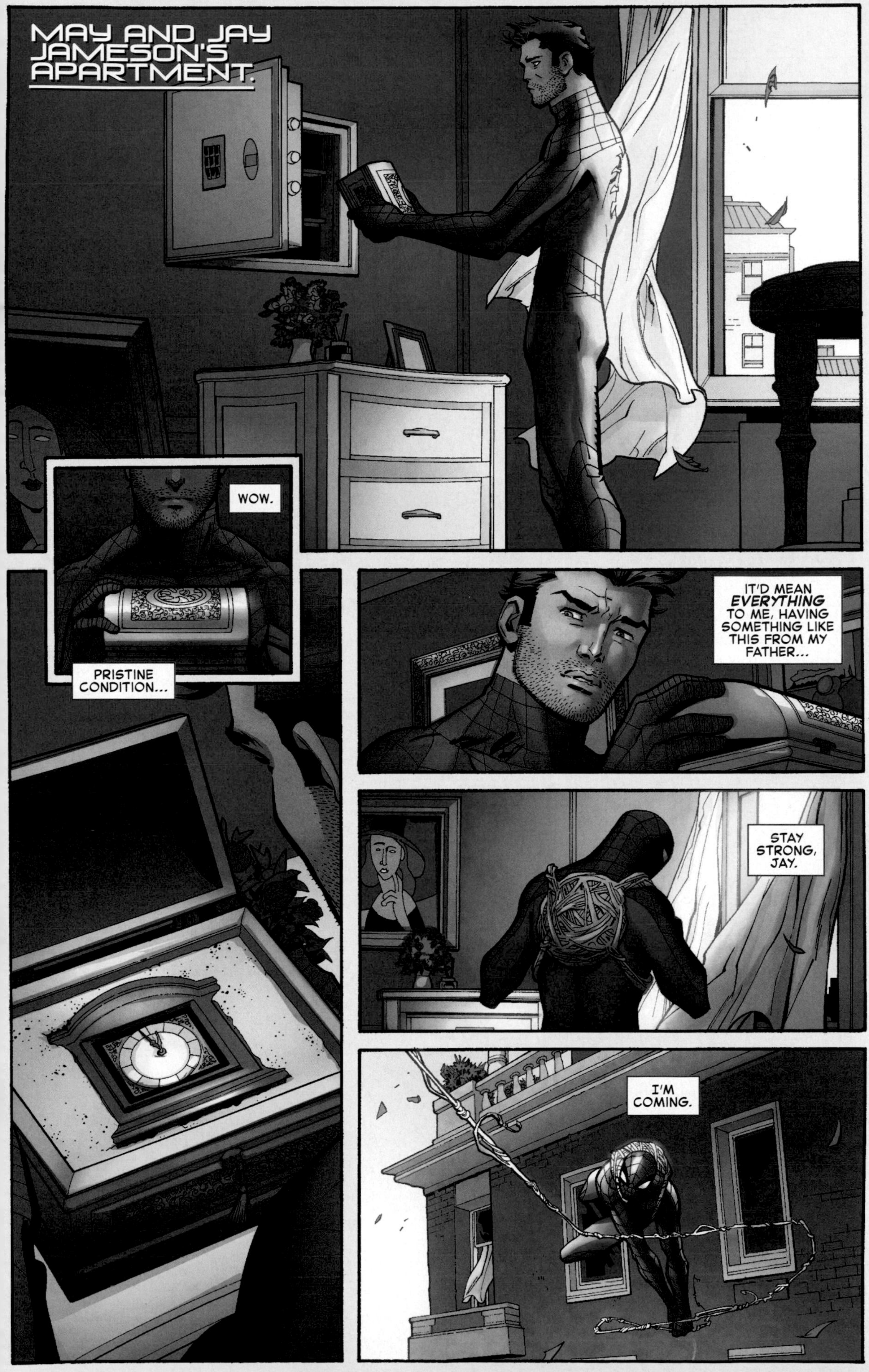
MAY AND JAY JAMESON'S APARTMENT.
WOW.
PRISTINE CONDITION...
IT'D MEAN *EVERYTHING* TO ME, HAVING SOMETHING LIKE THIS FROM MY FATHER...
STAY STRONG, JAY.
I'M COMING.

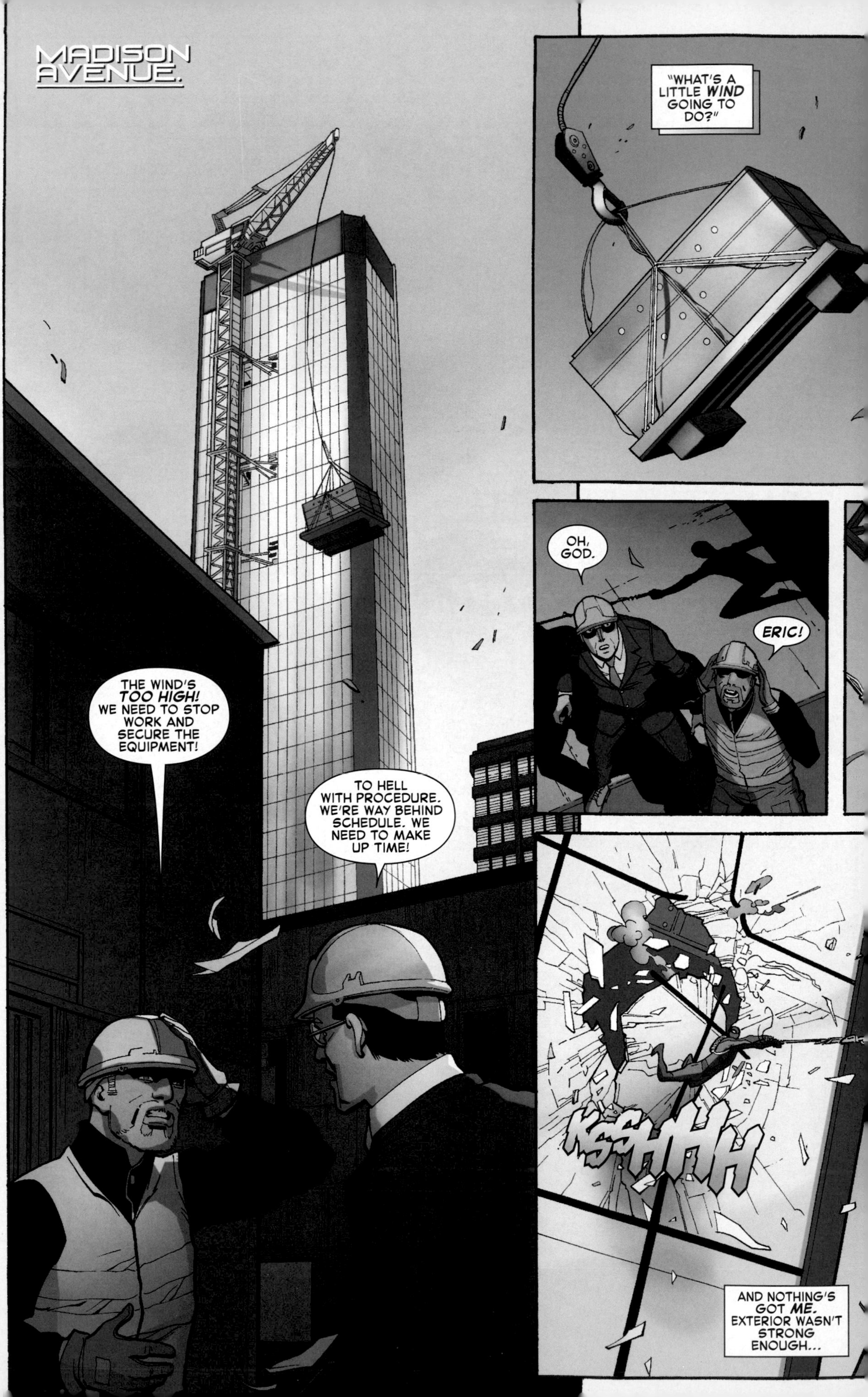
MADISON AVENUE.
THE WIND'S TOO HIGH! WE NEED TO STOP WORK AND SECURE THE EQUIPMENT!
TO HELL WITH PROCEDURE. WE'RE WAY BEHIND SCHEDULE. WE NEED TO MAKE UP TIME!
"WHAT'S A LITTLE WIND GOING TO DO?"
OH, GOD.
ERIC!
KSSHHHH
AND NOTHING'S GOT ME. EXTERIOR WASN'T STRONG ENOUGH...

RRRNNCCHH

BRRKNNCHH

KREEE

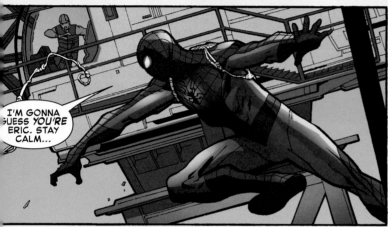

I'M GONNA GUESS *YOU'RE* ERIC. STAY CALM...

...I GOT YOU.

THWIP

THWIP

...LET'S PRAY THAT GIRDER *IS*.

THWIP

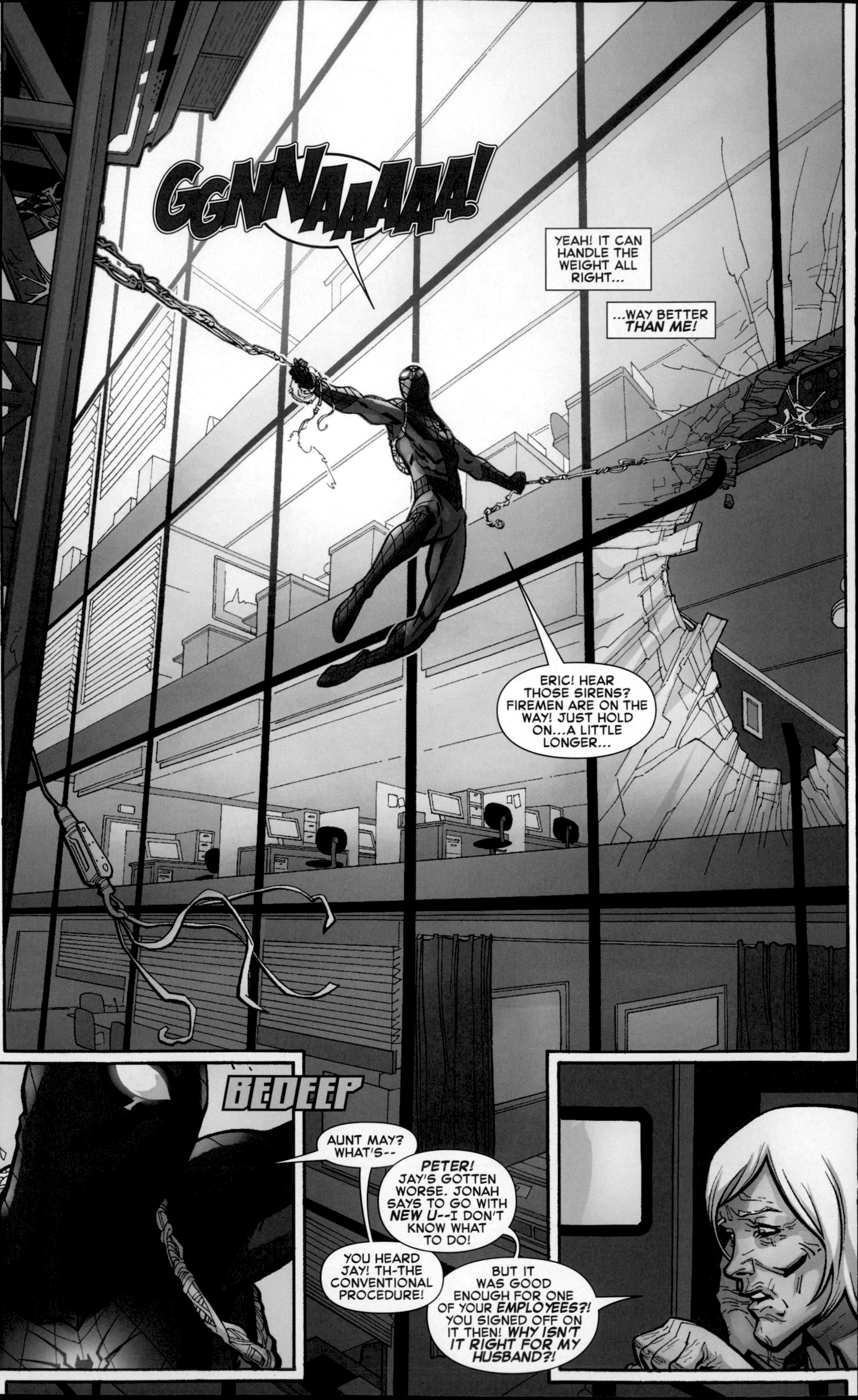
GGNNAAAAA!
YEAH! IT CAN HANDLE THE WEIGHT ALL RIGHT...
...WAY BETTER THAN ME!
ERIC! HEAR THOSE SIRENS? FIREMEN ARE ON THE WAY! JUST HOLD ON...A LITTLE LONGER...
BEDEEP
AUNT MAY? WHAT'S--
PETER! JAY'S GOTTEN WORSE. JONAH SAYS TO GO WITH NEW U--I DON'T KNOW WHAT TO DO!
YOU HEARD JAY! TH-THE CONVENTIONAL PROCEDURE!
BUT IT WAS GOOD ENOUGH FOR ONE OF YOUR EMPLOYEES?! YOU SIGNED OFF ON IT THEN! WHY ISN'T IT RIGHT FOR MY HUSBAND?!

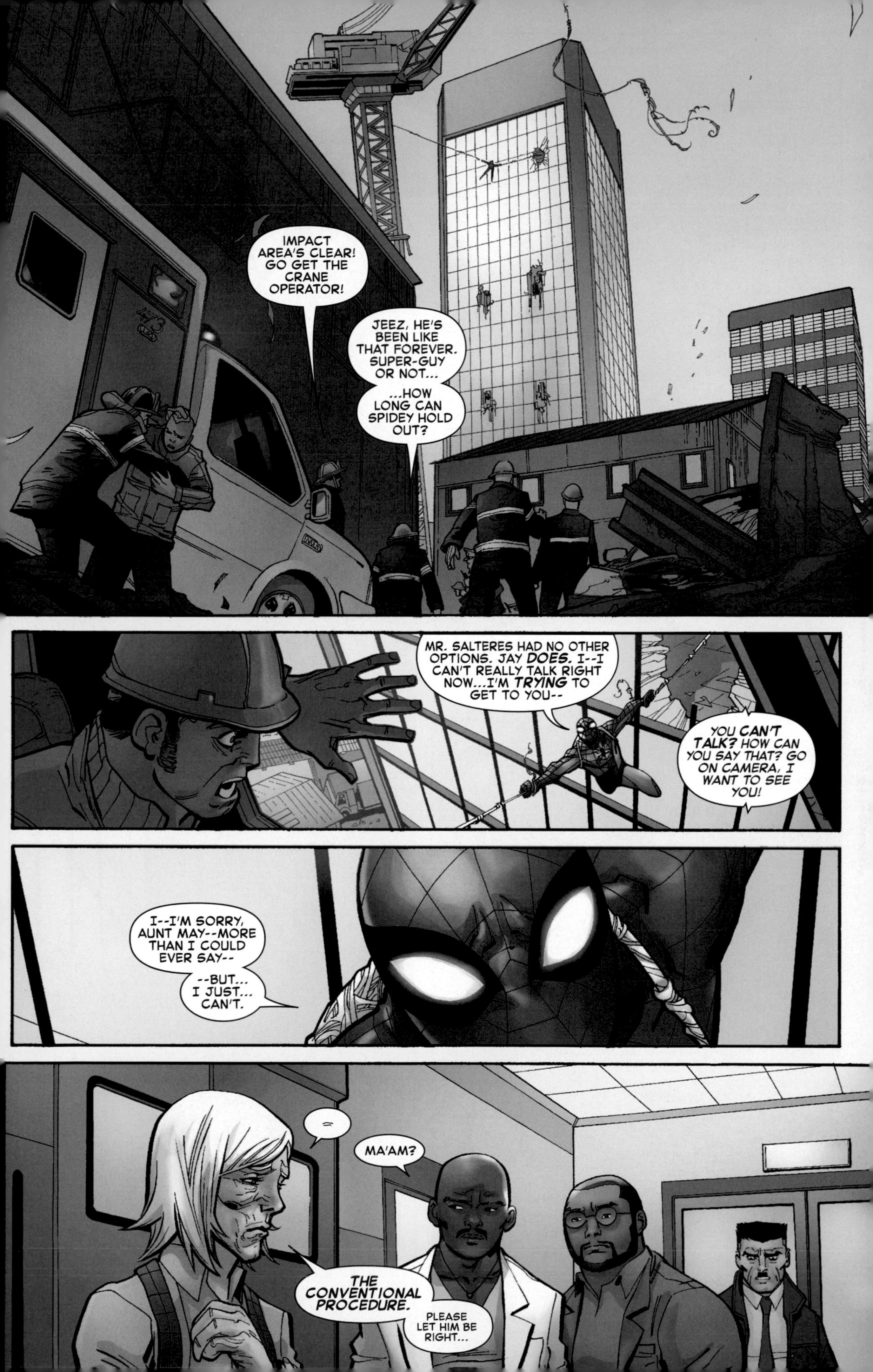
IMPACT AREA'S CLEAR! GO GET THE CRANE OPERATOR!
JEEZ, HE'S BEEN LIKE THAT FOREVER. SUPER-GUY OR NOT...
...HOW LONG CAN SPIDEY HOLD OUT?
MR. SALTERES HAD NO OTHER OPTIONS. JAY DOES. I--I CAN'T REALLY TALK RIGHT NOW...I'M TRYING TO GET TO YOU--
YOU CAN'T TALK? HOW CAN YOU SAY THAT? GO ON CAMERA, I WANT TO SEE YOU!
I--I'M SORRY, AUNT MAY--MORE THAN I COULD EVER SAY--
--BUT... I JUST... CAN'T.
MA'AM?
THE CONVENTIONAL PROCEDURE.
PLEASE LET HIM BE RIGHT...

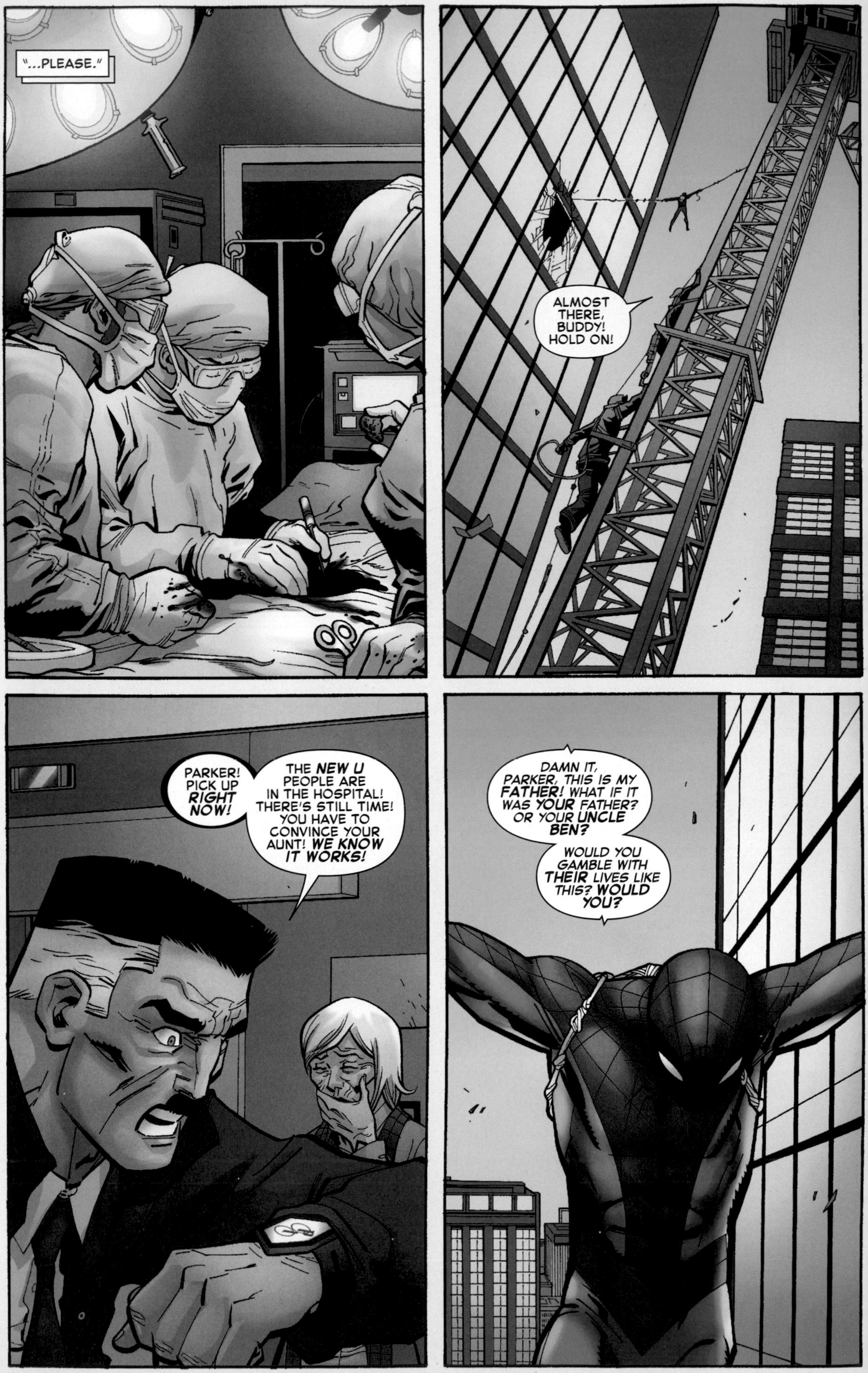
"...PLEASE."
ALMOST THERE, BUDDY! HOLD ON!
PARKER! PICK UP RIGHT NOW!
THE NEW U PEOPLE ARE IN THE HOSPITAL! THERE'S STILL TIME! YOU HAVE TO CONVINCE YOUR AUNT! WE KNOW IT WORKS!
DAMN IT, PARKER, THIS IS MY FATHER! WHAT IF IT WAS YOUR FATHER? OR YOUR UNCLE BEN?
WOULD YOU GAMBLE WITH THEIR LIVES LIKE THIS? WOULD YOU?

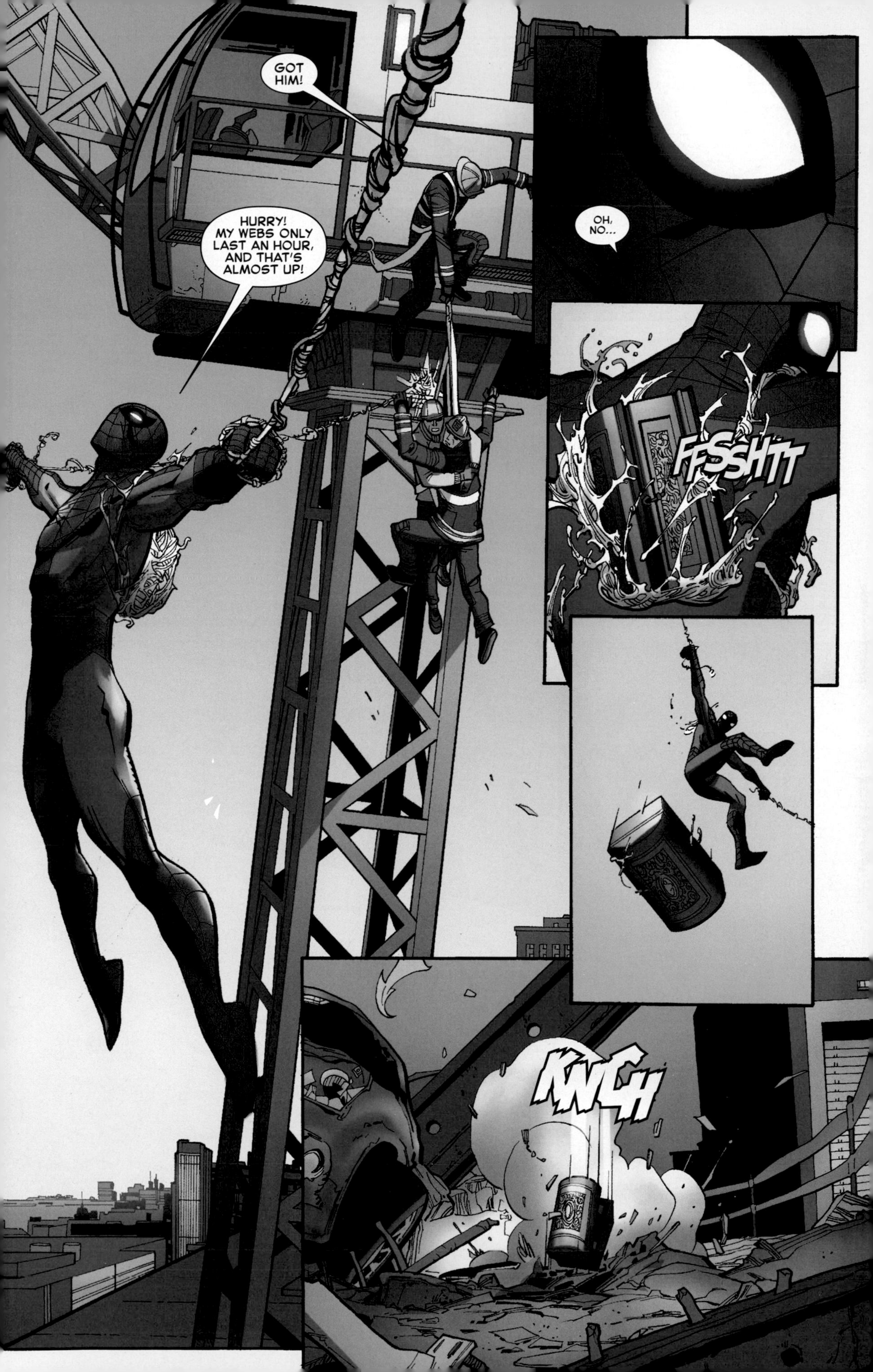
GOT HIM!
HURRY! MY WEBS ONLY LAST AN HOUR, AND THAT'S ALMOST UP!
OH, NO...
FFSSHTT
KNCH

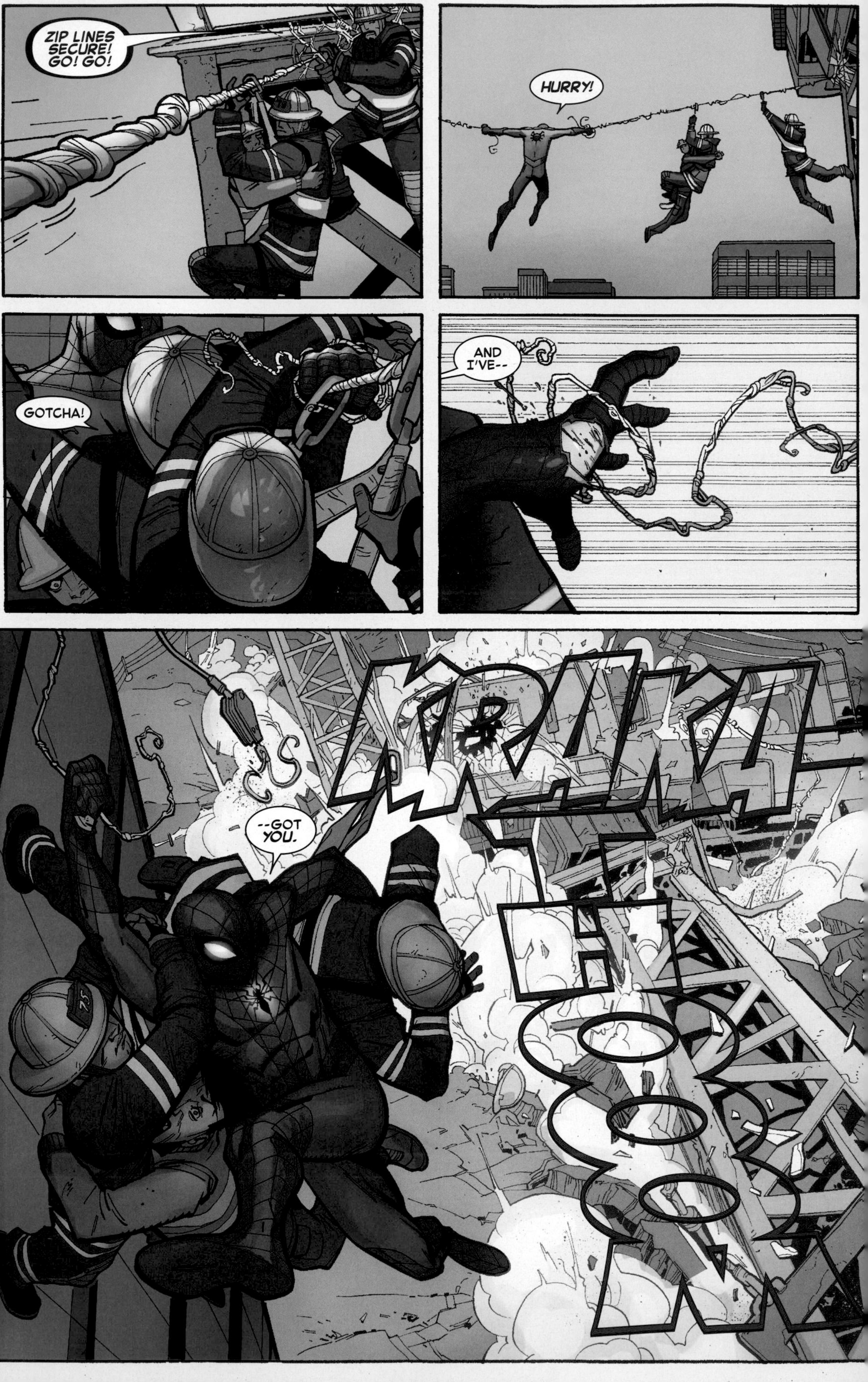
ZIP LINES SECURE! GO! GO!
HURRY!
GOTCHA!
AND I'VE--
KRAKA THOOOM
--GOT YOU.

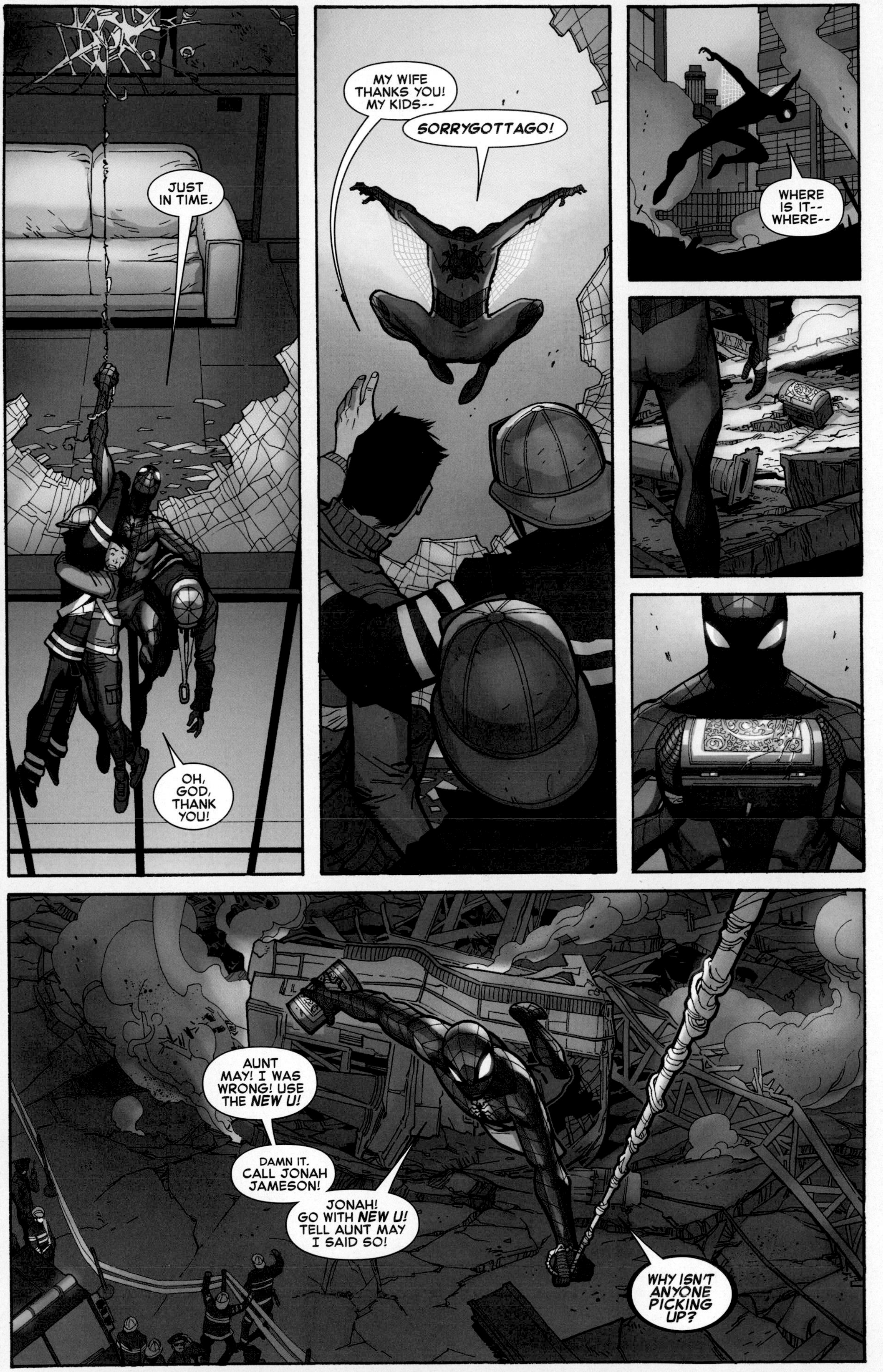
JUST IN TIME.
OH, GOD, THANK YOU!
MY WIFE THANKS YOU! MY KIDS--
SORRYGOTTAGO!
WHERE IS IT-- WHERE--
AUNT MAY! I WAS WRONG! USE THE NEW U!
DAMN IT. CALL JONAH JAMESON!
JONAH! GO WITH NEW U! TELL AUNT MAY I SAID SO!
WHY ISN'T ANYONE PICKING UP?

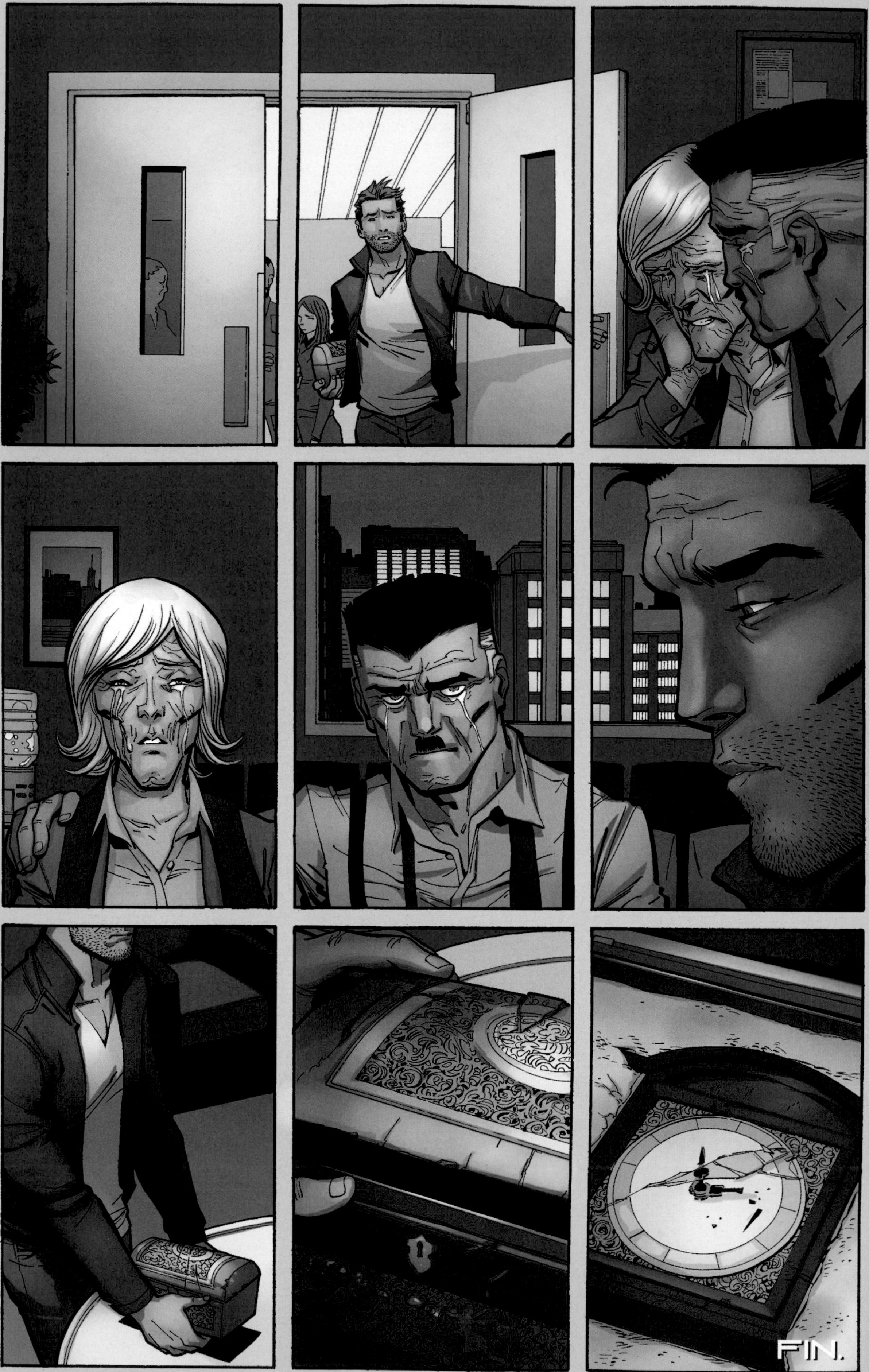
FIN.

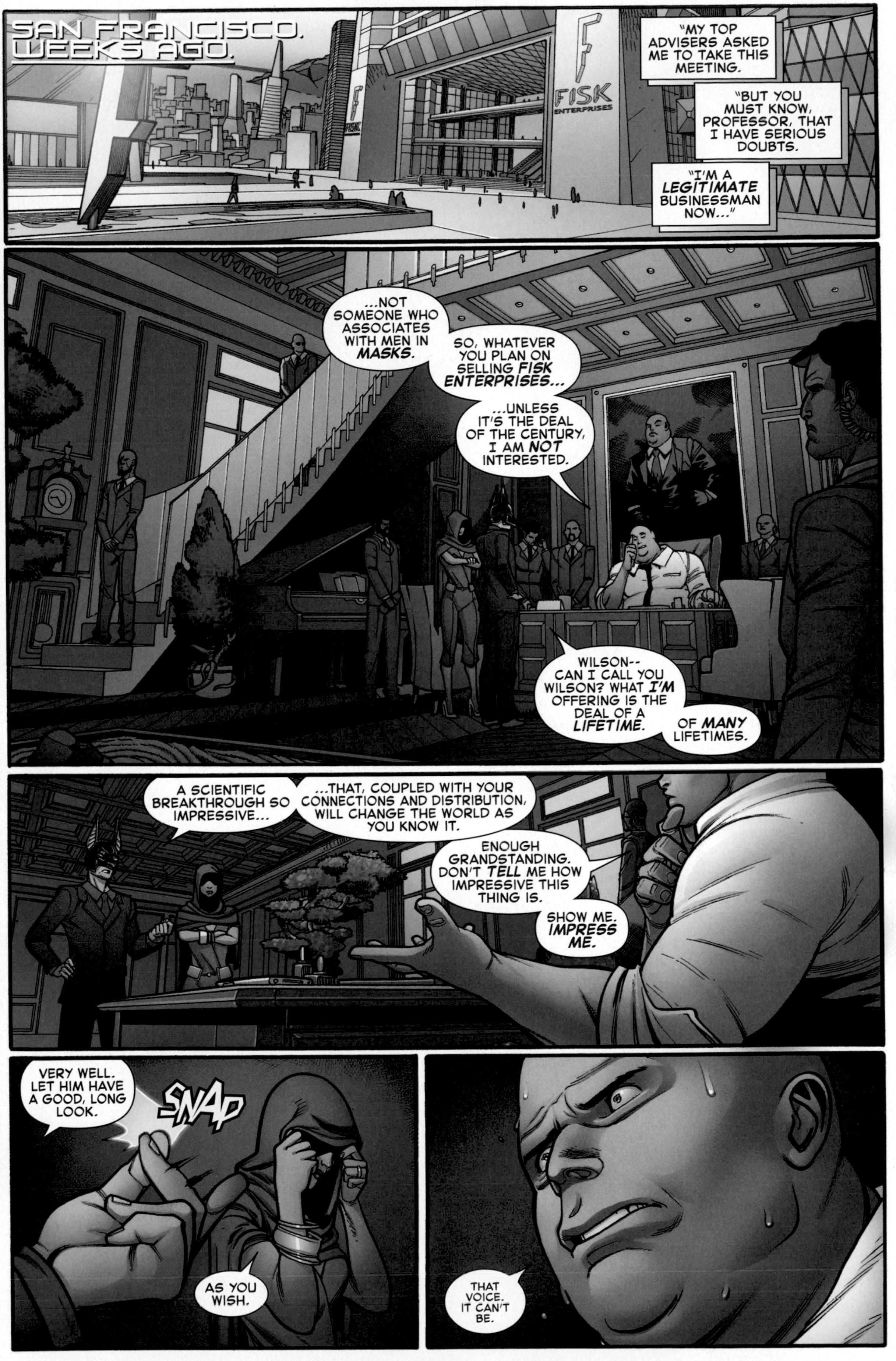
SAN FRANCISCO. WEEKS AGO.
"MY TOP ADVISERS ASKED ME TO TAKE THIS MEETING.
"BUT YOU MUST KNOW, PROFESSOR, THAT I HAVE SERIOUS DOUBTS.
"I'M A LEGITIMATE BUSINESSMAN NOW..."
FISK ENTERPRISES
...NOT SOMEONE WHO ASSOCIATES WITH MEN IN MASKS.
SO, WHATEVER YOU PLAN ON SELLING FISK ENTERPRISES...
...UNLESS IT'S THE DEAL OF THE CENTURY, I AM NOT INTERESTED.
WILSON-- CAN I CALL YOU WILSON? WHAT I'M OFFERING IS THE DEAL OF A LIFETIME.
OF MANY LIFETIMES.
A SCIENTIFIC BREAKTHROUGH SO IMPRESSIVE...
...THAT, COUPLED WITH YOUR CONNECTIONS AND DISTRIBUTION, WILL CHANGE THE WORLD AS YOU KNOW IT.
ENOUGH GRANDSTANDING. DON'T TELL ME HOW IMPRESSIVE THIS THING IS.
SHOW ME. IMPRESS ME.
VERY WELL. LET HIM HAVE A GOOD, LONG LOOK.
SNAP
AS YOU WISH.
THAT VOICE. IT CAN'T BE.

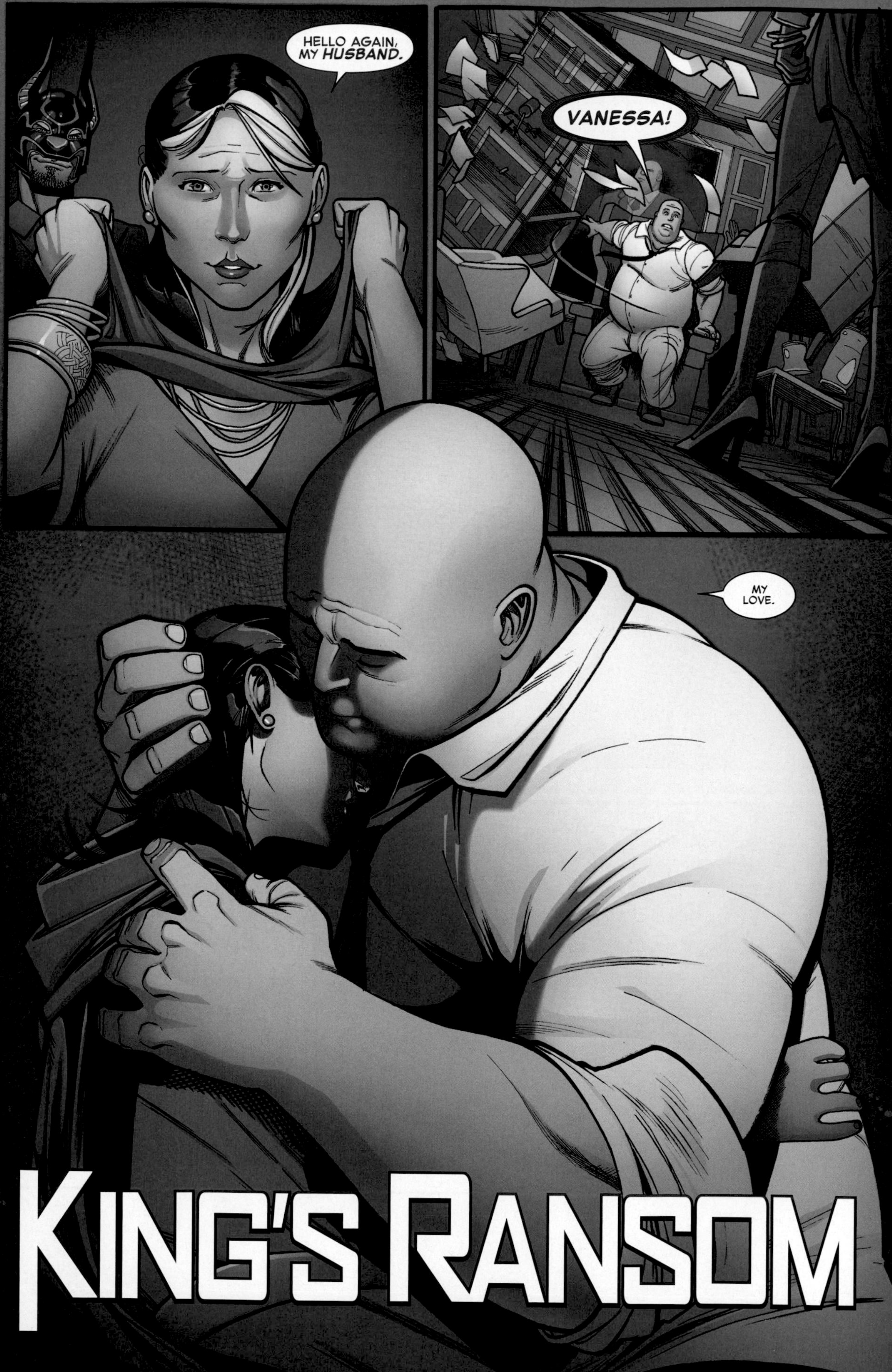
HELLO AGAIN, MY HUSBAND.
VANESSA!
MY LOVE.
KING'S RANSOM

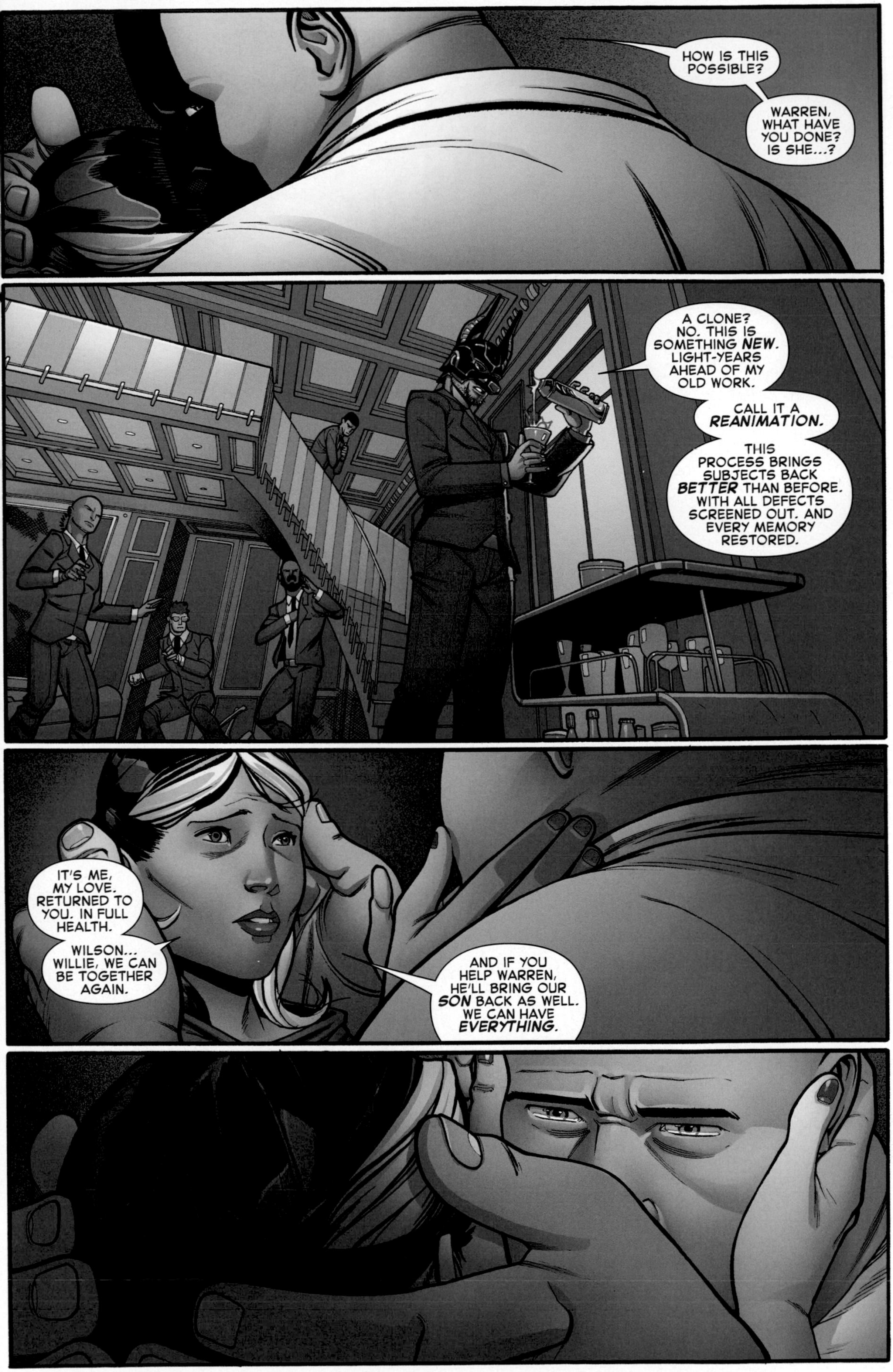
HOW IS THIS POSSIBLE?
WARREN, WHAT HAVE YOU DONE? IS SHE...?
A CLONE? NO. THIS IS SOMETHING NEW. LIGHT-YEARS AHEAD OF MY OLD WORK.
CALL IT A REANIMATION.
THIS PROCESS BRINGS SUBJECTS BACK BETTER THAN BEFORE. WITH ALL DEFECTS SCREENED OUT. AND EVERY MEMORY RESTORED.
IT'S ME, MY LOVE. RETURNED TO YOU. IN FULL HEALTH.
WILSON... WILLIE, WE CAN BE TOGETHER AGAIN.
AND IF YOU HELP WARREN, HE'LL BRING OUR SON BACK AS WELL. WE CAN HAVE EVERYTHING.

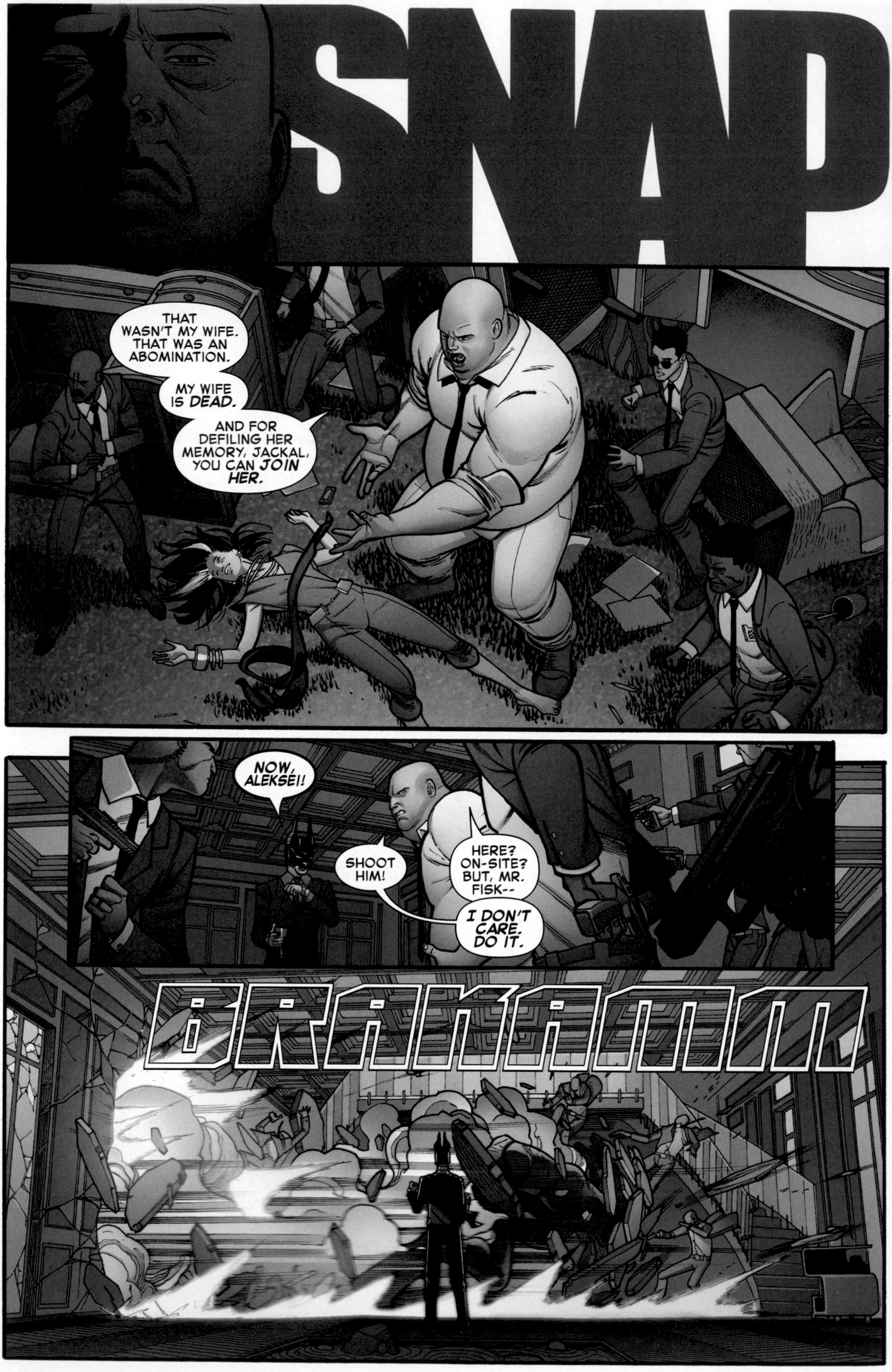
SNAP
THAT WASN'T MY WIFE. THAT WAS AN ABOMINATION.
MY WIFE IS DEAD.
AND FOR DEFILING HER MEMORY, JACKAL, YOU CAN JOIN HER.
NOW, ALEKSEI!
HERE? ON-SITE? BUT, MR. FISK--
SHOOT HIM!
I DON'T CARE. DO IT.
BRAKAOOM

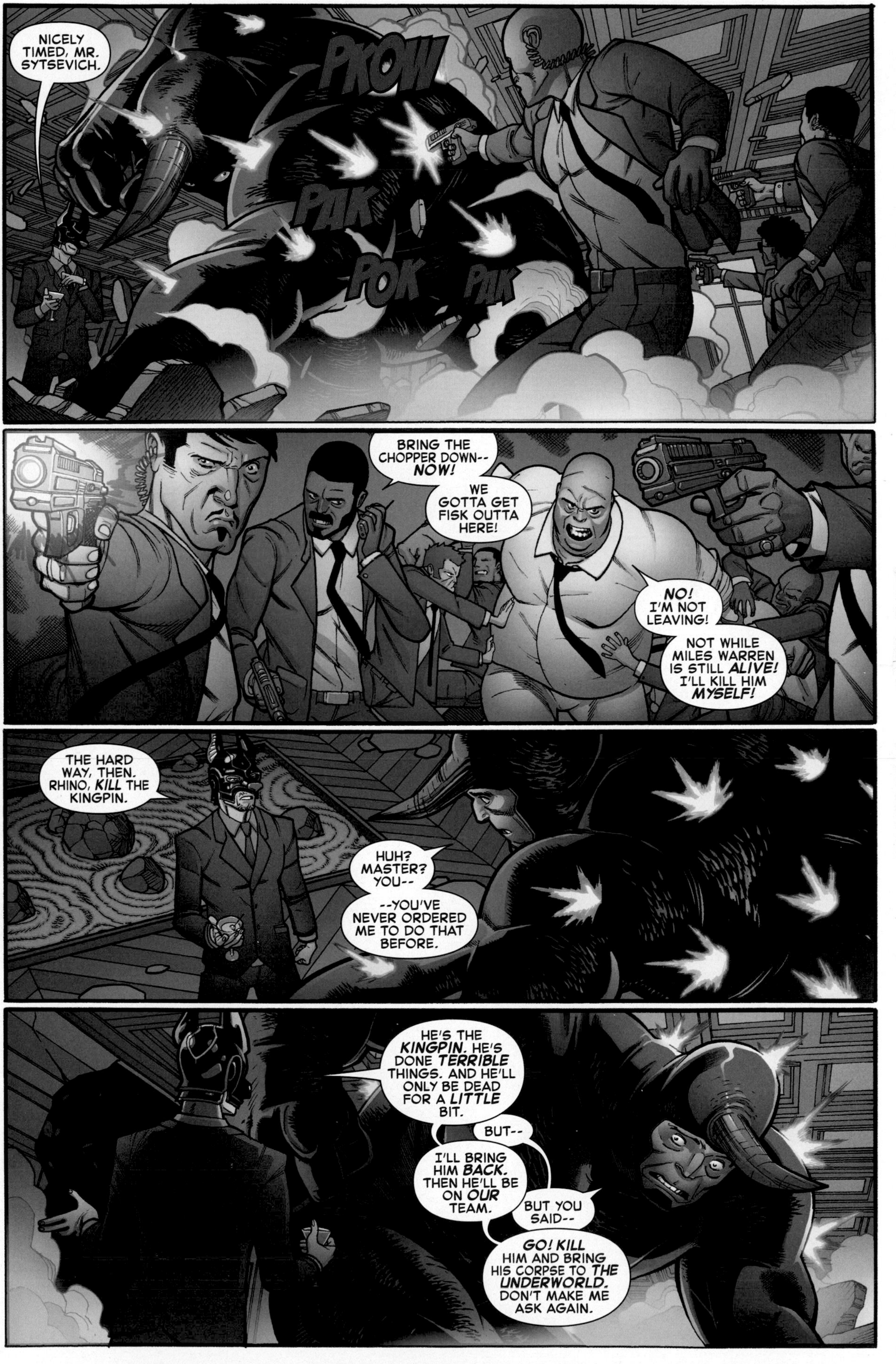
NICELY TIMED, MR. SYTSEVICH.
PKOW
PAK
POK
PAK
BRING THE CHOPPER DOWN-- NOW!
WE GOTTA GET FISK OUTTA HERE!
NO! I'M NOT LEAVING!
NOT WHILE MILES WARREN IS STILL ALIVE! I'LL KILL HIM MYSELF!
THE HARD WAY, THEN. RHINO, KILL THE KINGPIN.
HUH? MASTER? YOU--
--YOU'VE NEVER ORDERED ME TO DO THAT BEFORE.
HE'S THE KINGPIN. HE'S DONE TERRIBLE THINGS. AND HE'LL ONLY BE DEAD FOR A LITTLE BIT.
BUT--
I'LL BRING HIM BACK. THEN HE'LL BE ON OUR TEAM.
BUT YOU SAID--
GO! KILL HIM AND BRING HIS CORPSE TO THE UNDERWORLD. DON'T MAKE ME ASK AGAIN.

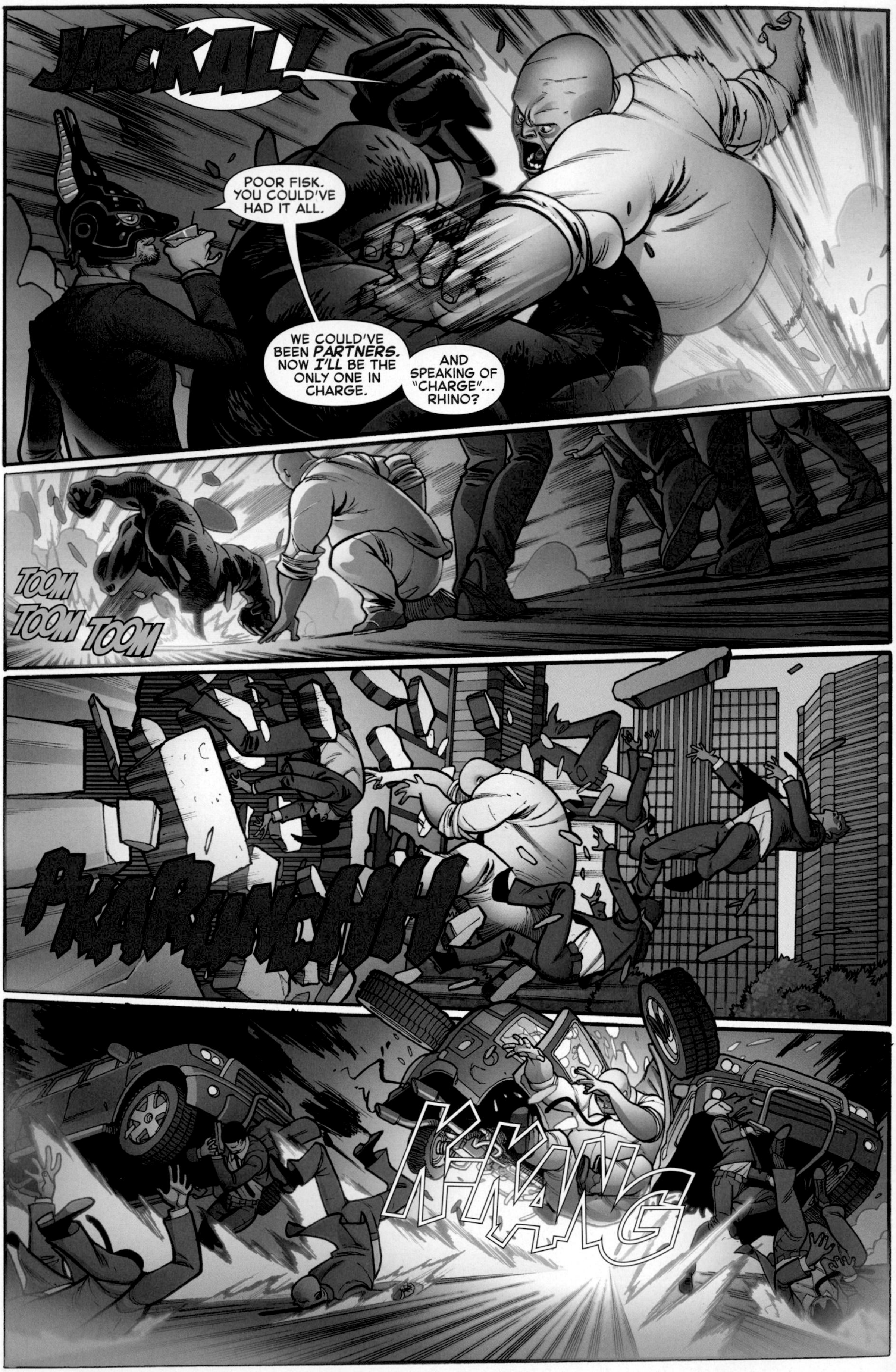
JACKAL!
POOR FISK. YOU COULD'VE HAD IT ALL.
WE COULD'VE BEEN PARTNERS. NOW I'LL BE THE ONLY ONE IN CHARGE.
AND SPEAKING OF "CHARGE"... RHINO?
TOOM TOOM TOOM
PKARUNCHHH
KHANG

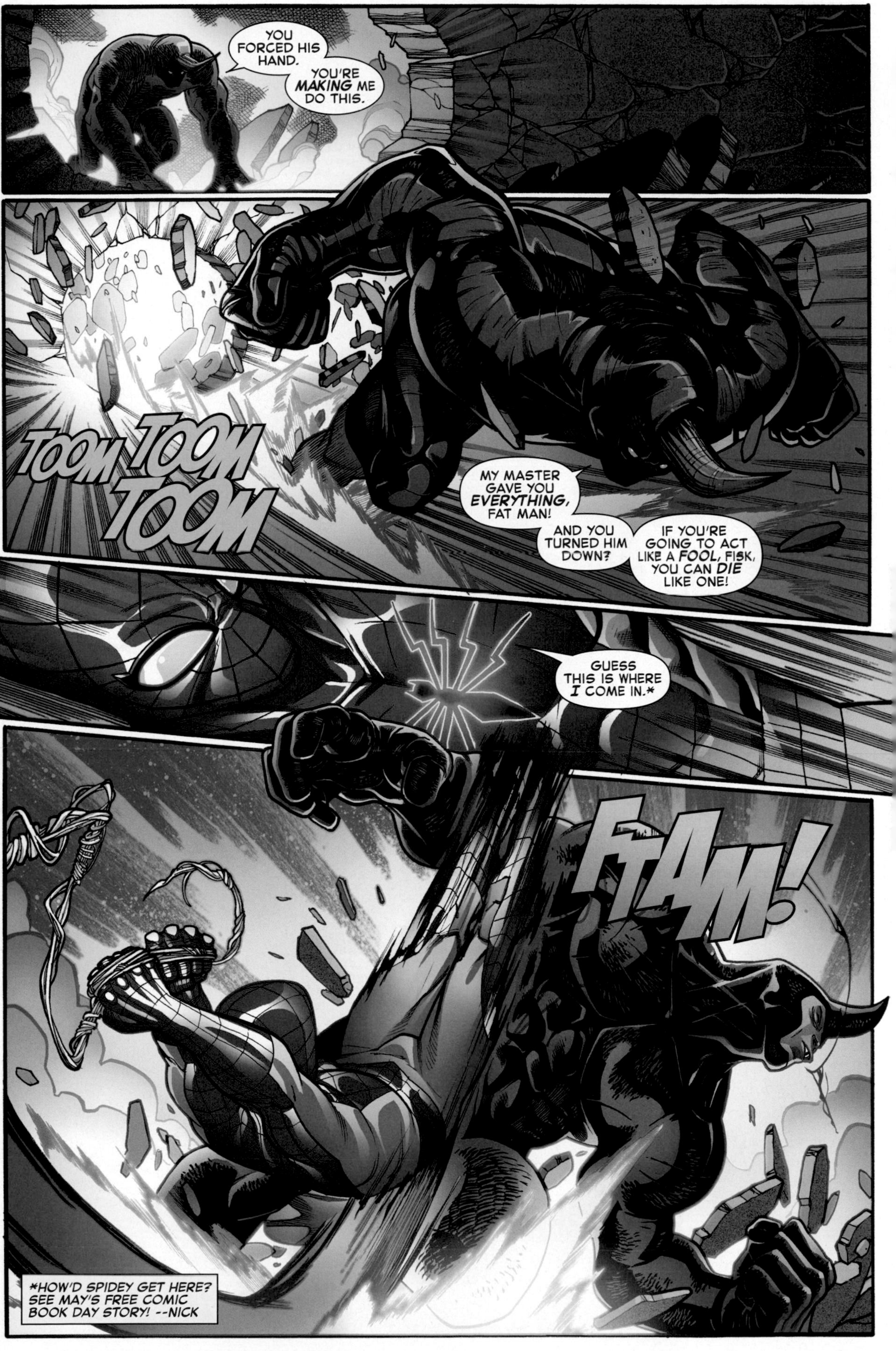
YOU FORCED HIS HAND.
YOU'RE *MAKING* ME DO THIS.
TOOM TOOM TOOM
MY MASTER GAVE YOU *EVERYTHING*, FAT MAN!
AND YOU TURNED HIM DOWN?
IF YOU'RE GOING TO ACT LIKE A *FOOL*, FISK, YOU CAN *DIE* LIKE ONE!
GUESS THIS IS WHERE *I* COME IN.*
FTAM!
*HOW'D SPIDEY GET HERE? SEE MAY'S FREE COMIC BOOK DAY STORY! --NICK

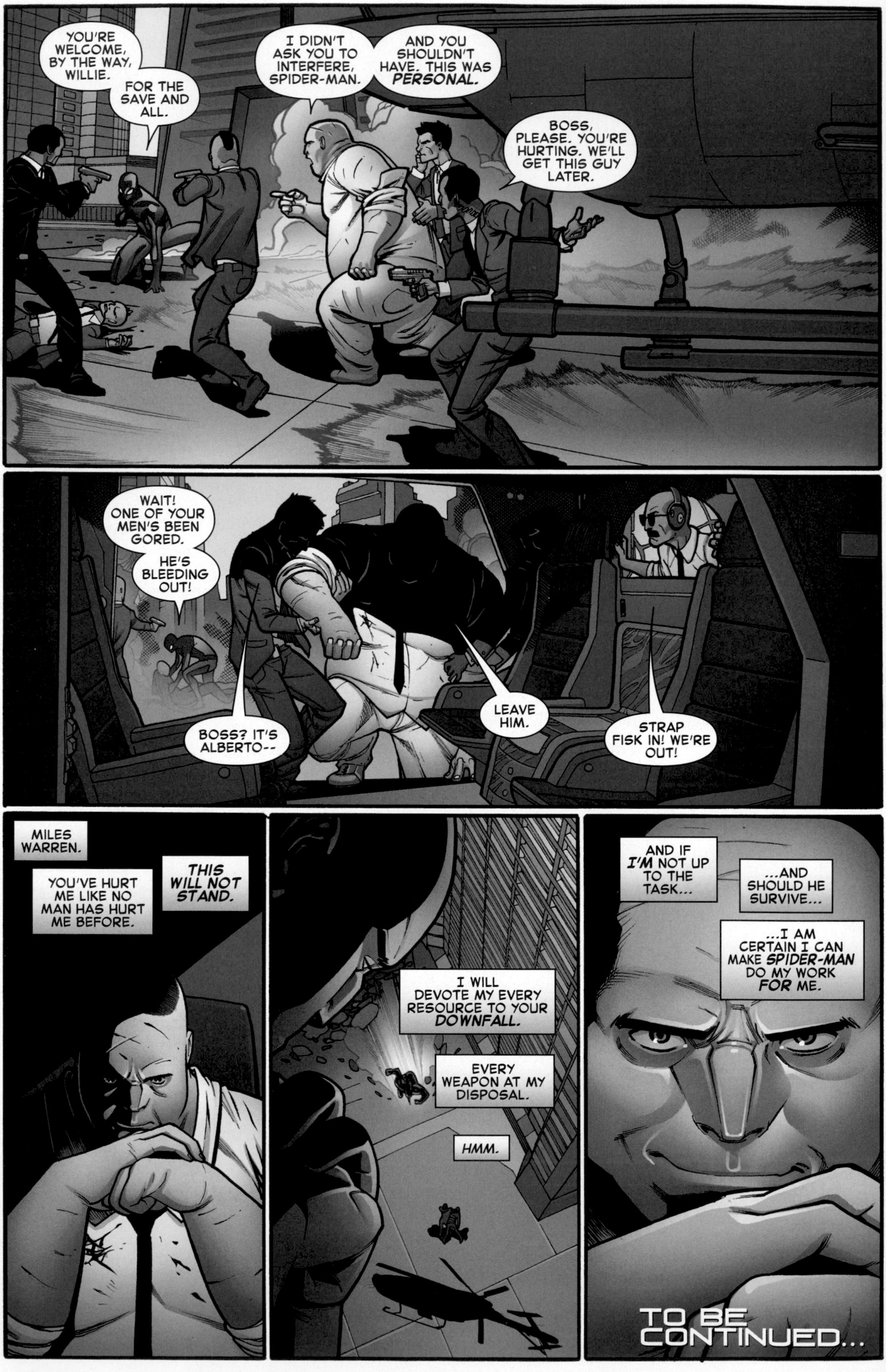
YOU'RE WELCOME, BY THE WAY, WILLIE.
FOR THE SAVE AND ALL.
I DIDN'T ASK YOU TO INTERFERE, SPIDER-MAN.
AND YOU SHOULDN'T HAVE. THIS WAS PERSONAL.
BOSS, PLEASE. YOU'RE HURTING. WE'LL GET THIS GUY LATER.
WAIT! ONE OF YOUR MEN'S BEEN GORED.
HE'S BLEEDING OUT!
BOSS? IT'S ALBERTO--
LEAVE HIM.
STRAP FISK IN! WE'RE OUT!
MILES WARREN.
YOU'VE HURT ME LIKE NO MAN HAS HURT ME BEFORE.
THIS WILL NOT STAND.
I WILL DEVOTE MY EVERY RESOURCE TO YOUR DOWNFALL.
EVERY WEAPON AT MY DISPOSAL.
HMM.
AND IF I'M NOT UP TO THE TASK...
...AND SHOULD HE SURVIVE...
...I AM CERTAIN I CAN MAKE SPIDER-MAN DO MY WORK FOR ME.
TO BE CONTINUED...

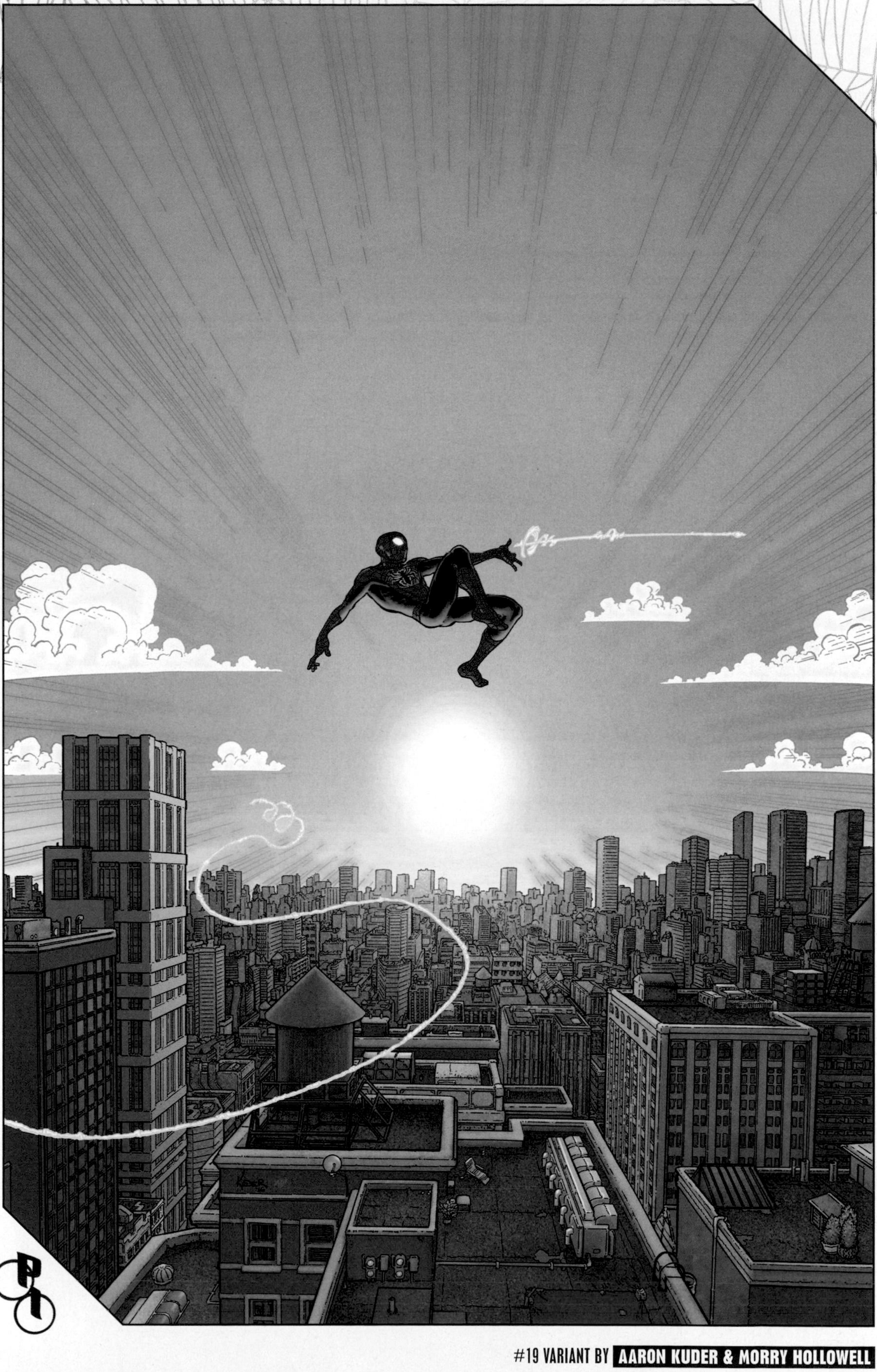

#19 VARIANT BY **AARON KUDER & MORRY HOLLOWELL**

AMAZING S

DEAD N

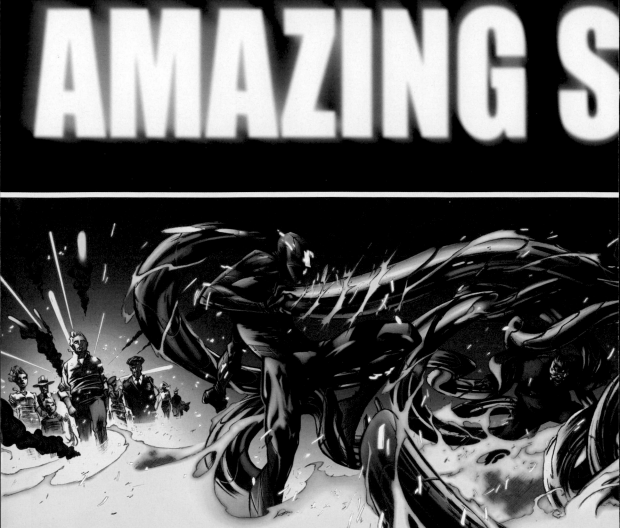

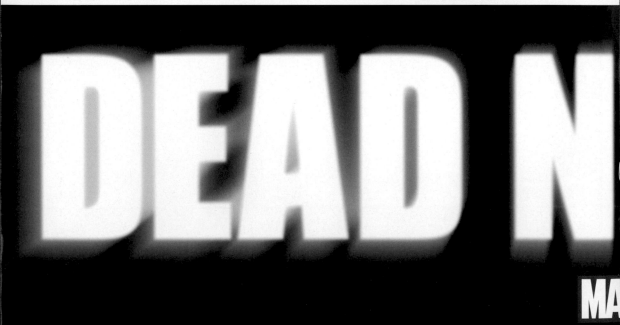

PIDER-MAN

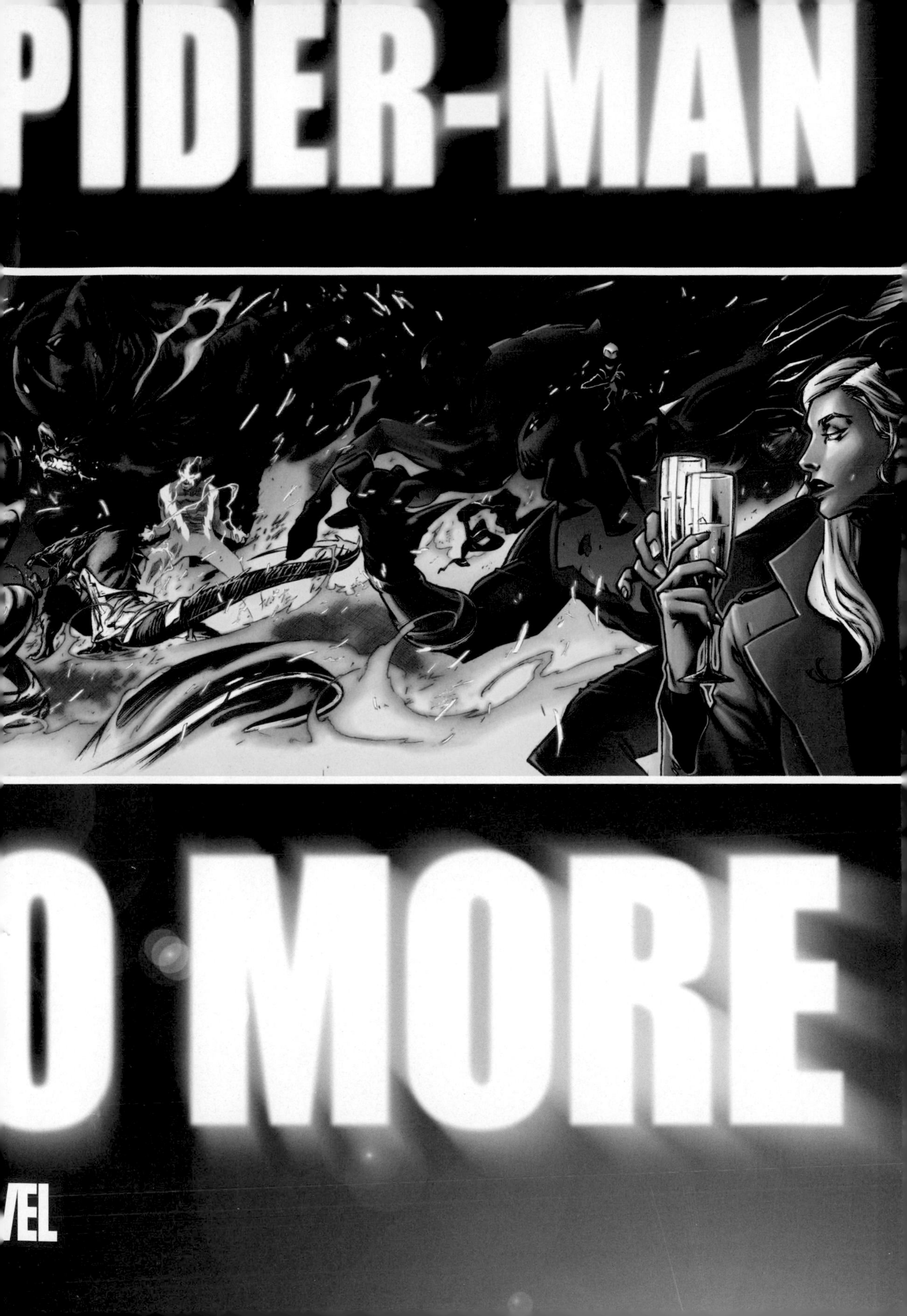

O MORE

VEL

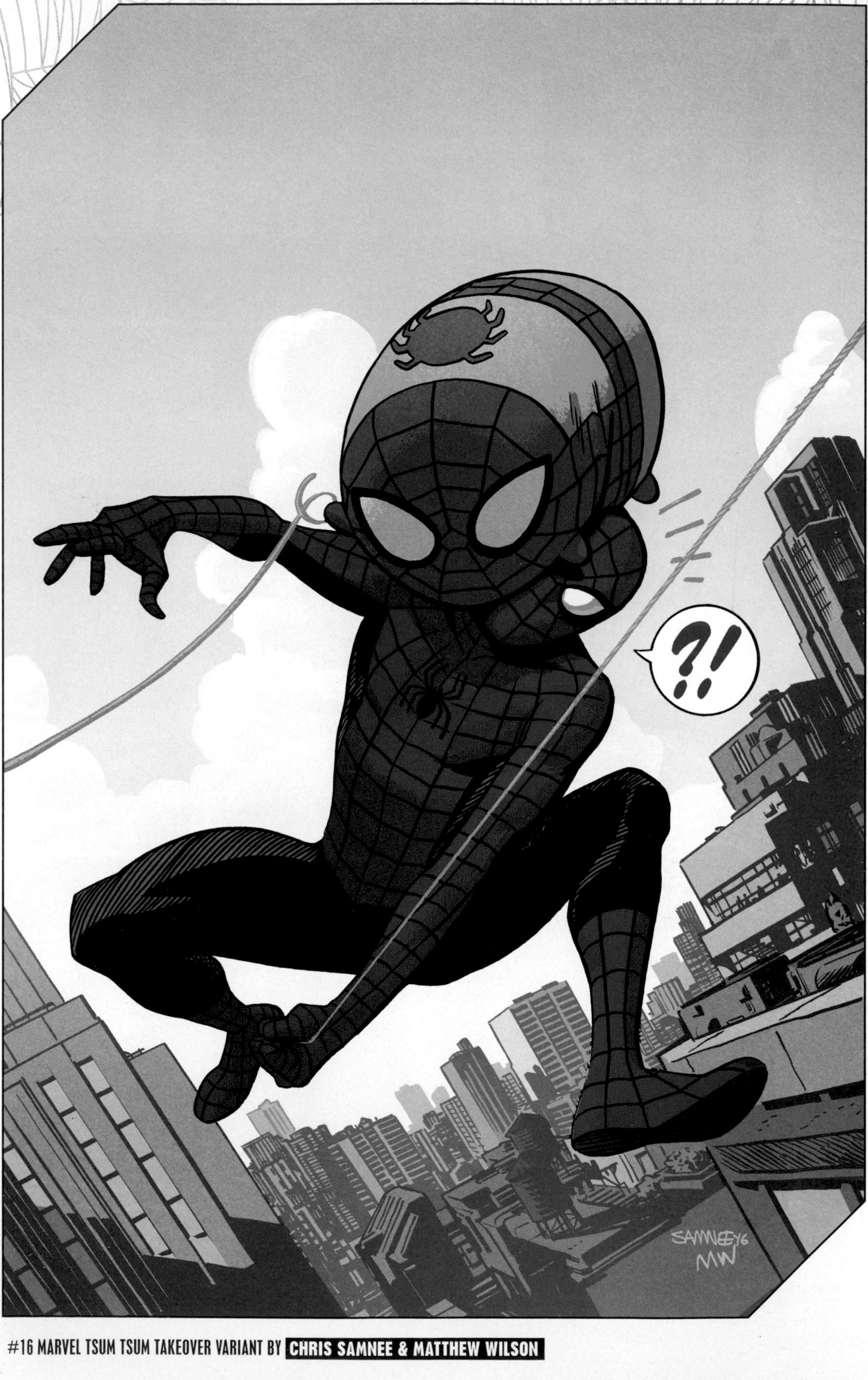
?!
SAMNEE '16
MW

#16 MARVEL TSUM TSUM TAKEOVER VARIANT BY **CHRIS SAMNEE & MATTHEW WILSON**